OVERTIME!

Also by Larry J. Sabato

Peepshow (with Mark Stencel and Robert Lichter)
The Party's Just Begun
Feeding Frenzy
Toward the Millennium – The Elections of 1996
American Government (with Karen O'Connor)
Dangerous Democracy
Campaigns and Elections
The Rise of Political Consultants
Goodbye to Goodtime Charlie
Dirty Little Secrets (with Glenn R. Simpson)

OVERTIME!

THE ELECTION 2000 THRILLER

Edited By

LARRY J. SABATO

University of Virginia
Center for Governmental Studies

New York   San Francisco   Boston
London   Toronto   Sydney   Singapore   Madrid
Mexico City   Munich   Paris   Cape Town   Hong Kong   Montreal

To my friends who are tirelessly working overtime to build the University of Virginia Center for Governmental Studies, and prove to the world that politics really is a good thing!

Publisher: Priscilla McGeehon
Senior Acquisitions Editor: Eric Stano
Senior Marketing Manager: Megan Galvin-Fak
Cover Designer/Manager: Nancy Danahy
Cover Photos: Copyright AP/Wide World
Senior Manufacturing Buyer: Al Dorsey
Printer and Binder: Courier Companies—Stoughton
Cover Printer: Phoenix Color Corp.

Please visit our website at http://www.ablongman.com

ISBN 0-321-10028-X

1 2 3 4 5 6 7 8 9 10—CRS—04 03 02 01

"There is no excitement anywhere in the world, short of war, to match the excitement of an American presidential campaign."

Theodore H. White

"Those who cast the votes decide nothing. Those who count the votes decide everything."

Joseph Stalin

"Not everything that can be counted counts, and not everything that counts can be counted."

Albert Einstein

CONTENTS

Overview of OVERTIME!

Larry J. Sabato
University of Virginia Center for Governmental Studies

The year 2000 gave us the election of the century. The first year of a new millennium featured a pedestrian campaign for president, but oh, what a thrilling election day! The results were such a cliffhanger and the 36-day post-election struggle for the White House was so engrossing that the contest transcended the two flawed major-party candidates, Vice President Al Gore and Texas Governor George W. Bush.

Already, the 2000 election has attained legendary status as the most exciting in well over a century. Yes, there were presidential nail biters in 1916, 1960, 1968, and 1976, as well as major upsets and historic landmarks in 1912, 1932, 1948, 1980, and 1992. But none of these, not even the fabled Kennedy-Nixon showdown in 1960, required decisive recounts or even a full day's delay in the press's declaration of the president-elect. None of these contests except 2000 produced a president with an Electoral College majority but no popular vote plurality. And most of all, none in all of history necessitated an extremely controversial Supreme Court decision that effectively decided the election's outcome.

The 2000 contest was a throwback to the nineteenth century more than the threshold election of the twenty-first. In America's 225 years, the only comparable presidential battles were fought:

- In 1800, when anti-Federalist ticket-mates Thomas Jefferson and Aaron Burr tied in electoral votes after defeating the reelection bid of America's second President, John Adams. The election was thrown to the U.S. House of Representatives, which took 36 ballots before finally electing Jefferson on February 17, 1801.[1]

- In 1824, when Adams' son John Quincy Adams lost both the electoral vote and the popular vote to Andrew Jackson. Adams still won election when the U.S. House decided the contest after the third-place finisher threw his support to Adams. Jackson came back four years later to score a landslide win over Adams.[2]

- In 1876 – the granddaddy of all disputed elections – when Republican Rutherford B. Hayes triumphed over Democrat Samuel Tilden only after a special congressional electoral commission awarded every disputed elector to Hayes by a vote of eight to seven, coincidentally the partisan breakdown of the commission. By this means, Hayes secured an electoral majority of exactly one vote, despite having lost the popular vote by over 250,000. (Neither Hayes nor Tilden ran again in 1880.)[3]

- In 1888, when Democratic President Grover Cleveland handily won the popular vote but narrowly lost the Electoral College to Republican Benjamin Harrison. Cleveland roared back in 1892, however, making Harrison a one-term president and becoming the only chief executive to be elected to nonconsecutive terms.[4]

Past is prologue, but in some respects the 2000 election exceeded the confusion, anger, and division of all four of these earlier elections *combined*. Television made the modern situation worse, and inescapably pervasive, exaggerating every dispute and speeding up the response time on all sides with a 24-hour news cycle, relentlessly driven by cable channels and talk shows. Also, the vicious controversies of the Clinton administration set the stage for the hyperventilating attack politics that characterized the weeks of recount maneuvering. The clear unpreparedness of Florida for the proctoscopic press scrutiny in the post-election period added to the destructive swirl generated by the state's second-rate election practices (now mainly corrected by model, progressive legislation passed in May 2001). At the root of it all was the voters' unexpected but manifest indecision, producing an election crisis that came down to a few hundred votes in only one state.

Just as we recounted both votes *and* memories of 1800, 1824, 1876, and 1888 during the Bush-Gore stand-off, so too will the 2000 election still be widely discussed a hundred years and more from now. Such a fascinating and dramatic vote deserves all the focused attention and analysis we can muster. This volume's team of distinguished authors – an unusual combination of political professionals, journalists, and academics – will provide that necessary scrutiny. First, Tom Fiedler of *The Miami Herald*, one of the 2000 election's best-situated eyewitnesses to history, sets the scene. Then this editor and Joshua Scott of the University of Virginia Center for Governmental Studies examine the nominating battles: who ran and who did not, how the primaries and caucuses unfolded, and why two campaigns triumphed at the conventions when the others did not. *The Washington Post*'s Chuck Babington takes the Bush and Gore campaigns from Labor Day to Election Day, explaining the ups and downs of "the trail" – from debate soup to the nuts of plans gone awry. Journalist Timothy Burger of *The New York Daily News* follows up with a fresh look into one of the Bush campaign's defining episodes, the last-minute revelation about the candidate's drunk driving conviction that nearly cost Bush the White House.

The editor then conducts an extended examination of the actual too-close-to-call results: what happened, who voted, and why, with all the accompanying "what-ifs." Political scientist Diana Owen of Georgetown University explores the news media's performance throughout 2000, not least TV's embarrassing election-night debacle in mis-calling Florida twice in the same evening. Focusing next on the election's "overtime" of five weeks, we hear the inside story of the Florida recount and *Bush v. Gore* from people at the top. Former Gore Chief of Staff Ronald Klain and his associate Jeremy Bash (both legal advisers for the Gore-Lieberman campaign) vividly describe the post-election efforts from the Gore team's perspective, while attorney George Terwilliger, III, of the Bush legal counsel team, describes the behind-the-scenes action in the Bush camp. Journalist Jake Tapper of CNN and *salon.com* also revisits the Sunshine State scene with new thoughts on this investigation of both post-election campaigns. Tapper made headlines with the publication of his book, *Down and Dirty: The Plot to Steal the Presidency* (Boston: Little, Brown and Co.) in March 2001. Finally, one of the nation's finest analysts, Rhodes Cook of the *Rhodes Cook Letter*, offers some concluding and insightful observations on a presidential election that may well be the closest thing in American history to a "perfect storm."

ACKNOWLEDGMENTS

I wish to thank all the contributors for their truly first-rate work under exceedingly tight deadlines; my editors at Longman Publishing, especially the talented and dedicated Eric Stano, whose political and publishing savvy earned him a well-deserved "Editor of the Year" recognition from his company, and Megan Galvin-Fak, the senior Marketing Manager for the Political Science division, whose exertions on coordinating and promoting this book are deeply appreciated; a team of superb staff and interns at the University of Virginia Center for Governmental Studies headed by the indispensable and marvelously talented project manager Joshua Scott, including Alex Theodoridis, Melissa Northern, Rakesh Gopalan, Catherine Giambastiani, Selene Mak, Adam Blumenkrantz, Jonathan Carr, and Tamsin Chance.

Overview of OVERTIME!

This volume is dedicated to the remarkable individuals who are helping to build the U.Va. Center for Governmental Studies into one of the most balanced, active, and respected political organizations in the country. Specifically, I want to thank U.Va. President John T. Casteen III and Executive Vice President Leonard Sandridge, as well as Gordon Burris, Fred Barnes, Sally Marquigny, William H. Fishback, Jr., and Sara Fishback, Eva Teig Hardy, James B. Murray, Jr., William H. Goodwin, Jr., Bruce Gottwald, Anna Thompson, W. Heywood Fralin, Joseph C. Palumbo, Richard F. Norman, R.K. Ramazani, Gilbert J. Sullivan, Mark Bowles, The Richard S. Reynolds Foundation, Randolph G. Flood, Ivor Massey, Jr., The Honorable L.F. Payne, and The Honorable Gerald L. Baliles. Your commitment to the Center will help ensure that current and future generations will understand that government works better when the political system works better. Always remember that "Politics Is A Good Thing!"

Larry J. Sabato
June 2001
Charlottesville, VA

NOTE

[1] For more information on the election of 1800, see Dumas Malone, *Thomas Jefferson as Political Leader* (Berkeley: University of California Press, 1963).
[2] For more information on the election of 1824, see Mary W. M. Hargreaves, *The Presidency of John Quincy Adams* (Lawrence, Kansas: University Press of Kansas, 1985).
[3] For more information on the election of 1876, see Paul Haworth, *The Hayes-Tilden Disputed Presidential Election of 1876* (New York: AMS Press, 1979).
[4] For more information on the election of 1888, see Homer Socolofsky, *The Presidency of Benjamin Harrison* (Lawrence, Kansas: University Press of Kansas, 1987).

CHAPTER 1

Introduction

The Encore of *Key Largo*

Tom Fiedler
The Miami Herald

For George W. Bush, Florida was supposed to be easy. In late October 1999, a year away from the presidential Election Day, a survey taken by *The Miami Herald* and *The St. Petersburg Times* showed the Texas governor sitting atop a near-landslide margin over Vice President Al Gore, the putative Democratic nominee. Nearly half of the state's likely voters, 49 percent, said they favored Bush, against just 34 percent lining up with Gore. That margin was confirmed a few weeks later when *Florida Voter Magazine* put Bush's lead at 52 percent to 39 percent.

And why not? Just a year earlier Florida voters had sent Jeb Bush, the presidential candidate's younger brother who lived in Miami, to the Florida governor's mansion in Tallahassee. And twice before—in 1988 and 1992—Floridians had backed the father, George H. W. Bush, in his campaigns for the White House.

But that cushion proved illusory, little more than a brief tease before playing hard to get. By January, when the candidates suited up for their primary campaigns, the yawning gap between the two front-runners began to close. For many reasons—a booming economy, concerns over school shootings, warming attitudes toward President Clinton—Bush's popularity slipped in Florida and nationwide while Gore's began to climb. Except for a brief flirtation with double digits in the days after the Republican National Convention in July, Bush would never build a lead that swelled much beyond that particular poll's margin of error.

So it was that clouds began to gather early in the year 2000, foretelling a stormy fall campaign that, from start to finish and beyond, would remain too close to call, not only through Election Day, but for five excruciating weeks beyond. The closeness of the contest defied every known measurement—except the one used by the U.S. Supreme Court, finally settling all doubt.

HOW FLORIDA VOTES

To understand how that came to be, it is necessary to understand the state at the center of the storm (see figure 1-1). The elements that made Florida the nation's battleground had been in place for years. Although (as one saying goes) Florida is in the South, it is not of the South. In fact, it's a little bit of everywhere, a bellwether of the nation's tastes, moods, and opinions. That shouldn't be a surprise. More than four of every five Floridians are from somewhere else—the Midwest, the Northeast, the Mid-Atlantic, and the South, for starters. But also they are from Cuba, Puerto Rico, Russia, Israel, Mexico, Haiti, Vietnam, China, and other points across the globe—each of those groups re-creating an Americanized version of its native land somewhere amid Florida's palms. In an almost uncanny way, these newcomers came in proportions that were roughly those of the United States as a whole. Also in rough proportion to the country is Florida's partisan breakdown, its mix of urban-suburban-rural, of white to black and Hispanic. Only in the category of age is Florida, a retirement mecca, skewed beyond the norm.

Within this system are natural constituencies that benefit each of the major parties. Republicans find a natural base in those lower Gulf Coast counties that have grown over the years with newcomers from the nation's Republican heartland. These are people who still say that "home" is Indiana, rural Michigan, downstate Illinois, Nebraska, Ohio, and Wisconsin. Many bring with them their midwestern, Rotary Club conservatism. The Republican Party also came to dominate the bedroom communities north of Orlando, and in those counties that trace an arc stretching east and southward to include the so-called Space Coast, the wealthy enclave of Vero Beach, and the affluent coastal communities of Stuart, Hobe Sound, Jupiter, and, of course, Palm Beach, towns where country-club Republicanism was handed down from generation to generation.

Figure 1-1.
Map of Florida

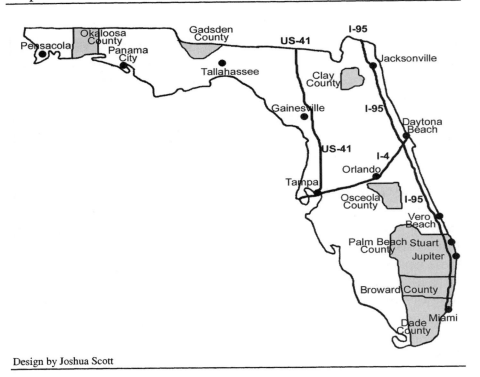

Design by Joshua Scott

And, giving the lie to the history of yellow-dog Democrat politics, GOP voters increasingly populate growing swaths of the Florida Panhandle, typically in concentric circles spreading outward from the many major military installations near Pensacola, Fort Walton Beach, Panama City, and Jacksonville. Many are recently retired career military families who plunge eagerly into partisan politics, predominately on the GOP's side. Years ago they formed an ideological alliance with the native white Floridians who, although born and bred to be Democrats, voted invariably for the most conservative candidate in state and national elections. In recent years, many of those old Democrats switched in droves—so much so that two North Florida counties, Okaloosa and Clay, in the 1990s began delivering GOP candidates their most lopsided victories.

The Democrats, too, had a base, although it has become more geographically concentrated in the past 10 years around the most densely populated urban areas—again, not unlike the national picture. Although whites in North Florida have become fickle in their loyalties (voting Democratic for county offices, GOP for state and national ones), African Americans remain loyal in the mostly rural counties. Gadsden County, the state's only majority-black county, still boasts that it was the only one of the state's 67 counties to go against Ronald Reagan in 1984. Democrats also continue to hold sway in the counties that are home to the state's two largest universities, located in Tallahassee (also the capital) and Gainesville.

From there, however, the Democrats must skip southward to the urban megalopolis of Southeast Florida, the densely populated corridor that stretches along Interstate 95—and old U.S. 1—from West Palm Beach to the northernmost cities of Miami-Dade County. Geographers long ago noted that most Floridians first came to the state as vacationers, usually by driving the most direct federal highway from where they lived to where they would end up in the Sunshine State. For midwesterners, that often meant U.S. 41, which begins in Wisconsin and winds its way down to Florida's west coast. For northeasterners, that was U.S. 1 and later Interstate 95, which begins in Bar Harbor, Maine, travels through Boston, New York, and Washington, D.C., and ends just south of downtown Miami. So it's no surprise that most of those who live in this teeming region imported with them their big-city ways, among them a taste for high-rise living, valet parking, major-league sports, nightlife, fresh-baked bagels, and, for many, liberal Democratic politics.

Although the Democratic Party's geographic reach has steadily eroded over the years, the density of the population along this stretch of I-95 can provide a counterweight sufficient to carry a statewide election. This is not to say that issues don't matter: Polls going into the 2000 campaign showed that Gore benefited among women and older voters all over the state because of his positions for abortion rights and for a strong federal contribution to Medicare and prescription drugs. But nobody would dispute that the Democratic base, its center of gravity, was what used to be called Florida's Gold Coast, with Broward County at its center. And it was here that the fiercest battles of both the regular campaign and the post–November 7 campaign would have to be waged.

Localities outside these partisan strongholds have become arenas for political dogfights. Miami-Dade County, the state's largest and most ethnically and racially diverse county, tends to lean Democratic in national and state elections, but just by a hair, and this tendency cannot be taken for granted. The county's largely Jewish and liberal Miami Beach precincts join with African-American neighborhoods to do battle with the Cuban-American enclaves in the central and western parts of the county. It was no accident that Al Gore made his final campaign appearance on the sands of South Beach in the wee hours of November 7, hoping (successfully, it would turn out) to tilt the advantage his way in the county where George W. Bush's brother had lived until moving to the governor's mansion.

A third region also plays a critical role in Florida elections, one that politicos describe simply as the I-4 corridor. This term describes those counties touched by Interstate 4 as it stretches between Tampa Bay on the west coast, through Orlando, and over to Daytona on the east. This region—formerly known for its citrus products and phosphate—is now one of the world's premier vacation spots, focused on Walt Disney World and countless other theme park resorts. Although originally powered by tourism, the region's biggest cities, especially Orlando, now are full-service commercial hubs driven by a kind of perpetual energy generated by their own growth. This region's explosive expansion has made its politics, once predictably Republican, unpredictable. In 1996, Bill Clinton stunned locals by carrying Osceola County, home to most of Disney World, and nearly winning Orange County, which encompasses metropolitan Orlando. One important reason: Tens of thousands of Puerto Ricans, both from the island and from greater New York, arrived in the area and carried along their preference for Democrats. This unpredictability made the I-4 corridor an instant battleground between Gore and Bush.

Each campaign was presented with an equation based on these dynamics, which needed to be solved to win the state. For Bush, victory lay in sweeping those GOP regions and, on the strength of his brother's ties, carrying Miami-Dade. For Democrats, the strategy was simpler still: Break even along I-4; hope that African-American antipathy toward Jeb Bush, who had abolished affirmative action programs in state contracting and university admissions, would hurt his brother; then blow the top off of all expectations in the Gold Coast's Democratic communities, especially the condominiums in Broward and southern Palm Beach counties. Democratic strategists knew that victory depended on the ticket winning by a landslide in those precincts so it could offset losses elsewhere. That was the formula that gave victory to Bill Clinton in 1996, and to the late Governor Lawton Chiles in 1994 against Jeb Bush—making Chiles the only Democratic governor of a major state to win election that year.

THE LIEBERMAN FACTOR

In the opinion of most analysts, including this one, Al Gore had only one hope of achieving the Democrats' goal: He needed to put Bob Graham, Florida's senior senator and a former two-term governor, on the ticket. And in fact, until the final hours of the veep hunt, Graham was in contention. But Gore, amazingly, found someone who arguably was even better: Joe Lieberman, the senator from Connecticut and—not coincidentally—an Orthodox Jew, the first named to a presidential ticket.

He embodied a political masterstroke, the perfect variable to satisfy that Democratic equation. Of all the assignments that fell to Lieberman to handle in the campaign, none was more important than campaigning in South Florida as if he were seeking a county commission seat. And that's precisely what he did, stalking the condominium precincts from Miami Beach to West Palm Beach while Jewish Democrats—sometimes weeping with joy at seeing one of their faith vying for the nation's second-highest office—treated him like a rock star. With Lieberman, not only could Jews vote their social consciences, but they could vote their hearts and souls, their very Jewishness. And vote they would do—although, they would learn later, not always properly.

From Labor Day to Election Day, polls in Florida, like those nationwide, seesawed back and forth, one going slightly for Bush, another for Gore, but never really straying outside the error margins. Yet one number seemed consistently to jump out of those surveys: Gore was trouncing Bush in those Jewish enclaves by two-to-one margins. Jim Kane, editor of the *Florida Voter Magazine*, told my colleague Mark Silva, two weeks before Election Day: "It's South Florida against the rest of the state." Florida, it appeared then, would pivot around which side did the better job of turning out its voters and rounding up absentee ballots. What nobody fully understood, however, was that victory would also turn on what those voters did with their ballots.

7

Tom Fiedler

THE PERFECT STORM

Of course, Florida mattered only because other factors conspired to make it so. Much has been said about Gore's failure to carry Tennessee, his home state, or Arkansas, that of President Clinton. And it's important to remind everyone that Ralph Nader walked out of Florida with nearly 100,000 votes—the vast majority of them more closely aligned with traditional Democrats than with the GOP. But just as it took myriad meteorological factors to come together in a catastrophic way to create Sebastian Junger's "perfect storm" described in the book of that name, it took myriad political factors to put Florida in the center of the 2000 presidential campaign's version of a perfect storm. But when it hit, the world took note—and its damage is still being assessed.

My phone calling started picking up signals of trouble shortly after noon on November 7. A longtime Democratic Party backer, George Dominicis, told me that he and his wife, a teacher, emerged from their polling place in Palm Beach County with a gnawing sense that they'd just participated in a disaster in the making. George is a sophisticated political participant, a prominent figure in Tallahassee and Washington, D.C. He told me that he couldn't say for sure whether he'd voted correctly because the ballot was virtually unfathomable.

His wife shared his unease. And, he told me, as he called around the county he was picking up the same signals from others. This was when I learned first about the "butterfly ballot," a design unique to Palm Beach County. Elections Supervisor Theresa LePore sketched it out herself in the hope that if all 10 presidential tickets were crowded onto two facing pages, with the punch holes along the center binding, elderly voters with limited eyesight could see the names better.

Today, no election analyst will say with a straight face that the butterfly design didn't cost Al Gore the presidency. Graphic designers have taken to showcasing the ballot as an example of how bad design can change history. An analysis by my newspaper, *The Miami Herald*, added detail to what others sensed: Voters in Palm Beach County were 100 times more likely than voters elsewhere in South Florida to vote for both Al Gore and Pat Buchanan, the Reform Party candidate, thus ruining their ballots as "overvotes."[1] What made it more painful for many elderly Jewish Palm Beach voters was Buchanan's reputation of insensitivity to their faith. One rabbi said with bitter humor that if Pat Buchanan ran again for president, the only one who'd follow him would be Simon Wiesenthal, the famed Nazi hunter. The mistakes were caused because the holes for Gore and Buchanan were adjacent to each other, in such a way that voters either mis-aimed or mistakenly thought they had to punch twice, once for Gore and once for Lieberman—the man they had waited desperately to make a mark for. *Palm Beach Post* reporters estimated that the butterfly ballot cost Gore about 6,600 votes in that county alone— over 10 times more than Bush's official 537-vote victory.[2]

But the horrors of the Florida election didn't begin and end in Palm Beach County. In the greater Jacksonville area, Duval County, African-American voters turned out in near-record numbers owing in part to a campaign to persuade them to vote for Gore and for Corrine Brown, the Democratic congresswoman, who is black. "Vote for Gore and Brown," went the mantra. So thousands of voters in predominately black precincts voted for Gore on the first page of their ballots, then turned to the next page and voted for Browne—Harry Browne, the Libertarian Party candidate for president. Their votes, too—as many as 9,000 under some estimates—went uncounted. The *Herald* found that of the 20 precincts in Florida that had the highest rate of spoiled ballots, 19 were in Jacksonville's mostly black neighborhoods. Statewide, nearly 1 in 10 of the ballots cast in black precincts were thrown out, arguably more than 90 percent of them for Gore. By contrast, about 1 in 37 ballots were disqualified in predominately white precincts.

That wasn't all, of course. Statewide, some 174,000 of the nearly 6 million votes cast on November 7 weren't counted. About 110,000 of those were so-called "overvotes." In these cases, the machine that scanned the ballots concluded that more than one candidate had been marked. Subsequently, several news media organizations, including my own, found that a hand examination of the ballots would have shown clear voter intent on nearly half. The remaining 64,000 or so uncounted ballots passed through tallying machines without registering a vote for anyone. Of course, many voters might be expected to find no stomach for any candidate and thus skip the line. But again, hand examinations found that more than half these ballots contained marks that were unread by the machines. How so? In those counties where punch-card ballots were used, those infamous chads got in the way of the tallying machines' sensors, or voters failed to dislodge the chad, leaving only dimples or pinpricks, through their own fault or that of a faulty "Votomatic" machine. *The Miami Herald*'s Martin Merzer wrote of the ingenuity many voters used to spoil their ballots, including one who tried to put a chad back into its slot with nail polish.[3] He also wrote of the North Florida woman who scribbled on the bottom of her ballot that, because she'd left her glasses at home, she couldn't read the names. So she politely asked that her ballot be marked for Bush. Of course it was tossed by the machine, which couldn't read her message.

Thousands of ballots were spoiled because voters took literally the printed words at the bottom of the page, "WRITE-IN CANDIDATE." So, even if they had already indicated their choice above, they dutifully wrote in the name again—thus spoiling their ballots. The concept of a "write-in candidate" was apparently new to them. In subsequent weeks, the news media turned up a cornucopia of other Election Day mishaps, including at least two "dead" people voting, many eager partisans voting more than once (usually by casting an absentee ballot in advance and then going to the precinct to vote again in person), and hundreds of former felons casting ballots in defiance (though apparently not intentionally) of state law. Former President Jimmy Carter was so horror-stricken by what occurred that he wrote: "I was really taken aback and embarrassed by what happened in Florida. ... If we were invited to go into a foreign country to monitor the election, and they had similar election standards and procedures, we would refuse to participate at all."[4]

Partisans can and will debate the meaning of all this for years to come. But two conclusions seem solid: (1) Despite the furor caused by the networks in making too-early victory projections, as well as the data-entry and vote estimation errors on election night, the facts seem to support the view that the Voter News Service's exit polls in Florida *were accurate to the extent that they measured what voters thought they had done*; and (2) The *Economist* magazine's editors had it right when they put George W. Bush on the December 16, 2000, cover under the headline "The Accidental President."

WHO REALLY WON?

There are two ways to phrase this question. The first is to add the words "according to the Constitution." The second is to ask, "Who would have won if the U.S. Supreme Court had not intervened?" The answer to the first question is clearly "George W. Bush"; the Electoral College and the Congress affirmed that fact. The answer to the second prompts a more equivocal response: "It depends on how and what you count."

It's important to recall that the U.S. Supreme Court intervened for the final time after the Florida Supreme Court directed the canvassing boards in 63 of the 67 counties to hand-count the "undervotes," those that the tallying machines had discarded as being blank. Three other counties had already finished their hand counts: Broward, Palm Beach, and Volusia. Within a day, however, the U.S. Supreme Court ordered a stop to all recounts, and, 48 hours later, the Court effectively handed the election to Bush by ruling that no hand tallies could be included because Florida lacked a uniform statewide standard for judging the disputed ballots. Of course there was no time left for Florida to devise such a standard, so the recount could not resume. The 537-vote margin that Bush had been awarded by Florida

11

Secretary of State Katherine Harris—the Bush campaign's state co-chair—became enshrined in history. Florida's 25 electoral votes would be cast for Bush the following week, making him president by two votes in the Electoral College.

But, the question was asked in living rooms and newsrooms around the country, "What would have happened if those 'undervotes' had been counted? What if the U.S. Supreme Court had stayed on the sidelines?" *The Miami Herald*, with *USA Today* and Knight Ridder newspapers (the *Herald*'s corporate parent), set out to answer that question. So did a second news-media consortium that included *The New York Times, The Washington Post, The Wall Street Journal,* and others. The *Herald*'s group filed public-records requests in every county, demanding the right under Florida law to examine these ballots. The group brought in the public accounting firm of BDO Seidman, LLP, to handle the ballot examination on the theory that the firm's expertise lay in being able to make fine judgments on detailed matters. The several-month-long examination produced a startling, and ironic, result: If the undervotes were tallied using the looser standard advocated by the Gore campaign in its arguments to the courts, Bush would have carried Florida by an even bigger margin than his official tally, actually tripling it to 1,665 votes. But if these undervotes had been counted using the strictest standard—the one advocated by the Bush campaign in its arguments—Gore would have won by the surrealistically infinitesimal margin of 3 votes.[5]

Then there was this further twist: The *Herald* group decided to look, too, at the undervotes that had already been tallied by Palm Beach and Broward counties. And using the same standards as each party had argued, Gore more than overtook Bush's lead. That analysis seemed to prove the U.S. Supreme Court majority's point, that Florida could not possibly conduct a credible recount because it lacked any consistent standard for counting these questionable ballots.

The final piece of this post-election tally came a few weeks later when the *Herald* group completed its review of the overvotes, those ballots that were tossed out because they showed what appeared to the machines to be marks for more than one candidate. Although these overvotes were never a part of the U.S. Supreme Court's decision making, they underscored the beliefs of many that Gore votes were disproportionately lost amid this blizzard of error. The worst of the overvote errors remained concentrated in Palm Beach County, where the voters were victims of the butterfly design. Thousands of other Gore votes were lost in the African-American precincts. At the end of this review, no fair-minded observer could doubt that if the ballots had reflected voter intent, history would be different.[6]

THE GOOD NEWS

Florida may carry for years its stigma of "Flori-duh." Months after President Bush moved into the White House, he organized a youth T-ball tournament on the South Lawn. This caused late-night comedian Jay Leno to quip that T-ball was a strange variation on baseball because nobody kept score, "sort of like Florida elections." But the humiliation of being under the national microscope for five weeks after November 7 with every wart revealed had a salutary effect. Prodded by Jeb Bush, the Florida legislature—with bipartisan backing—adopted an election reform package in early 2001 that addressed the most serious problems arising in the voting process. Punch-card machines, with their tendency to produce chads, were outlawed, to be replaced by optical-scan ballots and touch-screen machines, similar to standardized test sheets and ATM cash machines, respectively. The law also mandated a hand count of overvotes and undervotes in any election in which the margin was within one-fourth of 1 percent. And it directed the secretary of state, working with case law, to put forward a uniform statewide standard for dealing with disputed ballots.[7]

Ironically, had these provisions been state law on November 7, Al Gore would occupy the White House. But they weren't, and he isn't.

Tom Fiedler

Most longtime Floridians are familiar with the 1948 classic movie thriller *Key Largo*, starring Humphrey Bogart as a returning war veteran and hero, with Edward G. Robinson as Johnny Rocco, a mob boss who runs his town like a despot. The two men are thrown together in an oceanfront hotel just as a hurricane bears down on them. In one exchange, Bogart's upstanding character demands to know how Rocco could exert such control over local affairs. Here's Rocco's reply: "Let me tell you about Florida politicians. I make them out of whole cloth, just like a tailor makes a suit. I get their name in the newspaper. I get them some publicity and get them on the ballot. Then after the election, we count the votes. And if they don't turn out right, we recount them. And recount them again. Until they do."

Has life imitated art?

NOTES

[1] "Gore Lost 6,607 Votes Because of Butterfly Ballot," Associated Press, March 10, 2001.

[2] Joel Engelhardt and Scott McCabe, "Over-votes Cost Gore the Election in Florida: A Palm Beach Post Analysis of 19,125 Ballots That Were Punched More Than Once," *The Palm Beach Post*, March 11, 2001, p. A1.

[3] Martin Merzer, "Floridians Zany, Creative in Spoiling Their Battles," *The Miami Herald*, April 4, 2001.

[4] Jingle Davis, "U.S. Voting Standards Fall Far Short, Carter Says; Nonpartisan Panel Opens Hearings on Ways to Improve Accuracy and Fairness," *The Atlantic Journal-Constitution*, March 27, 2001, p. 3A.

[5] "Deadlock Again: Newspapers Find No Clear Winner in Ballot Review," Associated Press, May 10, 2001.

[6] Ibid.

[7] Florida Senate, January 1, 2002, *Relating to Elections*, Resolution # S1118.

CHAPTER 2

The Long Road to a Cliffhanger:

Primaries and Conventions

Larry J. Sabato and Joshua J. Scott
University of Virginia Center for Governmental Studies

The presidential election of 2000 will forever be remembered for the way it ended—the weeks of overtime uncertainty, the numerous counts and recounts, the infamous chads, the ensuing legal battles, and, finally, the unprecedented U.S. Supreme Court decision that awarded the presidency to Governor George W. Bush over Vice President Al Gore. This chapter, however, will take us back to the beginning, which set the stage for the razor-close November contest. We traverse the wild and bumpy road through the Democratic and Republican primaries, caucuses, and conventions to show how Bush and Gore became the chief contestants in the political match of the century.

OVERVIEW OF THE INTRAPARTY WARS

Vice President Gore, the former Tennessee senator and son of a Tennessee senator, who portrayed himself as a centrist "New Democrat," had served with President Bill Clinton since being chosen for the number two slot in 1992. Like most incumbent vice presidents who have run for president, Gore had the party leadership and establishment behind him in his efforts to succeed Clinton. He was intelligent (if not exciting) and a prolific fundraiser, and he was viewed by both supporters and opponents as one of the most active and influential vice presidents in history. Most importantly, he was inheriting the peace and prosperity of the Clinton-Gore administration, two fundamental keys that have decided election success or failure throughout history.

On the Republican side, Texas Governor Bush, son of the forty-first president of the United States, had become the clear front-runner for the party's presidential nod very early—partly because of a weak bench after successive presidential defeats. Affable and well liked, "Dubya" was perceived as a Washington outsider, but one with keen connections to the powerful party insiders and financiers who had aided his father. Fresh off a landslide 1998 Texas gubernatorial victory fueled in part by fairly strong Hispanic support, Bush espoused a message of "compassionate conservatism" and claimed that he would restore integrity and honor to the White House.

Both candidates obviously had a great deal going for them as they dispatched early contenders to become the front-runners. However, they also had sizable liabilities that allowed stiff primary competition to arise from somewhat unexpected sources. Bush, seen by some as all hat and no cattle, appeared to many observers as a smug, inexperienced candidate from a weak-governor state who was riding the coattails of his legacy. Throughout the first year of his campaign, Bush had not taken particularly well-defined stances on issues, and his frequent mistakes in grammar and pronunciation produced ridicule.

A large field of 10 Republicans ran for the nomination, but Bush's main opponent turned out to be Arizona Senator John McCain, a bona fide war hero and a maverick with populist appeal. McCain became the darling of the news media after he rode his "Straight Talk Express" bus to a shocking upset over Bush in New Hampshire.

Despite a few noteworthy victories, however, McCain was never able to translate his fawning press coverage into enough votes, and the wheels of the steely Bush bandwagon stayed in place.

Gore carried the burden of the public's contempt for the personal scandals and national embarrassments of that great American presidential polarizer, Bill Clinton. Gore also had a tarnished image due to the Buddhist temple fund-raising scandal of 1996 and his often exaggerated claims about his accomplishments. Moreover, he would have to prove to the voters that he was not the irritating, lecturing know-it-all and bloodless technocrat he often appeared to be. In order to win the election, Gore would have find a way to take credit for the successes of the Clinton-Gore administration while establishing himself as his own, more appealing man.

Gore was challenged for the nomination by former New Jersey Senator (1979–1997) and National Basketball Association Hall of Famer Bill Bradley. Although he was a plodding campaigner and a sleep-inducing speaker, Bradley managed to energize some of the liberal wing of the Democratic Party and provided a possible option for anti-Clinton Democrats. Although Bradley's campaign never caught fire, a few thousand more votes in New Hampshire to produce an upset of Gore *might* have changed the nomination equation, as we shall see.

In the late summer of 2000, Bush and Gore both selected vice presidential ticket mates who helped them counter their own weaknesses, and they also accepted the official nominations from their respective parties at the national conventions in Philadelphia and Los Angeles. During the extremely packaged and tightly scheduled four-day events, the Republicans preached inclusion and reached out to minorities and other nontraditional groups, while the Democrats formally passed the torch from Clinton to Gore. Both major party nominees recovered from primary wounds and both ran reasonably effective summer conventions, but neither managed to close the sale with the American people. For every plus, there was also a minus in most voters' minds, and this yin and yang persisted in the national consciousness to Election Day and beyond.

REPUBLICAN PRIMARIES: MONEYED CONSERVATISM BEATS MEDIA POPULISM

Governor Bush faced a much tougher road to the Republican nomination than many expected. His status as the perceived overwhelming front-runner prevented other Republican candidates from gaining much traction in the hunt for the nomination, including former Secretary of Labor and Secretary of Transportation Elizabeth Dole, former Tennessee Governor Lamar Alexander, billionaire publisher Steve Forbes, New Hampshire Senator Bob Smith, former Vice President Dan Quayle, Senator Orrin Hatch of Utah, Congressman John Kasich of Ohio, Gary Bauer of the Family Research Council, and former Ambassador Alan Keyes. As noted earlier, the only candidate who emerged from the field to challenge Bush was Senator John McCain. McCain's golden reputation as a campaign finance reformer and decorated Vietnam veteran (he had just published a national bestseller called *Faith of My Fathers,*[1] recounting his military service and his five years as a prisoner of war) made him the media's personal favorite. On the other hand, McCain's hot temper, large ego, and out-of-the-GOP-mainstream views on several subjects (including guns, campaign reform, and the Christian Right) made him a thorn in the side of many Republican leaders and activists.

Harkening back to William McKinley's "front porch campaign" of 1896, Bush received countless visits from state legislators to the Governor's Mansion in Austin, begging him to run for president. Why was Bush crowned so early as the Republican redeemer? First of all, his famous last name gave him immediate recognition among party voters and average citizens alike. Second, his record as governor of Texas was electorally potent, even among Democratic-leaning groups such as Hispanics, African Americans, and women.[2] Third, and perhaps most important to the often hierarchical GOP, there was no one of more senior service "in line" for the nomination.

The first showdown of the season occurred at the Iowa caucus, held on January 24, 2000. While Bush won the caucus, many were surprised at his meager percentage, which was far below expectations. He defeated two-time presidential contender Steve Forbes by 41 percent to 30 percent, an underwhelming margin especially because John McCain had decided not to run in the Hawkeye State. Still, the Bush team hoped for a bounce in the polls following their victory, as well as a potential backlash against McCain for skipping Iowa.

Nothing of the sort happened. The New Hampshire primary delivered the sharpest possible blow to Bush's run for the GOP nomination, and it arguably could have ended his White House hopes. In a shocking outcome some compared to that of 1996, when Pat Buchanan bested Bob Dole in the New Hampshire GOP primary, McCain pulled ahead of Bush by 18 points to win the state, 48.5 percent to 30.4 percent. (See table 2-1 for results of all the Republican primaries.) Although some analysts had belatedly believed that McCain might be able to pull off a narrow win, a blowout of such magnitude was thoroughly unexpected. In hindsight, pundits and reporters attributed Bush's massive defeat to the quality of his campaign, which had been endorsement-laden but lacking in substantive issues and personal contact, two essential elements of success in the fiercely independent Granite State. McCain's triumph immediately placed enormous pressure on the Texas governor to sharpen his message, boost his energy as a candidate, and confront McCain directly.

Bush did just that in South Carolina, abandoning his "compassionate conservative" label in favor of his new slogan, "a reformer with results." Bush also launched a furious frontal attack on McCain that worked. The Texan won the South Carolina primary on February 19 by a margin of 11 percentage points (53.4 % to 41.9 %), but the win came at a high price. Bush did what he had dearly hoped to avoid: He

Table 2-1.
Results of All the Republican Primaries

Date	State	Bush	McCain	Total Vote
February 1	New Hampshire	30.4	48.5	238,206
February 8	Delaware	50.7	25.4	30,060
February 19	South Carolina	53.4	41.9	573,101
February 22	Arizona	35.7	60.0	322,669
February 22	Michigan	43.1	51.0	1,276,770
February 29	Virginia	52.8	43.9	664,093
February 29	Washington	57.8	38.9	491,148
March 7	California	60.6	34.7	2,847,921
March 7	Connecticut	46.3	48.7	178,985
March 7	Georgia	66.9	27.8	643,188
March 7	Maine	51.0	44.0	96,624
March 7	Maryland	56.2	36.2	376,034
March 7	Massachusetts	31.8	64.7	501,951
March 7	Missouri	57.9	35.3	475,363
March 7	New York	51.0	43.4	720,000
March 7	Ohio	58.0	37.0	1,397,528
March 7	Rhode Island	36.5	60.2	36,120
March 7	Vermont	35.3	60.3	81,355
March 10	Colorado	64.7	27.1	180,217
March 10	Utah	63.3	14.0	91,053
March 14	Florida	73.8	19.9	699,503
March 14	Louisiana	83.6	8.9	102,912
March 14	Mississippi	87.9	5.4	114,979
March 14	Oklahoma	79.1	10.4	124,809
March 14	Tennessee	77.0	14.5	250,791
March 14	Texas	87.5	7.1	1,126,757
March 21	Illinois	67.4	21.5	736,857
April 4	Pennsylvania	73.5	22.7	643,085
April 4	Wisconsin	69.2	18.1	495,769
May 2	District of Columbia	72.8	24.4	2,433
May 2	Indiana	81.2	18.8	406,664
May 2	North Carolina	78.6	10.9	322,517
May 9	Nebraska	78.2	15.1	185,758
May 9	West Virginia	79.6	12.9	109,404
May 16	Oregon	83.6	---	349,831
May 23	Arkansas	80.2	---	43,755
May 23	Idaho	73.5	---	158,446
May 23	Kentucky	83.0	6.3	91,323
May 25	Alabama	84.2	---	203,079
June 6	Montana	77.6	---	113,671
June 6	New Jersey	83.6	---	240,810
June 6	New Mexico	82.6	10.1	75,230
June 6	South Dakota	78.2	13.8	45,279
	Total	**63.2**	**29.8**	**17,146,048**

SOURCE: Rhodes Cook, *The Rhodes Cook Letter*, May 2001.

abandoned his positive campaign and went "hard negative." Bush aired ads in South Carolina that attacked McCain as a hypocrite on campaign finance reform. There were even reports of Bush supporters calling Republican voters to tell them that McCain was "a liar and a thief and a cheat."[3] Bush's victory was marred by the media attention given to his negative campaigning and also by his visit to ultraconservative Bob Jones University (which at that time prohibited interracial dating among students). At the same time, the South Carolina campaign branded McCain as a liberal—a deadly label among Republicans—so Bush was thought to have the momentum heading into the next big-state primary, Michigan.

Bush was expected to win the Wolverine State, especially because of the strong endorsement he received from popular GOP Governor John Engler. However, Michigan's voters decided that they were not yet ready to end the nomination contest. Benefiting from strong turnout among Independents and even Democrats in the state (Michigan has an open primary), McCain pulled off another surprise victory, as well as an easy win the same day in his home state of Arizona. Ironically, a similar situation had occurred in Michigan during the 1980 Republican primary between Ronald Reagan and George Herbert Walker Bush (now known around the White House as President #41). In a reversal of roles, the elder Bush was the stubborn insurgent candidate troubling Reagan, the front-runner. Bush surprised Reagan with a win in Michigan, which revived the Bush candidacy and eventually helped lead Reagan to select Bush as his ticket mate. (Note that the younger Bush—President #43—made no similar offer to McCain; the personal dislike was much more intense between Bush Jr. and McCain than between Bush Sr. and Reagan.)

Looking south for sustenance once again, Bush turned the tables on McCain in Virginia a week later. Bush's opponent helped: The day before the February 29 Virginia GOP primary, McCain alienated himself from many hard-core Republican voters by attacking Christian conservative leader Pat Robertson as having an "evil influence" on the Republican Party.[4] Virginia Governor James S.

21

Gilmore, one of the co-chairs of Bush's national campaign committee, delivered Virginia's delegation to the Bush column with a solid but not overwhelming margin of 52.8 percent to 43.9 percent. The same day, McCain overwhelmingly lost both the Washington primary and the North Dakota caucus. McCain continued to slide downward, finally exiting from the race—but not the political landscape—on Thursday, March 9, after running out of money and suffering devastating defeats in eleven primaries on the previous Super Tuesday. Nonetheless, McCain still won in several New England Super Tuesday states (Connecticut, Massachusetts, Rhode Island, and Vermont), signaling Bush's weakness in that region.

Table 2-2.
The 2000 Primaries Revisited: Bush-McCain District Comparison

	Bush	McCain	Total
Congressional Districts Won	132	70	202
November Presidential Winner			
Bush	67	14	81
Gore	65	56	121
November House Winner			
Republican	71	20	91
Democrat	60	49	109
Independent	1	1	2
Region			
Northeast	36	27	63
Midwest	28	16	44
South	24	4	28
West	44	23	67

NOTE: Chart reflects congressional districts won between January 24,2000 and March 9, 2000, when McCain exited the race.
SOURCE: Rhodes Cook, *The Rhodes Cook Letter*, May 2001, p. 4.

Despite being overmatched by Bush in money and organization, John McCain won an eclectic array of congressional districts throughout the country, including four districts where, in November 2000,

Republicans picked up a seat from Democrats and four districts where Democrats picked up a seat from Republicans. (See table 2-2 for a comparison of Bush's and McCain's congressional districts.) One of McCain's most glaring liabilities (and the likely cause of his defeat) was the fact that he received almost no support from Republican leaders and strong-party identifiers and activists. "Outsider" status and worshipful media coverage could carry McCain only so far in an establishment-oriented, anti-press party. Yet McCain had made himself an enduring personal phenomenon, and in the process, he had exposed a number of Bush's flaws and caused substantial image problems for the Republican nominee. Some of these image difficulties, such as ideological placement of Bush on the "extreme right," have persisted into Bush's presidency.

DEMOCRATIC PRIMARIES: LIBERAL ESTABLISHMENT BEATS LEFTIST INSURGENTS

As the incumbent vice president in a time of peace and prosperity, Al Gore approached the 2000 election in the catbird seat. He had avoided challenges from Missouri Congressman and House Minority Leader Richard Gephardt (who decided to focus on reclaiming the U.S. House for the Democrats); Senators Bob Kerrey of Nebraska, John F. Kerry of Massachusetts, and Paul Wellstone of Minnesota; and civil rights leader and two-time presidential candidate Jesse Jackson. But the coronation was interrupted by former three-term Senator Bill Bradley of New Jersey. Bradley, popular with independents and more liberal members of the Democratic Party, stressed both campaign finance reform and universal health care coverage. Although a weak campaigner, Bradley was a proven fund-raiser who appeared (at least to some, for a while) to be the better option for very liberal Democrats, as well as for party members resentful about the Clinton scandals.

Yet despite some momentum and near equity in fund-raising in the early rounds, Bradley never seriously challenged Gore's bid for the nomination.[5] Throughout the short primary campaign, it became abundantly clear that although Gore had major flaws, Bradley was not the ideal candidate to exploit those weaknesses. He was never able to prove that he could provide the necessary leadership to win the general election better than Al Gore could.

In the January 24 Iowa caucus, Gore won a decisive 28-point margin over Bradley. Gore won every age and income group, and he was even judged a "stronger leader with better ideas" on campaign finance and health care reform, Bradley's chosen issues.[6] Heading into New Hampshire, Gore seemed unstoppable. Bradley also understood that if his campaign train were ever going to leave the station, it had to start in the New Hampshire terminal.

The Granite State's results turned out to be reasonably close, 49.7 percent for Gore to 45.6 percent for Bradley. But the New Hampshire primary solidified the belief that although Bill Bradley could win the support of anti-Clinton voters and well-educated white males, he could not garner enough support among core Democrats to carry the nomination. (See table 2-3 for complete results of the Democratic primaries.) Gore's coalition of Clinton supporters, union workers, and other voters who traditionally form the heart of the party[7] was just too strong. Even in New Hampshire, a state that has often been kind to insurgent Democratic outsiders (such as Eugene McCarthy in 1968, Gary Hart in 1984, and Paul Tsongas in 1992), Gore could not be defeated. Given this fact, one wonders what New Hampshirites would have done had they realized John McCain would win his GOP bid in a landslide. Would enough Independents have moved over to the Democratic side to produce *two* outsider victories—McCain *and* Bradley? The question is unanswerable, but the scenario seems likely.

After New Hampshire, Bradley continued his campaign, but his chances for victory had all but vanished. Gore handily defeated Bradley in California, New York, and other key Super Tuesday primaries. Bradley withdrew from the presidential race on March 9,

Table 2-3.
Results of All the Democratic Primaries

Date	State	Gore	Bradley	Total Vote
February 1	New Hampshire	49.7	45.6	154,639
February 5	Delaware	57.2	40.2	11,141
February 29	Washington	68.2	31.4	297,001
March 7	California	81.2	18.2	2,654,114
March 7	Connecticut	55.4	41.5	177,301
March 7	Georgia	83.8	16.2	284,431
March 7	Maine	54.0	41.3	64,279
March 7	Maryland	67.3	28.5	507,462
March 7	Massachusetts	59.9	37.3	570,074
March 7	Missouri	64.6	33.6	265,489
March 7	New York	65.6	33.5	974,463
March 7	Ohio	73.6	24.7	978,512
March 7	Rhode Island	57.2	40.6	46,844
March 7	Vermont	54.3	43.9	49,283
March 10	Colorado	71.4	23.3	88,451
March 10	Utah	79.9	20.1	15,687
March 11	Arizona	77.9	18.9	86,762
March 14	Florida	81.8	18.2	551,995
March 14	Louisiana	73.0	19.9	157,551
March 14	Mississippi	89.6	8.6	88,602
March 14	Oklahoma	68.7	25.4	134,850
March 14	Tennessee	92.1	5.3	215,203
March 14	Texas	80.2	16.3	786,890
March 21	Illinois	84.3	14.2	809,648
April 4	Pennsylvania	74.6	20.8	704,150
April 4	Wisconsin	88.5	8.8	371,196
May 2	D.C.	95.9	---	19,417
May 2	Indiana	74.9	21.9	293,172
May 2	North Carolina	70.4	18.3	544,922
May 9	Nebraska	70.0	26.5	105,271
May 9	West Virginia	72.0	18.4	253,310
May 16	Oregon	84.9	---	354,594
May 23	Arkansas	78.6	---	230,197
May 23	Idaho	75,7	---	35,688
May 23	Kentucky	71.3	14.7	220,279
June 6	Alabama	77.0	---	278,527
June 6	Montana	77.9	---	87,867
June 6	New Jersey	94.9	---	378,272
June 6	New Mexico	74.6	20.6	132,280
	Total	**75.7**	**20.0**	**14,024,664**

SOURCE: Rhodes Cook, *The Rhodes Cook Letter*, May 2001.

the same day as John McCain's swan song. Interestingly, he refused to endorse Gore formally for several weeks, and his manifest lack of enthusiasm for the vice president may have contributed to Ralph Nader's vote total in November.

Following his quick and relatively effortless elimination of Bradley, Gore was able to gain confidence and conserve a good deal of money in preparation for the campaign against Bush. Although Bush had raised $37 million by July 1999[8] and opted to become the first winning presidential candidate to forgo federal primary funding (and obligatory spending limits that came with it), he had to devote a great deal of money to wearing down the McCain campaign.

Gore went on to win every primary and caucus he contested, the first time a non-incumbent candidate had done so since Richard Nixon in 1960.[9] However, Gore seemed to take a break from the spotlight between the primaries and his convention, and he allowed Bush to unveil program packages on taxes, education, and Social Security without much response. Oddly, Gore may have lost ground to Bush by winning too easily over Bradley. Perhaps if he had struggled a little more in the primaries, he might have better understood the challenges ahead. The strategies and events of an election often have unpredictable consequences, and one can lose by winning and win by losing. Pundits confidently and instantly explain everything in the newspapers and on television, but maybe the unanswered questions remaining many months after the 2000 battle should remind us to pay little attention to the punditocracy.

Once the dust settled from the primaries and the intraparty acrimony subsided, both parties solidly backed their respective choices. Bush supporters understood that their candidate needed to renew his appeal to independent and moderate voters after being pushed to the right by McCain, but for the most part they believed the Clinton scandals and an itch for change gave them a good shot at the White House. Gore's camp believed that Bradley had left Gore relatively unscarred, and the Democrats were convinced that the ever-potent combination of peace and prosperity, plus a far more experienced candidate, would deliver unto them a third consecutive victory in November. As the indecisive fall results proved, both sides were mainly correct.

THE VEEP-STAKES: ADDRESSING THE PRESIDENTIAL CANDIDATES' WEAKNESSES

At a gut level, Americans had generally discovered the fundamental strengths and weaknesses of both candidates by the summer of 2000. Al Gore was viewed as the most qualified candidate for president, but he lacked any magnetism or charisma, as well as a sense that he was comfortable with himself—not to mention all the heavy Clinton baggage he carried. On the other hand, George W. Bush was personable and likable, but many Americans doubted that he was experienced, competent, or moderate enough to serve in the highest office in the land.

Both candidates did a commendable job of selecting running mates that helped to make up for their personal and professional limitations. On July 25, Bush tapped Dick Cheney, former White House Chief of Staff and former Secretary of Defense, to share his ticket. Cheney, a conservative former congressman from Wyoming, was simultaneously associated with both the moderate Gerald Ford–George Bush, Sr., wing of the GOP and the party's more rightist, Reagan wing. When chosen, Cheney had been serving as the head of George W. Bush's vice presidential selection process, which caused many to be surprised if not cynical at the search's outcome. Cheney was selected over a more politically useful Tom Ridge (moderate Governor of Pennsylvania, who would have likely contributed the Keystone State's 23 electoral votes to Bush) and ex-Missouri Senator John Danforth, another relative centrist. Yet Cheney brought to Bush's campaign the gravitas and experience in foreign policy and domestic matters that Bush sorely lacked. Bush's nomination of such a seasoned veteran—someone with an impeccable résumé—satisfied most Republicans and reassured most Americans. The decision demonstrated in part that Bush was looking past the politics of the election to the job of governing. Although the bland and understated Cheney (hailing from one of the least populous and most heavily GOP states in the nation) would bring Bush few additional votes directly, virtually everyone agreed that Cheney would make an excellent statesman and adviser to a President Bush. The major doubts raised by Cheney critics were his strongly conservative congressional voting record, his ties (like Bush) to big oil companies,[10] and his health (Cheney had already suffered three heart attacks prior to his selection). The questions about his health would resurface later in the campaign, and again in the interregnum following Election Day when Cheney had his fourth heart attack.

On August 7, Vice President Gore made public his dramatic selection for a vice presidential running mate: Connecticut Senator Joseph Lieberman, a longtime leader of the relatively moderate Democratic Leadership Council and the first Jewish major-party nominee in United States history. Lieberman emerged from a short list of potential candidates, which included Senators John Kerry of Massachusetts, John Edwards of North Carolina, and Evan Bayh of Indiana, as well as House Minority Leader Dick Gephardt of Missouri and New Hampshire Governor Jeanne Shaheen. Pundits emphasized the religious precedent as well as Lieberman's integrity and reputation as a strong moral leader. He was one of only a few Democratic senators who openly and seriously chastised Clinton during the impeachment trial, and thus many believed that he would help distance Gore from the Clinton scandals. Lieberman was also genial and charismatic, and he energized Democratic voters—and electrified Jewish voters in states such as Florida—in a way that Gore had never achieved on his own.

CONVENTIONAL WISDOM: THE PARTY CONCLAVES CREATE "TEMPORARY UNREALITY"

Earlier in the political history of the United States, national presidential conventions served to bring the party faithful together to select their nominee for the nation's highest office. Conventions were often exciting because of uncertainty, and they represented politics as an art in both its admirable and corrupt forms.[11] In the last forty years, however, conventions have evolved largely into spectacular, ritualistic artifices created of, by, and for the news media and the political necessities of the moment. Although candidates and parties in some years head into their respective conventions with the nomination undecided (such as 1976 for the Republicans and 1984 for the Democrats), most modern conventions are scripted theatrical parades organized for the sole remaining candidate, intended to unify and excite the party as well as influence the unaligned voters. The reality of modern conventions is precisely that they are *unreal* events. The party's architects project an image of their party to the public, and that image is usually comprised of half truth and half hypocrisy. The mirage of the modern convention therefore creates, if not temporary insanity, a temporary unreality that works magic on public opinion polls released at the conclave's end.

Although national conventions since 1960 have usually been covered in the national media as events whose outcomes have a critical impact on the November election, history has repeatedly shown that pre- and post-convention hoopla can be way off base and have little or no bearing on Election Day. For example:

- The 1968 Democratic convention ended amid severe factionalism and massive rioting in the streets of the host city, Chicago. Democratic nominee Hubert H. Humphrey was written off as politically dead in the aftermath of the convention, but he was able to revive his campaign and come within 0.7 percent of the popular vote to nearly defeat heavily favored Republican Richard M. Nixon.

- In 1976 Jimmy Carter received a major bounce from the Democratic Convention and led Gerald Ford, whose challenge from Ronald Reagan had divided the Republicans, by nearly 33 percentage points in the polls. Then Carter's lead shrank rapidly and he managed only a slim victory over Ford, 50.1 percent to 48 percent.

- Following a huge lift from his nomination of Geraldine Ferraro as the first female vice presidential candidate, Democrat Walter Mondale finished the 1984 party convention with a 2-point lead over the incumbent, Ronald Reagan, only to fall in a whopping landslide, losing by 17.7 percentage points and 49 states.

- In 1988, Democratic nominee Michael Dukakis led Vice President and Reagan heir George H. W. Bush by a wide margin in the polls following his convention, but he succumbed to Bush by a large margin (53.4% to 45.7%) in November.

- Bill Clinton boasted a mammoth lead in the polls following his upbeat 1992 Democratic convention and Ross Perot's simultaneous withdrawal from the race. But Perot's October reentry and support from an unanticipated 19 percent of the electorate for the quirky Texan created a much less convincing Clinton win than projected following the conventions. (Clinton received just 43 percent of the popular vote.)

Examples of this "living in the moment" sentiment abound from both the Republican and Democratic conventions in 2000. On August 3, 2000, the final night of the Republican convention in Philadelphia, CNN pundit Mark Shields followed George W. Bush's keynote address by commenting, "The debates, now, are clearly the

Democrats' fallback position. Democrats were counting on [Bush] to stub his toe, to fall on his face, here at the Convention, with his speech. They have to be sorely disappointed." The pundits were also quick to pronounce likely Democratic defeat for Gore after the first full day of the Democratic convention in Los Angeles. Reporter John King commented, "They're [the Democrats] not expecting as big a bounce out of this convention as they might have hoped for coming in." In reality, the Democrats came in hoping to get a bounce that would bring Gore even with Bush in the polls. The boost they got from the convention actually gave Gore his biggest lead of the campaign.

In fairness, CNN was hardly the only news organization to misdiagnose the impact of the media show on the outcome of the election in November. While CNN should be saluted for its around-the-clock, in-depth coverage of both conventions, being so entirely caught up in the spectacle of the conventions undoubtedly caused this network and others to severely overestimate the actual importance of these events.

REPUBLICAN CONVENTION: THE INCLUSION ILLUSION?

The Republican delegates arrived in Philadelphia in late July preparing for a different kind of convention. George W. Bush and his team descended on the City of Brotherly Love with a growing lead in the polls and a positive message of unity, progress, moderation, and inclusion. Held at the Comcast Spectator First Union Center from July 31 to August 3, the 2000 Republican convention marked the tenth time that Philadelphia had hosted a presidential nominating convention.

The Republican convention strategists attempted to shed the party's hard-right image and move themselves firmly into the moderate mainstream, an effort echoed in the convention's theme, "Renewing

31

America's Purpose. Together." The unconventional format focused on courting minorities without alienating the party's conservative base. The selection of Representative J. C. Watts Jr. of Oklahoma (an African American), Representative Henry Bonilla of Texas (a Hispanic), and Representative Jennifer Dunn of Washington as convention co-chairs was symbolic, as was the endless parade of minority speakers addressing the delegations over the four days of GOP brotherly (and sisterly) love.

Critics challenged the Republican claims of inclusion as phony, with Democratic vice presidential nominee Joe Lieberman stating, "Not since Tom Hanks won an Oscar has there been that much acting in Philadelphia."[12] A look at the Republican convention shows that the delegates were not really a mirror of America, but instead a mirror of the elite in America. Approximately 83 percent of the delegates to the Republican National Convention were white, while African Americans, Hispanics, and Asian Americans made up 8 percent.[13] The Democratic delegations, by comparison, were about 35 percent minority.[14]

The first night featured a diverse cast of speakers who hailed the "compassionate conservatism" of George W. Bush and a rousing challenge from the former Chairman of the Joint Chiefs of Staff, General Colin Powell, who forcefully urged the delegates to do more to live up to their legacy as the party of Lincoln. On a night devoted to the theme of leaving no child behind, Powell delivered a stirring call to arms, asking his party "to bring the promise of America to everyone" and praising Bush as a Republican who could "bridge the racial divides in America." Laura Bush, the candidate's wife, also addressed the convention on its first night.

The second night concentrated on energizing the Republican base across the country by recognizing the achievements of the three living Republican presidents, starting off with a video tribute to the GOP's reigning icon, Ronald Reagan. The short video brought tears to the eyes of many in attendance, and the nostalgia extended to former

Presidents Gerald Ford and George H. W. Bush, both of whom were present at the convention with their wives. Former Senate Majority Leader and 1996 presidential candidate Bob Dole and retired General Norman Schwarzkopf spoke about the importance of military readiness, and they honored veterans of America's wars. Condoleezza Rice, an African-American woman serving as foreign policy adviser to Governor Bush, discussed international relations. Rice was followed by Elizabeth Dole, who had been running her own presidential bid just a few months earlier.

The political highlight of the evening was a speech by Senator John McCain. The Arizona politician had a higher approval rating in the polls than either Bush or Gore and was especially favored by independents and ticket splitters, whose votes would decide the election. Considering McCain's rocky relationship with Bush, his endorsement was relatively enthusiastic. McCain told the cheering delegates and a national television audience that his erstwhile rival was a man "of courage and character" who would "confidently defend our interests and values wherever they are threatened." This "hail and farewell" is a staple of successful conventions: Losing candidates graciously withdraw and praise the victor, whether they genuinely offer the accolades or not.

The third day, Wednesday, August 2, was marred by an announcement of the hospitalization of former President Gerald Ford, who suffered a mild stroke late on the previous evening. Although Ford was in good condition, the extensive coverage of his situation over several days drew substantial attention away from the Bush message. Such is the intrusion of the real world into the unreal one of a convention.

Later that evening, vice presidential nominee Dick Cheney took the podium and delivered a blistering attack on Clinton and Gore for making Washington "a scene of bitterness and ill will and partisan strife." He assured the crowd in the convention hall and listeners across the country that a victory by Bush would "restore decency and integrity to the Oval Office." Cheney delivered the most partisan speech of the convention and effectively put some bite into the Republicans' feel-good convention,[15] firing up the crowd by repeatedly interjecting Clinton and Gore's 1992 campaign mantra, "It is time for them to go."

On the final night of the convention, the stage was set for George W. Bush to accept his party's nomination for president of the United States. Throughout the campaign, Bush had understandably been criticized for his lack of oratorical skill, and his address at the convention would be the most scrutinized speech to date. In a 50-minute address described varyingly as "confident," "successful," "magnificent," and "very presidential,"[16] Bush laid out his policy objectives, emphasized his belief in compassionate conservatism, and summarized his positions on key Republican issues, including abortion, tax cuts, military readiness, and retirement savings. He also soberly jabbed at Clinton and Gore, criticizing them for squandering opportunities: "This administration had its moment. They had their chance. They have not led. We will." The speech capped a tightly scripted and virtually bicker-free week, one clearly calculated to appeal to the independents, who told pollsters they were turned off by the more vicious forms of political warfare.[17]

Bush left Philadelphia with his party unified and his campaign team ready. Despite the lingering criticism that the convention's widely touted theme of inclusion was a political sham orchestrated to put a softer, more welcoming face on unyielding conservative principles, Bush succeeded in garnering an ample "bounce" in most polls following the Republican convention. Against the backdrop of Independence Hall and the Liberty Bell, and lulled by the temporary unreality of the event, Republicans ended the convention energized by their new nominee and overwhelmingly confident about their chances of recapturing the White House.

DEMOCRATIC CONVENTION: ELVIS HAS *FINALLY* LEFT THE BUILDING

Beginning 11 days after the Republican convention, the 2000 Democratic convention was held at the Staples Center in Los Angeles from August 13 to August 16. Organizers evoked memories of the 1960 Democratic convention (the last to be held in Los Angeles), where Massachusetts Senator John F. Kennedy was nominated. Unlike Kennedy, whose selection as the Democratic nominee to challenge two-term Republican Vice President Richard M. Nixon was not certain, Al Gore arrived in L.A. as the unrivaled heir to the mantle being passed by two-term President Bill Clinton. Gore had been lagging behind Bush in every poll leading up to the convention, and he hoped that a stellar performance and smooth passing of the torch would inspire Democrats.

Gore faced several important challenges at the convention. First, he had to escape the expansive shadow of his predecessor, Bill Clinton, whose eight years were indelibly marred by only the second impeachment trial in U.S. history. Gore had to convey to a large national audience that he was due credit for the accomplishments of the Clinton-Gore administration but was not to blame for the disgrace of Clinton's personal behavior. He had to come across as his own man, with an outstanding record and leadership abilities, and also as a person who was genuine and comfortable with himself. As former Clinton White House Chief of Staff Leon Panetta put it:

> Al Gore has to understand that first and foremost, he has to be who he is. If he can nail that down, then I think he will be in great shape. If he can't, if there's a sense that this is all kind of another programmed speech of some sort, then I think he's going to be in trouble. [18]

Amid extravagant pre-convention parties and fund-raisers by high-profile celebrities such as Magic Johnson, Hugh Hefner, and Barbara Streisand, Bill and Hillary Clinton at first stole the show and basked in the Hollywood spotlight. The convention's first day was inevitably theirs, too, as President Bill Clinton symbolically stepped aside for his vice president. Following a dramatic, televised entrance through a series of winding corridors, Clinton delivered an electrifying speech that chronicled the accomplishments of his administration and offered a sharp rebuttal to Republican criticism that he had squandered his presidency, claiming the nation's prolonged economic boom was "a matter of choice ... not a matter of chance." Clinton praised Gore as the candidate who would "keep our prosperity going," and he sought to give Gore a major boost by linking him to the economic prosperity and major foreign and domestic accomplishments of the previous eight years—a feat Gore himself had failed to achieve. Harking back to Ronald Reagan's now-famous 1980 campaign refrain, Clinton asked the delegates and the national audience, "My fellow Americans, are we better off today than we were eight years ago?" And then with cheers rising in the arena, he added, "You bet we are." Following the speech, Clinton left Los Angeles, to the relief of the Gore forces.

Although party officials shrugged off accusations that Clinton was stealing the spotlight from Gore, there was no question that the President was the center of attention until his departure. As one journalist commented following Clinton's address:

> Elvis has left the building. President Clinton, the Democratic Party's ultimate rock star, exited the stage Monday, leaving an adoring crowd begging for more. ... Now America will learn if the Democratic Party's new headliner can fill the void. Are Democrats getting Jimi Hendrix, an innovator who will lead the party in a new direction, or an Elvis impersonator? [19]

Democrats began to refocus for the second day of the convention. Just as the Republicans used the second night to energize their base voters, the Democrats brought out the lions of the liberal wing to encourage

Table 2-4.
Selected Contrasts in the 2000 Party Platforms

Democrats		*Republicans*
Democrats responsible for "longest economic expansion in American history."	**Economy**	"Inspired by Presidents Reagan and Bush," Republicans hammered into place the framework for today's prosperity and surpluses.
Tax cuts for middle-class families; enable families to "live their values by helping them save for college, invest in their job skills and lifelong learning, pay for health insurance, afford child care, eliminate the marriage penalty for working families, care for elderly or disabled loved ones."	**Taxes**	Replace the five current tax brackets with four lower ones; help families by doubling the child tax credit to $1,000; encourage entrepreneurship and growth by capping the top marginal rate, ending the death tax.
Support a woman's right to choose to have an abortion in all circumstances currently legal. "Respect the individual conscience of each American on this difficult issue."	**Abortion**	Support a constitutional amendment outlawing abortion in all circumstances. No specific mention of tolerance for other views on abortion.
"Democrats believe in using our prosperity to save Social Security."	**Social Security**	"Personal savings accounts must be the cornerstone of restructuring."
Support strengthening public schools. "Advocate raises for teachers and accountability for under-performing schools."	**Education**	Favor using federal money to help parents pay private school tuition. "Support increased local and state control of education."
"We support continued efforts ... to end workplace violence against gay men and lesbians. We support the full inclusion of gay and lesbian families in the life of the nation."	**Gay Rights**	"We do not believe that sexual preference should be given special legal protection or standing in the law."
Support mandatory child safety locks, and a photo license I.D., a full background check, and a gun safety test to buy a new handgun in America.	**Gun Control**	"Defend the constitutional right to keep and bear arms" and favor "mandatory penalties of crimes committed with guns."
Emphasize government regulation to protect the environment.	**Environment**	Emphasize consideration of private property rights and economic development in conjunction with environmental protection.
Oppose revival of the land-based missile defense system, known as Star Wars.	**Star Wars**	Favor development of the missile defense system.

SOURCE: Karen O'Connor and Larry J. Sabato, *American Government: Continuity and Change* (New York: Longman, 2001), p. 481.

the party faithful, such as Massachusetts Senator Edward Kennedy, Reverend Jesse Jackson, and defeated candidate Bill Bradley. Kennedy remarked that Gore was only the third Democratic nominee that he had supported for president as early and as strongly; the other two were his brothers, John and Robert Kennedy. With the delegates rising enthusiastically to join him, Jackson chanted, "Stay out [of] the Bushes!" Bradley roused the crowd with his speech, saying, "We don't window-dress diversity, we're the party of diversity. We don't declare ourselves to be compassionate, we've been acting compassionately for decades. ... Don't read our lips. Watch what we do."

In the only piece of official business at the convention, the delegates approved an economically centrist party platform pitched toward swing voters, but they reaffirmed the party's traditional liberal social stands on abortion, gay rights, and affirmative action. The platform endorsed Gore's policies on education, trade, Social Security, and health care. (For a comparison of key points in both parties' platforms, see table 2-4.)

The next night, vice presidential nominee Lieberman addressed the delegates. In a passionate yet often humorous speech, Lieberman promised to "work my heart out to make Al Gore the president of the United States." Al Gore also took the stage that night, much to the surprise of many of the delegates. Following the remarks of his daughter and campaign adviser, Karenna Gore Schiff, the vice president appeared on stage and hugged his daughter prior to the ritual roll call of the states.

Thursday night, the convention came to a close with the acceptance speech by Vice President Gore, with Tipper Gore first taking the stage to introduce her husband. In an effort to humanize Gore and make him seem less rigid, Tipper used a video album of family pictures that included testimonials of family friends. When the vice president ascended to the podium, he embraced his wife and planted what was soon to be known across the country and on the late-night talk shows as "The Kiss," a passionate display—some would say too passionate and showy—that distanced him further from Clinton by emphasizing that he was in love with, and entirely faithful to, his wife. Gore then stood before the crowd, asserting that he was his own man and would continue the nation's prosperity. He drew sharp contrasts with his opponent on issues such as tax cuts and Social Security. Unusually animated and energetic, Gore cast himself as a populist who would battle against powerful special interests to ensure "that our prosperity enriches not just the few, but all working families."

Gore's speech, and "The Kiss," did the trick. For the first time in several months, Gore surged past Bush in the national polls, and in a nearly sleepless post-convention trip down the Mississippi River, the Democratic nominee sustained and extended his convention momentum. The country seemed to be giving Gore a second, more positive look, and Democrats allowed themselves the luxury of optimism about November for the first time in a long time. "Temporary unreality" had struck the Democratic party like a super-charged bolt of lightning from the election gods.

REFORMING THE REFORM PARTY AND THE GREENING OF AMERICA

A couple of sideshows unfolded in the summer of 2000, one of which was to prove critical to the final result in the presidential contest. First, the environmentally conscious and far-left-leaning Green Party nominated consumer activist Ralph Nader for the second consecutive presidential election. Nader had not campaigned at all in 1996, but he had still received 0.7 percent of the votes nationwide. For 2000, however, Nader promised a vigorous effort—a pledge that correctly sent chills down the spines of Gore supporters. While Nader might well increase the pool of voters casting ballots for Democratic Senate, House, and gubernatorial nominees, he would almost certainly take votes away from Al Gore in November. How many? The early readings were frightening for Gore: Nader was securing 7 percent of the national vote and over 10 percent in critical Democratic-leaning states such as Minnesota, New Mexico, Washington, Oregon, and a number of others. Nader's presence may well have kept Gore too far to the ideological left in the fall to secure the necessary plurality for victory, and Nader's vote total—though far smaller than early projections—was enough to deny Gore the White House, as we shall see in Chapter 5.

At the same time, George W. Bush faced a threat from the right. Ross Perot had refused to run for a third consecutive presidential election—he had garnered 19 percent of the national vote in 1992 and 8 percent in 1996—but Perot still hoped to keep control of his Reform Party, which he regarded as centrist. But no major centrist candidate stepped forward to claim the mantle. Instead, the Perot forces generally backed John Hagelin, an advocate of transcendental meditation who was also the repeat presidential nominee of the very small Natural Law Party.

Hagelin's goal, embraced by Perot's closest associates, was simple: to stop two-time Republican presidential candidate Patrick J. Buchanan from grabbing control of the Reform Party—and the $12.6 million in public funds due the party for the general election campaign.[20] Hagelin and Perot were unable to stop Buchanan, however, and the loyal "Buchanan Brigades" produced an easy victory for the right-wing populist at the Reform Party national convention in Long Beach, California, on August 10-13, 2000. The Bush campaign deeply feared Buchanan's potential to disrupt the GOP nominee's effort, not least because of the damage Buchanan had done to President George H. W. Bush while challenging the elder Bush's re-nomination in 1992, as well as Buchanan's strong showing against Bob Dole in the 1996 Republican presidential primaries.

These fears would prove unfounded, however. Republicans were unusually united in their determination to end the Clinton-Gore regime, and the Reform Party was badly split by the Buchanan takeover. Buchanan and the Reform Party withered into irrelevance during 2000.

BACK TO THE FUTURE

Truth be told, there was nothing terribly special about the 2000 nominating battles and conventions. The Republican establishment got its preferred candidate, just as it has done every four years since 1968. John McCain lost like all other GOP insurgents, including Ronald Reagan in 1976, Jack Kemp in 1988, Pat Buchanan in 1992 and 1996, and Steve Forbes in 1996 and 2000. The party clearly learned from its landslide defeat in 1964 when it last nominated a pure insurgent, Barry Goldwater.

On the Democratic side, the incumbent party was also in no mood for insurgency, having finally regained the presidency in 1992 with a centrist-liberal Southerner. Gore appeared much the same, and he was the logical Clinton successor, whether he thought of himself in quite that way or not.

Just as the nomination battles produced the expected outcomes, so too did the conventions follow the modern script, from opening gavels to unrelenting propaganda over four long days to post-convention poll bounces. All in all, it had been a series of politically ordinary moments. Nothing in the preliminaries foretold this campaign's extraordinary end.

NOTES

[1] McCain's book,. *Faith of My Fathers,* was published by Random House in August 1999.

[2] In his 1998 Texas gubernatorial reelection, Bush received 49 percent of the Hispanic vote, 65 percent of the female vote, and 27 percent of the African-American vote. See David Koenig, "Exit Polling Sheds Light on Bush's Appeal to Hispanics," Associated Press, November 4, 1998. Later, some Texas experts questioned the exit poll's Hispanic proportion for Bush, insisting the Republican's Hispanic total was at least 10 points *lower* than reported.

[3] David S. Broder and Dan Balz, "Bush and McCain Clash; GOP Rivals Debate Blame for Negative Campaigning," *The Washington Post*, February 15, 2000, p. A1.

[4] See *The Hotline*, "McCain: A Defining Moment?," February 29, 2000.

[5] Jonathan Salant, "Bradley Outraises Gore, 2-1," Associated Press, December 29, 1999.

[6] For exit polls from the 2000 primaries and caucuses, see http://abcnews.go.com/sections/politics/2000vote/exitpoll_by_state.html.

[7] Ibid.

[8] Don Van Natta, Jr., "Bush Forgoes Federal Funds and Has No Spending Limit," *The New York Times*, July 16, 1999, p. A1.

[9] William G. Mayer, "The Presidential Nominations," in Gerald M. Pomper et al., *The Election of 2000: Reports and Interpretations* (Chatham, NJ: Chatham House, 2001), p. 33.

[10] At the time of his nomination, Cheney was the CEO of Halliburton Company, one of the largest oil companies in the United States.

[11] For a further discussion of political conventions, see Larry J. Sabato and Bruce Larson, *The Party's Just Begun*, 2nd ed. (New York: Longman, 2002).

[12] Joseph Lieberman delivered the line in his address at the Democratic National Convention in Los Angeles on August 15, 2001.

[13] Eun Kyung Kim, "The typical GOP delegate? White, educated and middle-aged," Associated Press, July 29, 2000.

[14] At the 2000 Democratic National Convention, 20 percent of delegates were African American, 10 percent were Hispanic, 3.4 percent were Asian or Pacific Islanders, and 0.4 percent were Native American. Data from the Delegate Profile (DNC 8/700 estimates) at http://www.cnn.com/ELECTION/2000/conventions/democratic/.

[15] Mark Barabak, "The Republican Convention; Cheney Takes Aim at Clinton, Gore; Bush Nominated," *The Los Angeles Times*, August 3, 2000, p. A1.

[16] See *The Hotline*, "White House 2000: Bush Speech: How It's Playing," August 4, 2000.

[17] Ibid.

[18] "Politics: Advice for Gore: Convince Americans, Where Your Heart Is," nationaljournal.com, posted August 12, 2000.

[19] Michael Griffin, "Will Gore Set Agenda or Follow Clinton's?" *Orlando Sentinel*, August 15, 2000, p. A1.

[20] Under the Federal Election Campaign Act, if a third party secures at least 5 percent of the vote in an election for president, as Perot did in 1996, then in the next presidential election, the party is entitled to a share of the Presidential Election Campaign Fund (public tax money allocated by the tax check-off on the federal 1040 form). That share is proportionate to the party's showing in the popular vote in the previous election.

CHAPTER 3

Campaigns Matter:

The Proof of 2000

Charles Babington
The Washington Post and washingtonpost.com

Americans inevitably will remember the 2000 presidential election for its extraordinary conclusion in Florida. For Al Gore, it's just as well. Maybe historians will devote less attention to the missteps and missed opportunities that cost him a presidency he should have won.

Gore defenders will point to the campaign's challenges, including the increasingly Republican nature of the South, the Plains, and the Rocky Mountain states; the historic difficulty of electing a vice president to the presidency; and, above all, "Clinton fatigue."

But a more compelling case can be made—and some of Gore's closest associates now endorse it—that the 2000 campaign was Gore's to lose. And he lost it mainly because he never found a way to exploit his greatest political asset: the remarkably strong economy that emerged during the Clinton-Gore administration. Gore could not sufficiently embrace that record because he devoted so much energy to distancing himself from Clinton and his scandals. Unable to tie himself closely to the Clinton presidency's many good features, Gore seemed to argue more for change than continuity. That turned his campaign into a massive contradiction: If change is more desirable than staying the course, why elect an incumbent vice president instead of a reasonably attractive governor from Texas?

It was, one top Gore adviser told me, "a message at war with itself."[1]

Unofficially, of course, Gore did win the election. He garnered 540,000 more votes nationwide than did George W. Bush. He almost surely would have carried Florida if the infamous butterfly ballot hadn't confused so many Democratic-leaning voters in Palm Beach County. Moreover, Gore would have won Florida, and perhaps New Hampshire, if Ralph Nader had not been on the ballot. But here are some equally telling facts. Exit polls showed that 61 percent of those who voted on November 7 felt the nation was heading in the "right direction," while only 31 percent felt it was on the "wrong track." Similarly, 56 percent said the country "needs to stay on course," while 41 percent said it needed "a fresh start."[2] Given those solid margins of contentment, why was Gore—probably the most hands-on, influential vice president in history—fighting for his political life in Iowa, Minnesota, Wisconsin, and Oregon? Why did he lose states Clinton had carried in 1992, including West Virginia, Nevada, New Hampshire, Missouri, and, most painfully, his native Tennessee (any of which would have given him the presidency)?

One answer is that substantial numbers of feel-good voters opted for Bush, the non-Washington challenger, instead of Gore, the second most important figure in the eight-year Clinton-Gore administration. Bush got more than a third of the "right direction" voters, and 29 percent of the "stay on course" voters. Combined with his predictably large harvest of "wrong track" and "fresh start" voters, they provided just enough electoral votes to win the election.

Gore lost many of the "right direction" voters because he didn't make a convincing case that they needed his leadership to keep the good times rolling. In short, he never wrestled his Clinton problem to the ground, never devised a strategy to associate himself with the administration's impressive accomplishments while minimizing the damage of Clinton's Monica Lewinsky scandal and subsequent impeachment.

"If Gore had said, 'I helped create one of the greatest economies in history,' the voters wouldn't have said, 'Oh, he must be for the girlfriend,'" said Paul Begala, a Clinton political adviser who also worked for Gore's campaign. Gore could not completely avoid the Clinton scandal taint, Begala acknowledged, but he could have found more artful ways to signal that he differed sharply with the president on moral issues even though he embraced the administration's policies. "He could have said, 'I'm a man of faith and family,'" Begala said. "People would have gotten it."[3]

Easier said than done? Sure. But consider Bush's challenge. He had to persuade the American people to change leadership at a time of record-high employment, plummeting crime rates, shrinking welfare rolls, low inflation, easy credit, the transformation of federal deficits to surpluses, a remarkable stock market run-up, and the United States' unquestioned role as the world's military and economic superpower. Incumbents, not challengers, dream of running on "peace and prosperity." Gore, the closest thing to an incumbent on the ballot, had both by the truckload.

Equally important is what was *absent* from the 2000 political landscape. It lacked the widespread public anger or anxiety of the sort that triggered the ousters of four earlier presidents: Johnson's (and therefore Humphrey's) Vietnam in 1968; Ford's Watergate pardon in 1976; Carter's gasoline shortages and Iran hostages in 1980; and George H. W. Bush's recession in 1992.

There was, of course, one gigantic problem with the Clinton-Gore administration: the Lewinsky scandal and Clinton's impeachment. Some Gore associates blame their loss squarely on the scandal (a notion Gore seemed to embrace when he confronted Clinton in a heated White House meeting after the election). Bob Shrum, a key Gore strategist, told a University of Pennsylvania panel in February

2001: "If there had been no so-called scandals, does anyone doubt who would be sitting in the Oval Office today?"[4]

But the campaign's fixation on Clinton's scandals—and Gore's sometimes ham-handed efforts to distance himself—often pulled the Gore-Lieberman ticket away from its most positive and potent theme. As one adviser to both Clinton and Gore told me, Gore's message "was weaker than what everyone expected him to run on: Keep the good economy going."[5] By spending so much time and energy differentiating himself from Clinton, Gore ensured that the general election would be fought largely on turf favorable to Bush: character issues, where the Clinton administration faltered, rather than economic issues, where it shone.

It may be unkind, even unfair, to attribute so much of George W. Bush's victory to Al Gore's miscalculations. With few exceptions, the Bush-Cheney team ran a smart and solid, if unspectacular, campaign. Unlike Gore, Bush stuck to a handful of easily understood themes. He didn't panic when Gore overtook him in the polls for much of September. Bush's most publicized missteps weren't fatal, for they didn't strike his chief vulnerabilities. (A microphone caught him calling a *New York Times* reporter a "major league asshole." But it had little impact, in part because the rap on Bush was that he was a bit dim, not a nasty person.) Bush bungled some facts in the three presidential debates, but the press and public paid more attention to Gore's sighs and exaggerations.

By any measure, Bush's accomplishment was impressive. He ran and won as an outside challenger in a time of widespread contentment with the status quo. He positioned himself to take advantage of any opportunity—including Gore's failure to reap the full benefits of that public contentment.

Top Bush strategist Karl Rove was self-serving, but perhaps also accurate, when he told the University of Pennsylvania gathering, "We should have gotten our brains beat" because of the strong economy.

Rove said he was grateful that Gore hadn't focused more on the nation's "extraordinary peace and prosperity."[6]

THE CLINTON DILEMMA

In a post-election defense of Gore's strategy, senior campaign adviser Carter Eskew wrote in *The Washington Post* that voter anger over Clinton's scandals was "the elephant in the living room" of the 2000 campaign. Resentment of Clinton, he said, ran especially high among the all-important "undecided and soft voters in most battleground states."[7] Gore couldn't draw these voters' attention to the administration's accomplishments, the campaign strategists concluded, without also refueling their anger over Clinton's personal behavior. Gore's best hope therefore was to say he was campaigning "as my own man," emphasizing populist themes for working-class people who felt passed over by the affluence of the 1990s.

Gore pollster Stan Greenberg, an architect of this strategy, said the vice president couldn't get far on "peace and prosperity" because voters felt he played a minor role in the robust economy. "Anything we tried to take credit for just did not work," Greenberg said.[8]

Some prominent Democrats, however, believe that Gore's concerns about Clinton's perceived toxicity became a self-fulfilling prophecy. The campaign didn't try hard enough or creatively enough, they contend, to maximize Gore's association with administration accomplishments while subtly reminding voters that Gore's personal behavior hardly mirrored Clinton's—certainly in terms of sexual propriety.

Greenberg and his colleagues "drew too strong a conclusion" from their poll findings, said Begala, the Clinton and Gore adviser. He argued that Gore, from the very beginning, should have put more emphasis on his role in administration policy-making, while adding,

"You ain't seen nothing yet." Instead, Gore spotlighted his efforts to distance himself from Clinton. Understandably, that became a major theme of press coverage, diminishing Gore's role in the administration's achievements.

"When Gore dropped the Clinton-Gore accomplishments out of his message," Begala said, "he just looked like another politician trying to tear down his opponent."[9]

Whatever the wisdom of such arguments, it is clear Gore charted his course long before Greenberg polled swing voters in the fall of 2000. Gore formally announced his candidacy in Tennessee with a June 1999 speech that drew as much attention to his testy relations with Clinton as to his policy proposals. *Washington Post* reporter Ceci Connolly's front-page story said:

> With its numerous references to conscience, goodness and decency, Gore's speech stood in distinct contrast to the Clinton administration credo of public values over private behavior and marked the 51-year-old Democrat's formal break from President Clinton. ... [Gore] is still struggling to find a way to both exploit the Clinton connection (strong economy, popular policies) and distance himself from the Clinton taint.[10]

Within days, it seemed that Clinton was almost as much a Gore opponent as were Bill Bradley and George W. Bush. A follow-up *Washington Post* story said:

> Long-simmering tension between advisers to President Clinton and Vice President Gore boiled over anew yesterday in a dispute about Gore's political strategy of trying to distance himself from Clinton's scandal-tarred personal life. The dispute is the latest example of the sniping and recriminations that have become common this year between the Clinton and Gore

> camps—a rivalry that is souring a once-smooth
> working relationship between the president and vice
> president and is becoming a significant stumbling
> block for Gore as his campaign tries to take off. ...
> One Clinton adviser said: "Gore's campaign is trying
> to make Bill Clinton their primary opponent. That is
> absolutely nutty."[11]

With so much early focus on his differences with Clinton, Gore could
not switch tracks and claim more credit for administration
achievements in the fall of 2000. Had he tried, the news media and the
Bush campaign would have hammered him for hypocrisy and lack of
convictions. In the election's closing days and weeks, Gore and his
aides barred Clinton from going into battleground states to campaign
for the ticket. They defended this controversial decision by saying
polls indicated the president's presence would do more harm than
good. In truth, Gore had closed off his options long ago, starting with
his 1999 announcement speech. Dispatching Clinton to Arkansas,
Florida, West Virginia, New Hampshire, or Nevada—states that some
Democrats felt the president could have saved for Gore—would have
triggered damaging national stories about Gore's strategic flip-flop,
top advisers to both the Bush and Gore campaigns said in post-
election interviews.

There's another strong hint that Gore's rejection of Clinton's
campaign help was rooted in matters that long preceded Greenberg's
polls in the autumn of 2000. In 1976, at age 27, Gore had forbidden
his father to campaign for him when he launched his first campaign—
for the U.S. House seat in Tennessee once held by Albert Gore, Sr. "I
must be my own man," Gore told his father, a former senator.[12] Those
words were almost identical to the ones Gore used in 2000 explaining
why he wanted minimal help from Bill Clinton. Several Gore
associates believe his decision was a complex mix of campaign
calculations and personal passions. Begala called the highly
publicized distancing from Clinton "a mistake of political strategy and
a massive psychological issue."[13]

Perhaps Carter Eskew was right. Perhaps Clinton's scandals were the elephant in the living room, too huge and odorous for Gore to overcome. Other Democratic activists, however, contend there was another monstrous presence, which might have trumped the elephant: the remarkably strong economy and the low crime rates and falling welfare rolls it helped spawn. Gore largely forfeited that gift, they lament, because it was tied to the man he would not embrace.

BUSH'S MOMENT OF PERIL

Since righting himself in the South Carolina primary and dispatching John McCain, Bush had run a smooth campaign, culminating in the GOP's well-choreographed convention in Philadelphia. But the Democrats' convention climax on August 17 triggered a four-week slide for Bush. After months of riding high, he fell behind Gore in virtually every poll, just as the serious campaign season began. Bush or his advisers made peculiar gaffes each time they seemed ready to regain their footing, and they spent precious hours on the phone trying to reassure supporters who saw their hopes slipping away. Mid-September would mark Bush's greatest moment of peril, when less steely campaigns might have panicked. "We told everyone the race would be even after the conventions," Bush pollster Matthew Dowd told me in a post-election interview. "But when we're 15 points up, nobody believes it. … When it happens, a bunch of people freak out and don't remember you told them it would happen."[14]

Bush's slide began with Gore's well-received convention speech and four-day boat trip down the Mississippi. The Bush team initially dismissed the riverboat cruise as silly, but later realized it was smart. It allowed Gore to campaign in heavily contested eastern Iowa, where Bush had not gone because airports couldn't accommodate his large plane. (Bush would lose Iowa by three-tenths of a percentage point.[15])

As the riverboat trip ended, a *Washington Post*/ABC News

nationwide poll found Gore with his first clear lead over Bush, 50 percent to 45. Less than two weeks earlier, Bush had led by 9 points. Suddenly, Bush seemed able to do little right. In Peoria, Illinois, he mangled the details of his signature $1.6 trillion, 10-year tax-cut proposal, forcing an aide to clarify his remarks to reporters. As August ended, the Republicans aired a harsh TV ad, challenging Gore's credibility by showing footage of his infamous 1996 Buddhist temple visit and mocking his claim that he helped create the Internet. Many felt the ad undercut Bush's self-portrayal as a "uniter, not a divider" and a new kind of Republican who wanted to "change the tone" of Washington's attack-driven politics. Democrats were so pleased that they canceled their own ad ripping Bush's Texas record. Democratic spokeswoman Jenny Backus said the party was happy to "watch the Republicans shoot themselves in the foot."[16]

The Bush campaign hoped to regain its balance on Labor Day, the traditional kickoff of general elections. But in Naperville, Illinois, a podium microphone captured Bush muttering to his running mate, Richard Cheney: "There's Adam Clymer, major league asshole from *The New York Times*." "Oh yeah," Cheney replied. "He is, big time." TV networks and newspapers wrestled with how specifically to quote Bush's vulgarity, but in every case the story overshadowed the campaign themes Bush had hoped to highlight.

A week later, an even stranger story broke. *New York Times* political writer Richard Berke had a front-page story noting that a GOP television ad attacking Gore included a split-second flash of the word "RATS."[17] The ad, criticizing the Democrat's proposal for a Medicare prescription drug benefit, said, "The Gore prescription plan: Bureaucrats decide." The flash—too brief to detect without running the ad in slow motion—featured the enlarged last four letters of "bureaucrats." Democrats called it a deliberate, sneaky slur. Bush called it an accident, denying any intent to send subliminal (which he repeatedly pronounced as "subliminable") messages to voters.

Once again, news coverage focused on a Bush campaign oddity rather than the nominee's message. Pollster Matthew Dowd later said: "All we wanted to do was put together three or four days in a row where we got good press or Gore got bad press. But every time we'd have a good day, something would happen, like the RATS ad or the off-mike comment."[18]

Alex Castellanos, the ad's producer, had a reputation for hard-hitting commercials. But he told me after the election that he didn't know every detail about the flashing graphics, which were assembled by a video production company near Philadelphia.

"I saw the final ad," Castellanos said, "but I did not see that one frame out of the 900 frames" in the 30-second spot. In the end, he said, the dustup over the ad "didn't move any [poll] numbers. But it wasted three days. I cost my candidate three wasted days."

Castellanos said he doesn't know whether his subcontractors deliberately included the word "RATS." "Did an editor at 2 in the morning think this was cute?" he said. "I never asked, because I didn't want to know."[19]

The video production company that assembled the ad for Castellanos was Shooters Post & Transfer, in Cherry Hill, New Jersey. Company officials declined to be interviewed about the RATS ad. However, two sources familiar with Shooters—which produces political ads for Democrats and Republicans—said a campaign consultant typically would be closely involved in editing such a commercial.[20] The RATS ad was created with a high-tech editing system known as Fire, made by Discreet Logic. Its features, according to the Shooters web site, included an "unlimited number of animatable layers of type" and retouching capabilities such as "customizable clone, blur, smear, shade, warp and wash airbrushes."[21]

In mid-September, soon after the RATS ad story broke, Gore reached his high-water mark. A Pew Research Center poll found voters reacting favorably to his populist emphasis on progressive tax policy, prescription drug benefits for the elderly, and better health care. The survey of 1,495 likely voters found Gore leading Bush, 48 percent to 43 percent.[22]

If there was a moment when the Bush campaign might have cracked, this was it. Gore's post-convention bounce had proved more than a blip. His lead in the polls was about to enter a fifth consecutive week—with the election less than eight weeks away. Bush's top advisers huddled in Austin, debating whether the governor should focus his attacks on Gore's issues or Gore's character. They decided they could not afford an either-or choice: Bush would have to pound away on both, simultaneously. "This is about issues," one adviser said, "but it's also about credibility."[23]

Bush launched his retooled strategy on September 18 in Kansas City, criticizing Gore's moderate tax-cut plan as "so targeted it misses the target." He didn't forget the character issue, telling Fox News: "I will not let this man distance himself from the previous administration."[24]

That was the sort of guilt-by-Clinton-association attack that Eskew and Greenberg felt was potentially potent. Begala and others had hoped Gore would counter with positive pitches about the Clinton-Gore administration's strong economic legacy. But in Las Vegas, Gore was sharpening a more negative message, saying big industries were gouging the little guy. Taking on one industry a day, he attacked managed-care companies, other health insurers, drug companies, and oil companies, arguing that he would protect Americans from powerful industries to which Bush was beholden.[25]

Democrats may argue for years whether Gore's emphasis on what's wrong, rather than on what's right, was the smart approach for an incumbent vice president. What's indisputable is that the next five days would bring a run of bad news and bad decisions for Gore, swinging the momentum back to Bush after a month of GOP stumbles.

Charles Babington

A TURNING POINT

The week of September 18 began with a *Boston Globe* story about Gore, pills, and a dog. Reporter Walter V. Robinson disputed an August speech in which Gore had claimed his mother-in-law paid $108 a month for the same arthritis medicine that the Gore family's dog used, at $38 a month.[26] Gore aides admitted the figures actually were estimates extrapolated from a report on prescription drugs. The story got wide attention, adding to Gore's reputation for exaggerated claims. Gore compounded the problem the same day, telling a Teamsters gathering that a favorite childhood lullaby was "Look for the Union Label." The song, Bush aides gleefully noted, was written when Gore was 27. Gore later said he had been joking, while a top aide said the vice president had confused the song with an earlier tune, "Don't Forget the Union Label."[27]

Gore made a bigger blunder on September 20, but this time his comments weren't accidental. After strenuous debate within the campaign, Gore publicly called on Clinton to release a portion of the Strategic Petroleum Reserve to help hold down heating-oil prices. Campaign aides knew the issue was politically risky because Congress created the reserve in the 1970s in the name of national security, not consumer comfort. Everyone knew that heating-oil prices were mainly an issue in the northeast, a must-win region for Gore. Energy Secretary Bill Richardson was among those urging Gore to tap the reserve, arguing that the nominee needed to be decisive and proactive in the emerging energy problem. Other insiders, including Treasury Secretary Lawrence Summers, tried to dissuade Gore, saying the move would look overtly political. Besides, they said, Clinton might decide to tap the reserve anyway.

Republicans pounced. Richard Cheney, campaigning in St. Louis, called Gore's decision "an expedient, crass political move that is not sound policy."[28] Gore added to his problems on September 22, telling reporters, "I've been a part of the discussions of the strategic reserve since the days when it was first established." As Bush noted the next day, "the reserve was established in 1975, two years before Al Gore even went to Congress."[29]

In the space of five days, Gore had been caught stretching the truth about his family's drug costs, a lullaby, and his role in creating an oil reserve. But none of these had the impact of his call for tapping the petroleum reserve, Bush advisers would say later. Juicy as that story was at the time, it soon faded from the news, as eyes turned to the upcoming debates. Looking back over the campaign's ebbs and flows, however, top GOP strategists said the oil decision proved to be a turning point. For weeks, they said, Gore had gotten many Americans to forget about his tortured defense of the Buddhist temple visit, and his break with Clinton on the Elian Gonzalez matter, which many saw as a blatant bid for Hispanic votes in south Florida. In one afternoon, Gore reminded voters of a side of him they didn't like.

"Gore started ticking down before the debates with the strategic oil reserve [issue]," said Castellanos. "People said, 'Oh, he's Clinton, he'll do anything to get elected.'"[30]

Dowd, the Bush pollster, said, "The Strategic Petroleum Reserve wasn't a big thing on its own. But according to our polling, it took away from the 'new Gore.' He did something the American public viewed as purely political. That was the first positive step to get us back on track."[31]

A top Gore strategist, who sided with the decision to tap the oil reserve, said campaign polling data suggested Gore "needed to do something" about rising energy prices. "We felt Clinton might do this anyway, so there was a sense of, 'Why not have Gore take a little credit?' We in the campaign underestimated the danger of that."[32]

With one bad week in September, Gore lost his edge on the eve of the three presidential debates, where many Democrats hoped he would put Bush away.

Charles Babington

THE DEBATES

Everyone knew the conventional wisdom. Gore was the experienced, pugilistic debater, the past conqueror of Ross Perot and Jack Kemp. Bush was the seldom-tested governor who mangled grammar and bobbled foreign leaders' names. Bush entered the first debate— October 3, in Boston—benefiting from low expectations. Still, Democrats hoped Gore could regain his form with a knockout punch.

It didn't happen. Bush held his own in an encounter that dwelt largely on tax cuts, Medicare, and prescription drugs. He gave a few questionable explanations of how his proposals differed from Gore's, but he committed no big blunders or gaffes. Gore was more aggressive, but with dubious results. He sighed audibly while Bush spoke, and he repeatedly asked for more rebuttal time, exasperating moderator Jim Lehrer. As for the Clinton-Gore administration's economic record, he basically kissed it off with one sentence: "We have this incredible prosperity, but a lot of people have been left behind."

Pundits and analysts generally agreed that the debate left the campaign unchanged. With momentum already shifting back to Bush, that was bad news for Gore, who needed to shake up the campaign dynamic. Things got worse when post-debate commentary turned largely to Gore's credibility. During the debate, Gore was cited for two relatively minor misstatements. When Gore said he had "not questioned Governor Bush's experience," Lehrer noted he had done so in an April interview. And Bush noted that during the Democratic primary, Gore had inaccurately said he co-sponsored the McCain-Feingold campaign reform bill.

Within a few days, reporters and campaign researchers uncovered two more alleged inaccuracies from the debate. Gore said a Florida man had written to him about his daughter's Sarasota high school being so crowded "they can't squeeze another desk in for her, so she has to stand during class." The school's principal said a desk was found for the girl fairly quickly. (The school system's superintendent eventually corroborated most of Gore's account, but by then the damage had been done.[33]) Later in the debate, Gore referred to the head of the Federal Emergency Management Agency, saying, "I accompanied James Lee Witt down to Texas" to inspect wildfires. Gore later acknowledged Witt was not on the trip.

If the nation had faced nuclear-flexing Soviets, urban riots, a recession, or a severe gasoline shortage—in other words, the types of dilemmas that animated some earlier campaigns—Gore's misstatements might barely have been noticed. Absent such issues, however, his credibility became a big topic. Bush told CNN that "Gore's pattern of exaggerations ... says something about leadership."[34]

On October 11, the day of the second presidential debate (in Winston-Salem, North Carolina), a *Washington Post*/ABC News poll found Bush leading Gore for "the first time since before the Democratic convention" in August.[35] The election was four weeks away.

In the second debate, Gore was so determined to avoid sighing and eyeball rolling that he seemed robotic at times. News accounts called the debate "extraordinarily civil"—again, not the best recipe for shaking up the campaign dynamic. This time, Bush was the one who made notable misstatements. Referring to a former Russian prime minister, Bush said some International Monetary Fund money had "ended up in Viktor Chernomyrdin's pocket." In fact, no such charges had been made. Bush also glossed over his role in blocking a Texas hate-crimes bill, and he wrongly stated that three (rather than two) Texas men were sentenced to death for a racially motivated murder. And yet Gore still made news on the credibility issue by apologizing during the debate for his earlier misstatements. "I'm sorry about that," Gore said, "and I'm going to try to do better."

Democrats fumed at what they saw as a double standard. The press and punditry flayed Gore for misstating facts, they said, but let Bush off with a slapped wrist. They had a point. But Gore, with boasts such as his Internet-invention claim, had established his reputation as an exaggerator years earlier. When he stretched the truth in the 2000 campaign, he reinforced people's preconceived notions of his faults. For George W. Bush in 2000, the danger of misnaming a foreign capital or leader was not as great as showing a fundamental misunderstanding of international policy. Although he bungled some facts in the Winston-Salem debate, those mistakes created few waves because they didn't reflect an inability to grasp the larger issues of the campaign.

By mid-October, polls suggested that Bush had gained the most from the first two debates, upending earlier expectations. Gore's top strategists grew testy, sometimes shouting at each other in strategy sessions about where and how their candidate should battle Bush. Campaign Manager William Daley, desperate to devise a way to stop the slide, put the strategists on a chartered flight back to the Nashville headquarters immediately after the second debate.

On October 17, the day of the last debate, a new *Washington Post*/ABC News poll showed Bush leading Gore by four points. "The poll showed that Gore has suffered a sharp drop in his credibility rating in recent weeks," the *Post* reported. "Last month, more than six in 10 voters said Gore was honest and trustworthy. Today, fewer than half shared that view."[36]

In the third debate—a town meeting format at Washington University in St. Louis—Bush restated his basic themes: Gore was "a big spender" who wanted a big government. Bush made no apology when moderator Jim Lehrer noted that much of his tax-cut plan would benefit the nation's wealthiest 1 percent. "Of course it does," Bush said. "If you pay taxes, you're going to get a benefit."

Near the debate's end, Gore turned to a theme he had largely ignored for months—the administration's economic record. "We have gone from the biggest deficits, eight years ago, to the biggest surpluses in history today," he said. "Instead of high unemployment, we now have the lowest African-American unemployment, the lowest Latino unemployment ever measured, 22 million new jobs, very low unemployment nationally. Instead of ballooning the debt and multiplying it four times over, we have seen the debt actually begun to be paid down." Gore hit the note again in his closing statement: "We've made some progress during the last eight years. We have seen the strongest economy in the history of the United States, lower crime rates for eight years in a row, highest private home ownership ever. But I'll make you one promise here: You ain't seen nothing yet."

Bush closed the debate the way he ended nearly every campaign speech, with a thinly veiled reference to Clinton's scandals. "Should I be fortunate enough to become your president," he said, "when I put my hand on the Bible, I will swear to not only uphold the laws of the land, but I will also swear to uphold the honor and the dignity of the office to which I have been elected, so help me God."

There, in the final minutes of the final debate, was the campaign in its essence. Bush's theme was familiar: The Clinton-Gore administration's scandals justified a change in leadership, even in the face of peace and prosperity. Gore's closing pitch was the one that Paul Begala and several other Democratic insiders had been urging for months. Was it too late?

THE FINAL SPRINT

With 20 days left, Gore decided to continue raising economic issues, telling voters the good times could disappear under Bush's tax-cut plan. He gave an interview on October 18 to Dan Balz and Mike Allen of *The Washington Post*. They wrote:

> Gore has been under pressure to refocus his campaign
> on the economy, but today he denied his reluctance to

talk about the gains of the past eight years was related to concerns within his campaign that such a strategy risked injecting President Clinton into the final days of the election. "Absolutely not," Gore said when asked whether he was reluctant to remind voters of Clinton. "All elections are about the future. I am proud of what I have been able to accomplish as part of this economic team that has brought about the strongest prosperity in the history of the country. But as I said at the convention, this election is not an award for past performance."

That same day, Gore reminded a Des Moines crowd that the Clinton administration had seen the creation of 22 million jobs, budget surpluses, even a drop in abortions. "Do we build on that foundation, or do we erode that foundation?" he asked.[37]

A day later, however, Gore seemed to shift his emphasis again. He told ABC's Regis Philbin that he hadn't conferred much with Clinton about his campaign "because it's something that you really have to do on your own."[38] Two days later, *The Washington Post* reported that friends of Clinton "said the president is bewildered that Gore is not more aggressively championing the administration's record and believes that it is a political miscalculation."[39]

With two weeks left, Gore decided to zero in on Bush's proposal to let workers divert some of their Social Security contributions to private investment accounts, such as stock funds. For months, Gore had contended the plan could force benefit reductions and jeopardize the entire program. His polls now told him many voters were concerned. Gore pounded his Social Security warnings into every battleground state with aggressive TV ads. "We think Social Security is enormously powerful," said campaign adviser Tad Devine. "That's why we've made a commitment to it."[40]

By October 25, most national polls showed the race tightening to a virtual tie. Bush decided to counterattack by hitting Gore squarely on the ethics issue. Before a raucous Pittsburgh crowd, he mocked Gore's 1996 claim of "no controlling legal authority" governing his questionable fundraising practices. Dwelling longer on Clinton's and Gore's scandals than he had all year, Bush said, "In my administration, we will ask not only what is legal, but what is right."[41]

With the election only days away, a major new poll indicated that Gore had failed to convince most voters that only he, not Bush, could keep the nation's prosperity going. Despite months of Democratic attacks on Bush's big tax-cut plan, only one-fourth of all voters felt it would hurt the economy, according to the survey by the Henry J. Kaiser Family Foundation and other institutions. Equally ominous for Gore, most voters felt Bush would be better at keeping U.S. jobs from moving overseas and at keeping the stock market rising.[42]

The campaign's final week was a frenzy of airport stops and TV commercials, fueled by the last of the millions of dollars both parties had raised. Each campaign brought about $23 million to that closing effort. But the Republican National Committee had somewhat more than the Democratic National Committee—$32 million to $26 million—for "soft money" ads (which were anything but soft in content).[43]

For the entire election cycle, Bush raised $193 million to Gore's $133 million. The RNC raised another $364 million; the DNC took in $242 million. The RNC's biggest source (nearly $90 million) was the finance/insurance/real estate industries, according the Center for Responsive Politics. That was the DNC's biggest source, too, but to the tune of a mere $41 million. The Democrats relied heavily on unions and lawyers to keep them competitive.[44]

Heading into the campaign's final weekend, most polls showed Bush holding a tiny edge. Then, on November 2, news broke that Bush had been charged with misdemeanor drunk driving in Maine in 1976, at age 30. Democrats alleged that Bush had covered up the incident, while Republicans cried "dirty tricks." Both campaigns were left to wonder what impact, if any, the eleventh-hour story would have. In the end, some Bush aides concluded it may have hurt the governor just enough to lead to the Election Day standoff. "Bush was doing OK going into the final weekend, until the DUI story hit," Alex Castellanos said. "That moved numbers. They lost a lot of steam."[45] (See Chapter 4 for more detailed coverage of the Bush DUI conviction.)

CONCLUSIONS

For nearly a year, Bush and Gore had largely ignored 33 states and vied for the 17 battlegrounds, including 5 of the nation's 10 biggest states: Florida, Pennsylvania, Michigan, Illinois, and Ohio. By Election Day, Ohio was in safely in Bush's camp, and Illinois was in Gore's. The election would turn on who could win the other three big states and several of the dozen smaller ones: Maine, New Hampshire, West Virginia, Tennessee, Iowa, Wisconsin, Minnesota, Missouri, New Mexico, Nevada, Oregon, and Washington. Gore had the tougher Electoral College challenge, and he nearly met it. He claimed Michigan and Pennsylvania, then Maine, Minnesota, and Washington. It would take several days to confirm his victories in Iowa, Wisconsin, New Mexico, and Oregon, all of which he carried by less than 1 percentage point. Bush took Missouri, Nevada, New Hampshire, West Virginia, and Gore's native Tennessee. Any one of those states would have given Gore the presidency, with or without Florida.

We will never know if Gore would have picked off one of those states had he devoted more of the campaign to touting the administration's eight-year record. But exit polls show that Gore made precious little headway on the route he chose instead: trying to ease voters' concerns about his character and the administration's ethics. When voters were asked what quality matters most in a president, the biggest group—24 percent—said honesty. And among those voters, Bush crushed Gore, 80 percent to 15 percent. Gore in turn clobbered Bush among voters wanting an experienced leader. The exit polls suggest that Gore might have won handily had he somehow neutralized the character question. When asked which nominee "would say anything to get elected," 48 percent of the voters said both or neither. Gore easily outpolled Bush among these people, who presumably saw neither nominee with a decisive edge in terms of character. Gore's downfall? Among the remaining voters, twice as many felt "only Gore" would say anything to get elected.[46]

In the end, maybe it all came down to Bush's Texas chumminess and Gore's standoffish, dodgy nature. "Gore is velcro. He's the kind of guy that bad stuff sticks to because he's not likable," said Alex Castellanos, drawing on campaign focus groups. "Gore gives you nothing of himself. So at the end of the day, he's expendable."[47]

Perhaps Gore could do little to make himself more likable, but he could control his campaign's focus and main themes. He decided to devote much of his attention, overtly or subtly, to a subject Bush was happy to engage—character and ethics. Ultimately, as the exit polls and vote tallies show, Gore got relatively little payoff. The strategy allowed Bush, meanwhile, to keep the spotlight off the weakest card in his hand: the robust economy of the previous eight years.

NOTES

[1] Interview with the author, May 15, 2001.
[2] Exit poll data, Voter News Service, November 2000.
[3] Interview with the author, May 17, 2001.
[4] Richard L. Berke, "Gore and Bush Strategists Analyze Their Campaigns," *The New York Times*, February 12, 2001, p. A19.
[5] Interview with the author, May 18, 2001.

[6] Richard L. Berke, "Gore and Bush Strategists Analyze Their Campaigns," *The New York Times*, February 12, 2001, p. A19.

[7] Carter Eskew, "The Lessons of 2000," *The Washington Post*, January 30, 2001, p. A17.

[8] Richard L. Berke, "Gore and Bush Strategists Analyze Their Campaigns," *The New York Times*, February 12, 2001, p. A19.

[9] Interview with the author, May 17, 2001.

[10] Ceci Connolly, "'Restless' Gore Launches Campaign of 'Values,'" *The Washington Post*, June 17, 1999, p. A1.

[11] John F. Harris and Ceci Connolly, "Rivalry Between Clinton and Gore Camps Gets Heated," *The Washington Post*, June 27, 1999, p. A2.

[12] Bill Turque, *Inventing Al Gore* (Houghton Mifflin: 2000), p. 113.

[13] Interview with the author, May 17, 2001.

[14] Interview with the author, May 14, 2001.

[15] Richard L. Berke, "Gore and Bush Strategists Analyze Their Campaigns," *The New York Times*, February 12, 2001, p. A19.

[16] Howard Kurtz, "GOP Goes on Attack in New Ad," *The Washington Post*, September 1, 2000, p. A1.

[17] Richard L. Berke, "Democrats See, and Smell, Rats in GOP Ad," *The New York Times*, September 12, 2000, p. A1.

[18] Interview with the author, May 14, 2001.

[19] Interview with the author, May 7, 2001.

[20] Interviews with the author, May 2000.

[21] Shooters web site, www.shootersinc.com.

[22] Thomas B. Edsall, "Populism 'Working' for Gore," *The Washington Post*, September 15, 2000, p. A18.

[23] Dan Balz, "Can Bush Prevent an '88 Repeat?" *The Washington Post*, September 17, 2000, p. A1.

[24] Dan Balz, "Bush Begins to Stress Differences with Gore," *The Washington Post*, September 19, 2000, p. A8.

[25] Mike Allen, "With Trustbuster Echoes, Gore Goes After Big Business," *The Washington Post*, September 19, 2000, p. A1.

[26] Walter V. Robinson, "Gore Mistates Facts in Drug-Cost Pitch," *Boston Globe*, September 18, 2000, p. A6.

[27] Mike Allen, "Bush Labels Gore's Remarks 'Misleading,'" *The Washington Post*, September 24, 2000, p. A14.

[28] Robert E. Pierre, "Going on the Attack, Cheney Finds Groove," *The Washington Post*, September 23, 2000, p. A14.

[29] Mike Allen, "Bush Labels Gore's Remarks 'Misleading,'" *The Washington Post*, September 24, 2000, p. A14.

[30] Interview with the author, May 7, 2001.

[31] Interview with the author, May 14, 2001.

[32] Interview with the author, May 5, 2001.

[33] Mike Allen, "Republican Father of the Standing Student Stands Up for Gore's Debate Description," *The Washington Post*, October 10, 2000, p. A5.

[34] Ceci Connolly and Terry M. Neal, "Nominees Carry Debate Themes Back on Road," *The Washington Post*, October 5, 2000, p. A18.

[35] Dan Balz and Claudia Deane, "Bush Overtakes Gore in Poll," *The Washington Post*, October 11, 2000, p. A1.

[36] Dan Balz and Richard Morin, "Bush Has Slim Lead on Eve of 3rd Debate," *The Washington Post*, October 17, 2000, p. A1.

[37] Dan Balz and Mike Allen, "Gore Pins Hopes on Economy," *The Washington Post*, October 19, 2000, p. A1.

[38] Ellen Nakashima and Eric Pianin, "President Laces Into GOP, Bush," *The Washington Post*, October 20, 2000, p. A1.

[39] Mike Allen and Ellen Nakashima, "Clinton, Gore Paths Unlikely to Cross Before Election Day," *The Washington Post*, October 21, 2000, p. A14.

[40] Dan Balz, "Gore to Attack Bush in Ads on Social Security," *The Washington Post*, October 22, 2000, p. A1.

[41] Mike Allen, "Bush Promises 'Responsibility Era," *The Washington Post*, October 27, 2000, p. A12.

[42] Dan Balz and Richard Morin, "Gore Has Yet to Make Sale on Economy," *The Washington Post*, October 27, 2000, p. A1.

[43] John Mintz, "Politics: Gore, Bush Nearly Even in Campaign Cash," *The Washington Post*, October 29, 2000, p. A25.

[44] Center for Responsive Politics web site, http://www.opensecrets.org/2000elect/index/AllCands.htm.

[45] Interview with the author, May 7, 2001.

[46] Exit polls, Voter News Service, November 2000.

[47] Interview with the author, May 7, 2001.

CHAPTER 4

In the Driver's Seat:

The Bush DUI

Timothy J. Burger[1]
New York Daily News

The buzz on the press bus started right after an afternoon rally at DuPage Community College in the Chicago suburb of Glen Ellyn. Five days out from the closest-ever U.S. presidential election, a local Fox TV affiliate in Maine was reporting that Governor George W. Bush had been arrested for drunk driving there some years ago. Communications director Karen Hughes would hold a briefing to explain when we got to the airport.

It was unclear at first if this was just one of those rumors that would occasionally sweep through the press corps. But sure enough, when the bus stopped at O'Hare Airport early on that chilly, windy evening of November 2—almost eight years to the day from Bill Clinton's first election to the White House—any doubts were erased. Instead of being led back to the safe belly of the campaign jet Bush had dubbed "Responsibility One," we were solemnly assembled in a surreal scene on the runway between the bus and the plane surrounding a little spot of tarmac where a mess of hot mikes was waiting for Hughes to meet the press.

In what would arguably be the most important press conference of her

Timothy J. Burger

life, a particularly tense Hughes admitted around 5:30 p.m. on live television that a 30-year-old Bush had been arrested in Kennebunkport on September 4, 1976, over Labor Day weekend for drinking and driving. He paid a $150 fine and had his driving privileges in Maine suspended after pleading guilty on October 15 of that year. During the press conference, Hughes stated:

> This was a mistake. This is something he is not proud of. Drinking and driving is wrong. It's a mistake he has made in the past and he's not proud of this. I think as a parent he knows this is something that does not set a good example. His own daughters did not know. Mrs. Bush is calling to let them know now.

Promptly pivoting into attack mode, Hughes began trying to fling the ugly story back onto the Gore campaign, saying, "I think the timing of an announcement like this, coming out four or five days before the election, about an incident that happened 24 years ago about which even the governor's daughters did not know, is certainly questionable."

"I hope that a mistake the governor made 24 years ago would not have an impact in the final days of this election," she added. Hughes had voiced the question that was suddenly on everybody's mind: Would the unprecedented last-minute revelation change the course of history?

A QUESTION OF BLAME

Aboard Air Force Two, Al Gore's consigliere, Chris Lehane, knew he would be facing questions like those raised by Hughes in Chicago. About fifteen minutes from landing in El Paso, Texas, en route to a rally in Las Cruces, New Mexico, Lehane had just gotten "this urgent call" from communications director Mark Fabiani, informing him "that a story had just moved on the wires saying X, Y and Z."[2] Lehane told me in May 2001 that he promptly peppered Fabiani on whether the Gore campaign could be blamed for leaking the report. "Obviously, the first tough question I was going to get was 'Did you guys have anything to do with this?' ... We did a quick canvass and no one seems to be aware of the campaign having anything to do with this. I then said, 'It's not going to take people long to start pointing fingers,' and he said, 'Yeah, basically it is what it is.'"

Worse still for Lehane, he is a native of Portland, Maine, just up the road a piece from Kennebunkport. Lehane knew the deflection the Bush campaign would attempt and that the suspicions of his opponents and the press would quickly point to him. But Lehane denied any role in the revelation. In the world of Lehane's trademark Irish-Italian rapier wit, his alibi came down to this, drawing a chuckle from Fabiani: "At that point, I said, 'I guess the best defense is [that] if I had given it out, I would have done it a lot sooner and I wouldn't have given it to Fox,'" the network with a reputation in some circles for schmoozing Republicans and spanking Democrats. "Bush's big vulnerability was that people weren't sure he was up to the job," Lehane fretted to me. "If it had hit three or four weeks earlier, it could have been the election. ... We would have at least won New Hampshire, if we couldn't get Florida."[3]

But now, Lehane had to tell Gore about the new wrinkle in a tumultuous campaign. The vice president took in the bizarre news impassively.

"Without missing a beat, he said, 'I guess I should do a press conference on this.'" Lehane was aghast.

"Sir, I don't think that's a good idea," the aide said. "And I looked at him and he had already started smiling. He had winked at the guys behind me. ... It was obviously very deadpan."

But as Lehane briefed Gore on the details, telling him, "I was going to say, 'It's not appropriate to comment at this time,'" everyone in the vice president's cabin knew it was just the calm before the storm.

Air Force Two landed, followed by the press plane. The press descended on Lehane. "It was the mother of all gaggles, and it was 150 press surrounding me."

INTOXICATING POLITICS

On September 4, 1976, Bush was hauled in after Officer Calvin Bridges saw him swerve onto the shoulder of a small local road just after midnight. Bush had been out for a night of drinking in a local bar with Australian tennis star John Newcombe, a longtime family friend, and Newcombe's wife. No one would quantify it at the time, but after Bush had safely won the election, Newcombe would be quoted by the online *London Telegraph* in March 2001 saying that Bush had downed about six beers—and cheerfully adding that he "went underground for several days" after the story broke to avoid being questioned by the media and potentially hurting Bush's campaign.[4] Bush would register 0.10 percent in a blood-alcohol test at the police station, though the Associated Press reported that other evidence released by the Maine secretary of state's office hinted that Bush's readout could have been as high as 0.12 percent.[5] (Either way, Bush registered significantly higher than the 0.08 percent blood-alcohol level allowed under a Texas law that the then-governor had signed in May 1999—with what was, in hindsight, an understandably low level of fanfare.) Also in the car had been Bush's 17-year-old sister, Dorothy, and her boyfriend at the time.

This incident was apparently a big part of what Bush had meant when he doggedly avoided answering specific questions about his party-boy days and instead made the vague but intriguing confession early in the campaign: "When I was young and irresponsible, I was young and irresponsible."[6] But it would conveniently take the Bush campaign precious days to spin out the details, such as exactly who was in the car (the name of Bush pal Pete Rousel was later added), whether Dorothy and her boyfriend were minors, and other elements of the long-ago evening.

Now, Bush and his wife, Laura, were scrambling to beat the media to telling their twin daughters, Jenna and Barbara, who were both 18 and college freshmen, an embarrassing story about their father that had pointedly been kept from them. Indeed, setting a good example for the girls would be the reason Bush gave for keeping the arrest secret until it came out in the media. "He talked to his daughters pretty quick after" the news hit, one Bush source said.

Needless to say, the Bush team was also mounting a supreme effort for political damage control. The story might have been devastating for any campaign, even if Gore allies weren't already working overtime to sow the seeds of doubt about Bush's gravitas and forthrightness about his past. It was compounded by the fact that Bush running mate Dick Cheney had admitted to two drunk-driving offenses in the early 1960s, when he was in his twenties.

Earlier in the day, the whole Bush team seemed to feel victory was theirs. Even the famously intense Hughes was joking around lightheartedly. When the campaign jet's takeoff on the way to Chicago was delayed because mechanics had discovered a faulty brake, she joked about the pilot's widely remarked-upon penchant for hard landings. "The way we land on this plane, who needs the brakes?" she said, after the plane was pronounced airworthy even with one set of brakes on the blink. "With seven sets of brakes, the Bush campaign is on to victory," she laughed. "No stopping us now."

Bush, meanwhile, had been coming in from rallies pumped up and reporting that he felt like he was connecting with his audiences as never before. "You sensed something different. ... He talked about, 'There's a lot of enthusiasm on our side,'" said one knowledgeable Bush source. "There was a sense of feedback from the crowd."

The DUI revelation seemed to put everything in doubt. In Austin, "people were just shell-shocked. Up until that point, things were just clicking," said one source. "All of a sudden this hits, and there was just dead silence" at campaign headquarters. "This was a body blow."

But it was a late hit, of which the media and the public tend to be deeply suspicious. The Bush team deftly took every opportunity to turn the nasty story back on Gore by immediately and repeatedly questioning its timing and origins, even before it emerged that a former Democratic candidate for governor of Maine had dished out the public but previously unpublicized information. They continued the accusations even though no evidence emerged that direct Gore operatives were responsible.

After Hughes's press conference, we clambered back on the plane. Our filing time had been an unusually long hour and 40 minutes at DuPage Community College—but the story of the day had changed. All the writers fired up their laptops. Some grabbed candy bars from the ready supply on board. A few reporters popped the usual evening beer for the flight to the Wisconsin State Fair Grounds in West Allis, a Milwaukee suburb, and another rally. At that point, it looked like Hughes's comments might be all that the Bush campaign would have to say on the matter. But at the front of the plane, Bush aides huddled to plot the next move.

Although Gore joked about holding a press conference, there was little he could really do. It was Bush who had to face the music that night. While it looked like the campaign might try to fend us off with the Hughes briefing, it was clear inside Team Bush that the candidate had to deal with the problem himself. "The decision was made, 'He has to get out there.' It was a question of when," said one knowledgeable Bush source. The idea was to do it at day's end. "Do the events that we had outlined that day and then have him talk afterwards so it didn't seem like we were screwing up the schedule," as one Bush operative put it. After tense talks on the flight to Milwaukee and the State Fair Grounds, the Bush high command arranged for the governor to address the story himself outside, after the rally.

Bush entered the rally to the pounding strains of Van Halen's "Right Now" and his other usual theme songs. Music from the Oak Ridge Boys had warmed up the crowd, and supporters waved signs around the arena with upbeat proclamations such as "W Wins Wisconsin" and "Character Counts." Bush gave his usual stump speech to the crowd of enthusiastic Republicans—most, if not all, of whom were blissfully unaware that their front-running presidential candidate's back was against the wall.

In some good news for Bush, supporters of the governor who were standing near the press corral reacted in angry disbelief when asked if they'd heard the DUI story on the news, immediately blaming the media and Gore for trying to tear down their man.

I asked a couple of the Bush backers there whether they had heard about the story—having been penned in place to await Bush, they hadn't—and what they thought of it. "It sounds like dirty politics, that's what I think," said a man who would give only his first name, Bill, and his age, 57. "When you're losing, you go negative and you dig in the dirt. That's what Gore's doing," Bill continued, on message even though he could not yet have heard the Bush campaign's prompt suggestion that politics was behind the story. "If you think that's bad, what about the arms deal between the Russians?" he added, referring to late-in-the-campaign reports that Gore had helped negotiate an arms trade compromise involving Russia and Iran.

Bush, meanwhile, said nothing of the matter in his remarks. But as the rally finished, we were hurriedly herded outside the Fair Grounds cow barn to a roped-off exit where the mikes were once again set up, flooded by television lights. After a few minutes, an almost serene Governor Bush emerged, wife Laura at his side, to face press questions for the first time in at least a month.

"Thank you all for—obviously there's a report out tonight that 24 years ago I was apprehended in Kennebunkport, Maine, for DUI. That's an accurate story. I'm not proud of that," he said. "I've oftentimes said that years ago I made some mistakes. I occasionally drank too much and did on that night. Was pulled over. I admitted to the policeman that I had been drinking, paid a fine. I regret that it happened. But it did. I've learned my lesson. I mentioned, many of you know, that I quit drinking alcohol in 1986. It was the right decision for me to make—then. Be glad to answer a few questions."[7]

Bush insisted he had never tried to conceal the incident. Asked why it hadn't come out until now, he said he had simply "made a decision that as a dad I didn't want my girls [to know about it when I] told them not to drink and drive. Decision I made. ... I didn't want to talk about this in front of my daughters. I told my daughters they shouldn't be drinking and driving," Bush said in an answer that almost seemed to foreshadow the trouble those daughters would court a few months later.

Then he pivoted into accusation mode, saying, "I think that's an interesting question: Why now?" He hammered the theme again when asked whether the episode was relevant to his candidacy. "No," he said. "I think the people knew that I had been straightforward, that I had made mistakes in the past. This happened 24 years ago. I do find it interesting that it's come out four or five days before an election. I've been straightforward with people saying that I used to drink too much in the past and straightforward with people saying that I don't drink now."

Bush repeated the theme again when asked what kind of night he'd had that could have led to such excess. "How many beers? Enough," he chuckled, "to have been in violation of the law. I can't remember how many beers—it was 24 years ago. And that's the interesting thing about this. Here we are with four days to go in the campaign."

Bush insisted that he had never lied about the incident, saying, "Yes I

76

was" when asked whether he'd been truthful about it—though the next day Wayne Slater, the Austin bureau chief of *The Dallas Morning News*, would assert that Bush had once told him he had never been arrested for anything other than a couple of well-known 1960s college pranks.[8] Bush also said he hadn't taken a field sobriety test. "No. I admitted I was wrong," he said when asked about that, though put in context it seems that Bush may have misunderstood or misheard the question. But aides would concede a day or so later that he had done so. "He did do one at the station, [a] walking a line type of thing," said campaign spokesman Dan Bartlett.[9]

Asked whether voters had a right to know about this arrest, Bush said:

> I told the people I had made mistakes in the past. And this was a mistake I had made in the past. I also told the people that in the past I had drunk too much at times. This was the case. And [as] I mentioned to you I'm a dad ... trying to teach my children right from wrong. I chose the course [for] my daughters, I was going to tell them they shouldn't drive and drink. And, uh, that's the course of action I took.

Hughes tried to end the session, but Bush continued. "And I'm the first to say that what I did was wrong. ... And I think the people of America will understand that. I think the interesting thing is, is that why five days before an election?" I asked Bush: "Why do you think it's happening now?"

"That's your job. I've got my suspicions," Bush said, ending the press conference. It would be the last time that Bush would make himself available for press questions before the November 7 election—and the last time he would field questions on his still murky history from the days when, by his own description, Bush had been "young and irresponsible."

The next day, Hughes implicitly linked the story to the reputation

Clinton-Gore allies had for slinging mud at their political enemies. "I think the American people are tired of this kind of 'gotcha' politics, are tired of this kind of last-minute dirty tricks, and I think the Democrats owe the American people an explanation," she said in another tense tarmac news conference. This impromptu grilling came together at the Kent County International Airport in Grand Rapids, Michigan, as Hughes tried to refute Slater's allegation that Bush lied to him about not being arrested since 1968. At the time, Slater did not print Bush's response to his question because he did not feel that it was newsworthy.

In comments that now bring to mind the subsequent alcohol-related legal scrapes of the First Twins in Austin in 2001—Jenna's April arrest and her alleged effort, accompanied by Barbara, to buy alcohol with a fake ID in May[10]—Hughes talked at length about Bush's decision not to disclose the DUI because of "his desire as a father to set a good example for his own daughters, [who were] at a very impressionable age. ... He had made a decision as a father that he did not want that bad example for his daughters."

Campaigning for Bush in Louisiana, Dorothy Bush, who had been in the car when Bush was arrested, had a similar take: "Here we are four days before Election Day and suddenly this comes out. I think that's unusual," she told a local reporter. "I think the opponent may have some fingerprints on it."[11]

Bush's parents would also defend him. Barbara Bush, who had been quoted during her husband's 1988 campaign saying nonchalantly that she assumed her children had tried drugs, called the story "much ado about nothing." Former President George H. W. Bush called the episode a "little hiccup here at the end of this campaign," and fumed as he pounded a lectern at an appearance while praising his son for having "changed his life" and saying that Democrats in Maine were acting for Gore. "Give me a break," the elder Bush said.

Other supporters chimed in as well. "Don't be distracted by the little sniping that comes in from the flanks," former General Colin Powell told supporters at a rally with Bush in Dearborn, Michigan, on November 4. For his part, Governor Bush followed the dual track of blaming the Democrats for the story even as he repeatedly said he took responsibility for his actions and had learned his lesson.

After the issue had settled in overnight, Bush used an 11 a.m. appearance at a rally at a Christian college in Grand Rapids, Michigan, as a sort of confessional. "It's become clear to America over the course of this campaign that I've made mistakes in my life," he said to great applause. "But I'm proud to tell you, I've learned from those mistakes," he said, continuing somewhat inexplicably to say that "that's the role of a leader—to share wisdom, to share experience with people who are looking for somebody to lead."

"I believe most Americans are going to come to the conclusion that this is dirty politics, this is last-minute politics," Bush told Fox later that day in a previously scheduled interview—with the network that had exposed his secret the night before—during a stop in Saginaw, Michigan. "I don't know whether my opponent's campaign is involved, but I do know that the person that admitted doing this at the last minute was a Democrat in Maine."

Such talk prompted Gore campaign chairman William Daley to issue a statement angrily denying any involvement by the vice president's team: "This charge is wrong. ... It is made without proof or evidence. It is time for Governor Bush's campaign to stop hurling charges and start accepting responsibility."

It would also emerge that when called for jury duty in 1996, Bush had failed to disclose the DUI conviction on a written jury questionnaire. Campaign aides said the document had been completed by an aide. Bush was struck from that jury when it was discovered that the case on which he would be sitting involved a drunk-driving charge. Alberto Gonzales, then the governor's counsel and now the White House counsel, got Bush off the case by arguing that Bush faced a conflict since he might later have to rule on clemency for the defendant after serving on the jury.

Since this argument might have been raised as soon as Bush was called for jury duty, the last-minute argument by Gonzales raised questions for some as to whether the objective was actually to help Bush avoid having to disclose his own DUI—though the judge agreed that Bush appeared to have "an inherent conflict." Before the nature of the case was known, the Associated Press wrote the following as Bush reported for jury duty on September 30, 1996: "'My message is that's a feeble excuse to say I'm too busy or too important,' the governor said. 'If you're going to live in a democracy and take advantage of a fantastic system, you need to participate.'"[12]

After Bush was dismissed, the October 9, 1996, *Austin American–Statesman* story included the following:[13]

> As he left the courthouse, Bush continued to offer nonspecific answers on his former drinking habits. "I did not have a perfect record as a youth," he said. "When I was young I did a lot of foolish things. But I will tell you this—I urge people not to drink and drive." Later Tuesday, Bush spokeswoman Karen Hughes said he would have answered the drinking-related questions under oath, but would not respond to the same questions if posed by reporters.

But November 3, 2000, had dawned with Bush's credibility questioned by Slater, *The Dallas Morning News* reporter. Slater said he had asked Bush in 1996 whether he'd been arrested since 1968, and that Bush replied, "No." He then added, "Well, wait a minute, let's talk about this," before Hughes cut off the interview.

Hughes ventured back into the press section of the Bush campaign plane to take the temperature of the press on the morning of November 3, only to find Slater fielding questions about his recollection that Bush had lied to him. Hughes immediately tried to refute the story. "That conversation was off the record, wasn't it, Wayne?" she snapped. Slater insisted it had not been. "I disagree with that. I walked up to the conversation and stopped the conversation," Hughes said. She then disappeared to the front of the plane and returned to say, "The governor disagrees with that. The governor does not believe he said that. He has not addressed that issue."

Slater's story in the October 9, 1996, *Dallas Morning News* included the following:[14]

> On Tuesday, after his dismissal, the governor was asked by reporters if he had ever been arrested for driving while intoxicated. "I do not have a perfect record as a youth," he said. "When I was young, I did a lot of foolish things. But I will tell you this, I urge people not to drink and drive. It's an important message for all people to hear," he said. "I don't drink, and I hope others don't drink and drive as well."

The session on the plane was off camera. When pressed to address the issue for television, Hughes excused herself, saying she wanted to put on some lipstick. But she never returned and would only go on camera a little later, under duress, surrounded on the tarmac.

There, Hughes would insist that Bush has no recollection of saying "no" to Slater's question. But she went on to accuse Slater of engaging in "some illogic." Hughes insisted that Bush must have been truthful either way, since after the interview, Slater "was clearly left with the impression—an accurate impression—that the governor had been involved in some incident involving alcohol."

Later, some at the Dallas paper—whose editorial page is one of the more conservative in Texas—would sense a strong chill from the Bush campaign and transition, though this feeling faded a bit once Bush moved into the White House.

In the coming days, the Bush campaign would fill in a few gaps in the story. Bartlett told me Bush did not recall buying alcohol for his underage sister that night and that Dorothy Bush Koch told the campaign that her brother had not done so. Bartlett indicated that Bush hadn't done any drinking with his younger sister at all, saying that the evening proceeded along the lines of a bunch of Bush family members attending "a large party" in Kennebunkport before hitting various bars. Bartlett said Dorothy Bush and her then-boyfriend split off to get something to eat, before rejoining the group to catch one of the most infamous rides home in political history. Bush also said through Bartlett that he was not handcuffed for his ride to the police station.[15]

Among the many questions raised by the episode was which senior aides knew about the incident, and when—particularly Hughes, whose iron fist controlled the flow of statements by, and information about, the candidate. Hughes conceded she'd known about the arrest but never would say how long she'd been aware of it. "This was not known to many people, but I have known about this before," Hughes said in Chicago on November 2. Whether aides had unsuccessfully urged Bush to disclose the DUI earlier or to try to keep it quiet was left to the fertile imagination.

REPERCUSSIONS IN THE GORE CAMP

When Lehane first faced the press for the Gore campaign following the DUI announcement, he was barraged with demands for the campaign's reaction, but kept declining comment. "That was one of those moments where you just roll the dice completely … and the whole thing's going to pivot on how you answer," he said later.[16] "You've had no time to do the due diligence that you would like to," but an answer of some kind was required. News accounts of that night cite Lehane as saying, "It's inappropriate for us to comment on it. It's something we are not familiar with."

And as he waded through the press questions, "for a moment towards the end ... I actually thought I was going to emerge without the question being asked." But then a reporter lobbed it in: Did the Gore campaign have any role in digging up the arrest? "This is just not something the Gore campaign is involved in, in any way, shape or form," Lehane said. The press corps virtually ignored Gore's campaign event that night in favor of the DUI story, and once the group reboarded the planes, "rumors were running amuck."

Lehane then warned Gore:

> At some point people are going to start blaming us just based on where I'm from. And [Gore] said something like, "I assume we have nothing to do with this," in which case I assured him that I certainly didn't and I [would] assume the campaign did not have any involvement. He just nodded. He actually was very calm about the whole [episode]. We were literally all exhausted at this point.[17]

But the rumor mill was just getting in gear. The next day, Lehane said he had to do battle against "all sorts of crazy rumors that the Bush people were stewing," adding that "other reporters were saying" they were getting information and allegations from the Bush camp. Lehane declined to name which reporters were making these statements, however, saying he'd agreed to keep that confidential. He said that one of his favorite rumors was "that I had taken a secret trip to Maine when Lieberman had been there the week before, when I did all this research and figured all this stuff out."

And the allegations didn't stop with Chris Lehane. His sister, Erin, an attorney in Portland, immediately came under fire, too. It started as she left her home to go for a run early on the morning of November 3. Her husband, Julius, asked, "Did you hear that DUI story that broke last night?" Jokingly, he added, "I hope Chris had nothing to do with this. Ha ha," she told me in May 2001. The joking ended the minute she got to her office at Curtis Thaxter Stevens Broder & Micoleau in Portland.

"I got off the elevator at work and the receptionist said, '*The New York Times* is on the line for you, Fox News is on the line for you.' ... I turn on my computer and I have already at this point 30 emails of people telling me what scum I am, telling me to repent. One told me to check into the Betty Ford Clinic."[18]

Lehane said her email address had been posted on a conservative Internet bulletin board. The incoming messages ranged from "Are you the *&#hole lawyer who leaked the story about G. W.?" to "Honorless" to "You are a pig" to "Thanks for your help with the Bush's campaign" [sic]. Lehane said the Bush supporters "got every public record available about me within moments. They had a wedding announcement, they had my [running] race times."

When some email messages appeared to amount to threats, another attorney in Lehane's firm called the U.S. attorney and the FBI quickly stopped by. "They came and took my computer files. They offered me protection, they gave me a caller-ID box to record all the calls that were coming in at home, and they told me not to go home that night," she said. "We stayed out till about 11:00 at night and then we got mad." Lehane's concern about her dog prompted her and her husband to go home. "Julius slept with a nine iron. ... I got threats all day, I got calls all day. Fox News called to confirm the story even after they had reported it. I tried to get a copy two weeks later and [a transcript service she was referred to by Fox] said they burn all their tapes."

Danielle Gorash, the testy spokesperson for Fox's Washington bureau, said in an e-mail message that the network had properly reported out the story. While Fox did mention Erin Lehane's name on the air, "we at no time said that she had anything to do with the story," she said.[19]

GORE'S FINAL STATEMENT

Gore eventually addressed the matter himself when questioned by the media. "I am not engaged in personal attacks. He is and has been," Gore said of Bush November 3 on *NBC Nightly News*. Asked by Tom Brokaw whether the DUI saga would "have any impact" on Bush's ability to serve as president, Gore carefully avoided trashing Bush for the incident, but also would not fully let the governor off the hook. "Tom, I don't really have any comment on this. I—you know, I think people see that for what it is, something that happened a long time ago. But I don't know all of the details, and all I know is this: Our campaign had absolutely nothing to do with it, and I am talking about the issues."

THE FALLOUT

While Bush didn't personally take any more questions on his arrest, the story inspired a raft of questions from some reporters, some about the incident in Kennebunkport and some more generally about Bush's old penchant for having a good time.

Hughes was asked, for example, whether Bush has had problems with substances other than alcohol; he was the only major 2000 presidential candidate to refuse to disclose during the campaign whether he'd ever tried cocaine, for example. Hughes was vague in her response: "The governor has acknowledged in the past that he has made mistakes." But tips, leads, and rumors flew fast and furious after Bush's arrest was revealed—too late, really, to be thoroughly checked out and, if true, published fairly. A common theme: Had Bush been treated in this or that substance abuse rehabilitation center?

"That is a totally ridiculous, partisan rumor being spread by partisan Democrats," campaign spokesman Scott McClellan fumed at me when I asked about one such story during a November 3 stop in

Morgantown, West Virginia. He said Bush had "never" visited a particular facility named by one source. On November 4, another Bush campaign spokesman, Dan Bartlett, gave me a definitive answer to a question that had long been whispered about, but was never legitimized until the DUI surfaced. Bartlett said Bush told him he "has never been in any sort of treatment center for any reason" as a patient.[20]

A MEDIA FAILURE?

Bush clearly did not want the story out. But his decision not to reveal this embarrassing chapter of his life was hardly to blame for the fact that it was almost not revealed to voters before November 7. With all the questions and investigation by news organizations and others into Bush's background, it was really a story that the media had no excuse for not finding—a whole lot sooner. As Katie Couric more politely put it on *The Today Show* November 3: "Given that reporters have been looking for years at the governor's background, why did they never find this before?"

Indeed. The story was waiting to be found in public records available to anyone who had the sense to check what should have been an obvious place—where the candidate was known to have vacationed as a younger man in the Bush family version of the Kennedys' beloved Hyannis.

And once the story broke, many news outlets were unsure how to play it in the campaign's crucial waning hours. Even *The Washington Post* didn't know what to do with it. The newspaper that made Watergate the root moniker for virtually all subsequent political scandals initially put the story inside—until "the story gathered steam during the night on the news wires," according to the November 4 edition of *The Los Angeles Times*.[21]

"In the end, after a lot of discussion back and forth ... I decided that this was front-page news pure and simple," editor Leonard Downie told the *Times*. It took some cogitation, Downie explained, to get to the point where it "struck me as a newsworthy decision, to not disclose this when there was a long-standing issue about his personal conduct in the past." It also turned out that a Maine newspaper, the *Portland Press Herald*, had stumbled on the story some time earlier, but for some reason deemed the story unfit to print.[22]

Officer Bridges had dreaded that he would someday be asked about what would become his most famous collar, and he gave an interview about that night to the Associated Press only after the Bush campaign implored him to do so. Under the circumstances, Bridges' side of the story was probably helpful to Bush. "The man was, and I say this without being facetious, a picture of integrity. He gave no resistance. He was very cooperative," Bridges said.[23] Bridges would later tell the *Boston Globe* that the only rank-pulling that went on came when Newcombe said to the officer, "'Do you know who you just arrested? ... That's George Bush.' And I went, 'Geez, what's going to happen?'"[24]

The *Globe* also quoted Bridges as recalling a poignant moment that followed much later, when former President Bush thanked him for arresting his 30-year-old son. At a 1993 rally, Bush had approached Bridges, "smiled broadly," and shook his hand. "He said, 'You are the officer who arrested my son.' ... And he told me that it was the best thing that could have happened to his son. It really was the crescendo of my career ... that he thanked me. I felt that I had helped."[25]

"AWAITING FURTHER ORDERS"

Aboard the Bush press bus on the hour and 45-minute nighttime drive from Pittsburgh to the November 3 rally in Morgantown, my cell phone rang. "There's another one," a normally good source said in an urgent tone. "Another what?" I asked. "Bush had another DUI—in Texas."

"Don't get me started," I said. The rap sheet for that one was already framed on my office wall back in Washington.

About three weeks earlier, in mid-October, I'd become aware that a George Bush, Jr., had a DUI arrest in Galveston, Texas, in August 1976. I had a personal trip to hear a band in Austin already planned for the weekend of October 21, so I told my editors that if they gave me a couple of extra days out there and staked me for the extra travel, I'd check it out. Fortunately, I'd offered the obvious caveat: "Remember, I'm making no promises here. It could just be some poor bastard with the same name."

Sunday night—after a weekend of enjoying the music and barbeque of Austin while wondering in the back of my mind whether the documents in my luggage were a political A-bomb or not worth the paper they were written on—I flew to Houston, then drove to Galveston and put up in a $60 room in a La Quinta with a view of the Gulf of Mexico. The next morning, I was at the courthouse, where the records didn't show any more than I already knew: George Bush, Jr., had been nabbed on a DUI that he pleaded guilty to on November 2, 1976—24 years to the day before President Bush's DUI would later be disclosed in the heat of the 2000 campaign. He paid a fine of $150 and spent 15 days in jail, according to the papers. But there was no date of birth or other identifying information to nail down who the guy really was—certainly no middle initial. A clerk said the Galveston County sheriff's office, next door, should have the rest of the file if it still existed.

Over there, I handed the piece of paper to Deputy John Pruitt, Jr., who looked at it, saw the name, and laughed. "And you really think you're going to find something?" he asked. He told me to have a seat while he searched the archives. A few minutes later, he came back with the file. The negative of the mug shot didn't look much like Governor

Bush. And according to the description, while the defendant in question was described as five foot eleven, about the same height as George W. Bush, George Bush, Jr., was nine years older than the 2000 Republican nominee for president of the United States. In addition, he had been born in Louisiana, and he was also categorized in the more detailed—and decidedly Old South—sheriff's file as "Negro."

I thanked Pruitt, scurried back to my rental car, headed for the first waterfront blackened oyster joint I could find, and left my boss a voice mail from the parking lot: "It was the wrong George Bush. Awaiting further orders." Needless to say, my head almost exploded when the real story came out barely two weeks later.

"WE'VE ALL BEEN THERE BUT WE HAVEN'T BEEN CAUGHT"

Polls suggested that voters did not care much about the revelation, and Bush supporters interviewed at the rallies that came immediately afterward gave a hint of this—even in states that Bush would go on to lose, such as Michigan and Wisconsin.

"We've all been there but we haven't been caught," retired insurance adjuster Carl Gaerig, 77, said in Dearborn, Michigan, on Saturday, November 4. "He didn't hurt anybody." A Marine veteran of the Battle of Okinawa—and, according to family folklore, a descendant of Yankee great Lou Gehrig—Gaerig also said he didn't blame Bush for trying to keep the drunk driving arrest quiet. "Nothing to be proud of. You don't advertise it," Gaerig said.[26]

But some Bush aides wonder if it cost the president the popular vote. As one Bush source put it, "You got the Christian Right and you got 'honor and integrity,'" a major part of Bush's standard speech trying to cast himself as the ethical antidote to the Clinton-Gore scandal years. The DUI story "stopped whatever momentum you might have had."

Bush's chief strategist, Karl Rove, insisted right up until the election that Governor Bush was on track to win 320 electoral votes. Insiders say he meant it, but that he must have been spinning off the last round of tracking polls, which were taken before the arrest story took root, as one source put it. "I think Karl's numbers got thrown out of whack," said one Bush source. "We stopped tracking ... so we were literally flying blind the last few days." When Rove kept citing his 320-vote prediction—49 electoral votes more than are needed to win and enough, obviously, to have avoided the 36-day recount—despite the arrest story, "it may have been a false sense that we had addressed [the story] head on. ... But you didn't have anything to back it up with, check it with."

For all the decades of family history, grooming, fund-raising, and planning that got Bush and Gore to Election Day 2000, it was a last-minute blast from the past, detonated in an already superheated 24-hour news environment that would leave them both limping across what they thought would be the finish line: November 7.

NOTES

[1] Timothy J. Burger, a correspondent in the Washington bureau of the *New York Daily News*, traveled with the Bush campaign for two months, including the then-governor's final push on November 2 through 6, as part of the *News* team coverage of the 2000 elections.

[2] Interview with the author, May 2001.

[3] Interview with the author, May 2001.

[4] Michael Shelden, "I Could Have Been the Next Monica," *The Daily Telegraph,* March 9, 2001, p. 25

[5] Larry Margasak, "Alcohol an Issue in Bush Campaign," Associated Press, November 3, 2000.

[6] Michael Kramer, "Snow in August: Candidate George W. Tries to Stem the Cocaine Avalanche," August 22, 1999, p. 45.

[7] The author's transcription of Bush's November 2, 2000 press conference:
"Thank you all for—obviously there's a report out tonight that 24 years ago I was apprehended in Kennebunkport, Maine, for DUI. That's an accurate story. I'm not proud of that. I've oftentimes said that years ago I made some mistakes. I occasionally drank too much and did on that night. Was pulled over. I admitted to the policeman that I had been drinking, paid a fine. I regret that it happened. But it did. I've learned my lesson. I mentioned many of you know that I quite drinking alcohol in 1986. It was the right decision for me to make—then. Be glad to answer a few questions.
Q: Why is it out now?
A: "It came out now because ... I made a decision that as a dad I didn't want my girls [to know when I] told them not to drink and drive. Decision I made. I didn't want to talk about this in front of my daughters. I told my daughters they shouldn't be drinking and driving. I think that's an interesting question—why now?"
A: "No, the girls did not know until tonight. I talked to them."
A: "I did not spend time in jail."
Q: Is it relevant in any fashion to W's candidacy?
A: "No, I think the people knew that I had been straightforward, that I had made mistakes in the past. This happened 24 years ago. I do find it interesting that it's come out four or five days before an election. I've been straightforward with people saying that I used to drink too much in the past and straightforward with people saying that I don't drink now."
Q: Was he truthful under past questioning?
A: "Yes I was."
Q: "How did you think you could get away with keeping this secret?"
A: "I'm not trying to get away with anything [chuckling]."
Q: Is he concerned that this would renew questions on whether he's been candid about his social history?
A: "I've been very candid about my past. I said I've made mistakes in the past. People know that. They've thought about that. They've made their dec—they're making their minds up now. They've seen me as the governor of the State of Texas. I've upheld the honor and integrity of my office. It's a regrettable incident and I find it interesting that four or five days before the election it's coming to the surface. The only thing I can tell ya is I told the people of my state I used to drink. I quit drinking. I'm not going to drink. I haven't had a drink in 14 years."
Q: Had Bush or his family taken any actions to hide this?
A: "None whatsoever. ... I told the guy I had been drinking and 'what do I need to do?' And he said here's the fine."
Q: Did he recall what he'd been doing that night that led to that kind of excess?
A: "I was drinking beer, yes, with John Newcombe. How many beers? Enough to have [chuckling] been in violation of the law. I can't remember how many

beers—it was 24 years ago. And that's the interesting thing about this. Here we are with four days to go in the campaign."

A: "There was no court. I went to the police station. I said 'I'm wrong.'"

Q: "Was there any kind of a field sobriety test?"

A: "No. I admitted I was wrong."

A: "My father? As I recall he wasn't very happy about it."

Q: "Are there any more 'mistakes' of this kind or a similar nature waiting to be discovered?"

A: "No."

Q: Didn't people have a right to know since he was running for highest office in the land?

A: "I told the people I had made mistakes in the past. And this was a mistake I had made in the past. I also told the people that in the past I had drunk too much at times. This was the case. And [as] I mentioned to you I'm a dad ... trying to teach my children right from wrong. I chose the course [for] my daughters, I was going to tell them they shouldn't drive and drink. And uh that's the course of action I took. [Karen Hughes tries to shut it down now.] And I'm the first to say that what I did was wrong. ... And I think the people of America will understand that. I think the interesting thing is, is that why five days before an election?"

Q: "Why do you think it's happening now?"

A: "That's your job. I've got my suspicions."

[8] Anne E. Kornblut, "Bush Camp Fires Back on Drunk-Diving Story," *Boston Globe*, November 5, 2000, p. A35.

[9] Interview with the author, November 4, 2000.

[10] In early May 2000, Jenna Bush pleaded no contest to a charge of being a minor in possession of alcohol. Then on May 31, 2000, Austin police officers announced that President Bush's 19-year-old twin daughters (Jenna and Barbara) allegedly tried to purchase alcohol at a restaurant using someone else's identification card. See Natalie Gott, "Police Say Bush Daughters Tried to Buy Alcohol with Fake ID," Associated Press, May 30, 2001.

[11] Keith O'Brien, "Bush's Sister Plays Down Arrest for Drunken Driving," *The Times-Picayune* (New Orleans), November 4, 2000, p. 10.

[12] "Gov. George W. Bush Is on His Way," Associated Press, October 1, 1996.

[13] Ken Herman, "Bush Gets Bumped from Jury Panel," *Austin American–Statesman*, October 9, 1996.

[14] Wayne Slater, "Defense Lawyer Strikes Bush from Jury Pool in DWI Case," *Dallas Morning News*, October 9, 1996, p. A22.

[15] Interview with the author, November 4, 2000.

[16] Interview with the author, May 2001.

[17] Interview with the author, May 2001.

[18] Interview with the author, May 11, 2001.

[19] E–mail to Larry J. Sabato, May 24, 2001.

[20] Interview with the author, November 4, 2000.

[21] Josh Getlin, Jeff Leeds, "Coverage of Bush's '76 Arrest Called 'Disgraceful,'" *Los Angeles Times*, November 4, 2000, p. A22.

[22] Mark Jurkowitz, "The Media; DUI May Give Press a Hangover," *Boston Globe*, November 4, 2000, p. F1.

[23] Tom Raum, "Bush, Cheney Had Drunken Driving Arrests," Associated Press, November 2, 2000.

[24] Beth Daley, "President Bush Once Thanked Maine Office," *Boston Globe*, November 4, 2000, p. A10.

[25] Ibid.

[26] Interview with the author, November 4, 2000.

CHAPTER 5

The Perfect Storm:

The Election of the Century

Larry J. Sabato
University of Virginia Center for Governmental Studies

There have been many close presidential elections, but never before—
and maybe never again—will there be one as excruciatingly tight as
the election of 2000. A contest that attracted more than 105 million
Americans to the polls essentially came down to a few hundred
ballots in one state: a margin of less than one-thousandth of 1 percent
of the national vote. Almost anything could have changed the
outcome—a candidate staying in Florida to work the polls on Election
Day, a few more well-placed television ads, a last-minute
endorsement by some well-known local pol, or a thousand other
plausible possibilities.

But "would have, could have, should have" does not count in the
harsh world of elections. A vote is a vote is a vote, as Gertrude Stein
might have said had she been in politics. In this chapter, the focus will
be on an analysis of the votes cast throughout the nation on November
7, 2000.

The kaleidoscope of voting patterns that emerged on that day will lead
to a deeper understanding of what Americans did and why they did
it—and how, most of all, they came to such an indecisive conclusion

95

in electing the country's forty-third president (not to mention a 50-50 split in the U.S. Senate and a near-tie in the U.S. House of Representatives. [1])

PAINT BY THE NUMBERS: AMERICA AT THE POLLS

The 105,402,138 Americans whose votes were officially tallied on November 7, 2000, split this way:

Candidate	Total Votes	Percentage
Al Gore (D)	50,996,064	48.4
George W. Bush (R)	50,456,169	47.9
Ralph Nader (Green)	2,882,708	2.7
Patrick Buchanan (Reform)	448,847	0.4
Harry Browne (Libertarian)	386,024	0.4
Howard Phillips (Constitution)	98,000	0.1
John Hagelin (Natural Law)	83,520	0.1
Others/Write-ins	50,806	---

The raw numbers are revealing. Not only did Al Gore secure 540,000 more popular votes than George W. Bush, but Ralph Nader's liberal Green Party constituency of almost 2.9 million voters unquestionably cost Gore the election. This is true even if one assumes that most of the nearly 1 million predominately conservative voters who cast ballots for Pat Buchanan, Harry Browne, and Howard Phillips would have chosen George W. Bush in a pure Gore-Bush matchup. New Hampshire (where Bush won by nearly 7,000 and Nader received 22,000 votes) and Florida (where Bush won by 537 and Nader garnered over 97,000 votes) would both surely have tipped to Gore without Nader in the race.

Had Nader been absent, Gore would easily have captured Iowa, Minnesota, New Mexico, Oregon, and Wisconsin, which he won by paper-thin margins. By contrast, the conservative third-party candidates probably cost Bush only New Mexico, by 336 votes out of almost 600,000 cast.[2] Yet even here, Nader cut into Gore's strength far more; the Green candidate captured over 21,000 votes, compared to the conservative trifecta's 4,000. (See official vote by state and region in table 5-1.)

REGIONAL DIVISIONS

Regionally, the South was the heart of Bush country and the indispensable key to his disputed election (see table 5-1). All 13 Southern states backed Bush, even Gore's home state of Tennessee; Bush crushed Gore in the Volunteer State with 55 percent of the votes to Gore's 43 percent. Bush also narrowly won the Midwest, 49 percent to Gore's 48 percent. Thanks mainly to a big California victory (54% to 42%), Gore carried the West, 48 percent to Bush's 46 percent. In the Northeast, Gore smashed Bush by an even larger margin than Bush had won the South: 56 percent for Gore to 39 percent for Bush. Overall, then, the Northeast gave Gore a 4,066,903-vote plurality, and Gore won the West by 454,450 votes. Bush's Southern plurality of 3,670,822 votes and Midwest edge of 310,636 votes left him exactly 539,895 votes behind Gore nationally—with millions of "undervotes" and "overvotes" left uncounted, of course. (An undervote had no recorded vote for president; an overvote registered votes for two or more presidential candidates—part of Florida's indelible national civics lesson in 2000.)

ELECTORAL VOTES: "TOLERANT" VS. "TRADITIONAL"

Constitutionally, there is no such thing as the national popular vote. Only the Electoral College vote matters, which Bush won in a squeaker, 271 to 267, with 270 necessary for election. As figure 5-1 shows, the 2000 election was a starkly regional one.

97

Table 5-1.
2000 Official Presidential Vote

NORTHEAST	Bush (R)	Gore (D)	Nader (G)	Rep.-Dem. Plurality	
Connecticut	561,094	816,015	64,452	254,921	D
Delaware	137,288	180,068	8,307	42,780	D
Maine	286,616	319,951	37,127	33,335	D
Maryland	813,827	1,144,008	53,768	330,181	D
Massachusetts	878,502	1,616,487	173,564	737,985	D
New Hampshire	273,559	266,348	22,188	7,211	R
New Jersey	1,284,173	1,788,850	94,554	504,677	D
New York	2,403,374	4,107,697	244,030	1,704,323	D
Pennsylvania	2,281,127	2,485,967	103,392	204,840	D
Rhode Island	130,555	249,508	25,052	118,953	D
Vermont	119,775	149,022	20,374	29,247	D
West Virginia	336,475	295,497	10,680	40,978	R
Washington, D.C.	18,073	171,923	10,576	153,850	D
Northeast Total	**9,524,438**	**13,591,341**	**868,064**	**4,066,903**	**D**
MIDWEST					
Illinois	2,019,421	2,589,026	103,759	569,605	D
Indiana	1,245,836	901,980	18,506	343,856	R
Iowa	634,373	638,517	29,374	4,144	D
Kansas	622,332	399,276	36,086	223,056	R
Michigan	1,953,139	2,170,418	84,165	217,279	D
Minnesota	1,109,659	1,168,266	126,696	58,607	D
Missouri	1,189,924	1,111,138	38,515	78,786	R
Nebraska	433,862	231,780	24,540	202,082	R
North Dakota	174,852	95,284	9,486	79,568	R
Ohio	2,350,363	2,183,628	117,799	166,735	R
South Dakota	190,700	118,804	---	71,896	R
Wisconsin	1,237,279	1,242,987	94,070	5,708	D
Midwest Total	**13,161,740**	**12,851,104**	**682,996**	**310,636**	**R**

NOTE: Votes for Nader in Georgia, Idaho, Indiana, and Wyoming were write-ins. A dash (-) indicates candidate was not on the ballot and did not receive any write-in votes.

George Bush won every state that fell into the column of 1996 GOP nominee Bob Dole, and he picked up 11 Clinton states from four years earlier: Arizona, Arkansas, Florida, Kentucky, Louisiana, Missouri, Nevada, New Hampshire, Ohio, Tennessee, and West Virginia. At the same time, Bush fared far less well than his father in the 1988 election. Bush Sr. prevailed in 40 states with 426 electoral

Table 5-1.   (continued)

SOUTH	Bush (R)	Gore (D)	Nader (G)	Rep.-Dem. Plurality	
Alabama	941,173	692,611	18,323	248,562	R
Arkansas	472,940	422,768	13,421	50,172	R
Florida	2,912,790	2,912,253	97,488	537	R
Georgia	1,419,720	1,116,230	13,273	303,490	R
Kentucky	872,520	638,923	23,118	233,597	R
Louisiana	927,871	792,344	20,473	135,527	R
Mississippi	572,844	404,614	8,122	168,230	R
North Carolina	1,631,163	1,257,692	---	373,471	R
Oklahoma	744,337	474,276	---	270,061	R
South Carolina	786,892	566,039	20,279	220,853	R
Tennessee	1,061,949	981,720	19,781	80,229	R
Texas	3,799,639	2,433,746	137,994	1,365,893	R
Virginia	1,437,490	1,217,290	59,398	220,200	R
South Total	**17,581,328**	**13,910,506**	**431,670**	**3,670,822**	**R**
WEST					
Alaska	167,398	79,004	28,747	88,394	R
Arizona	781,652	685,341	45,645	96,311	R
California	4,567,429	5,861,203	418,707	1,293,774	D
Colorado	883,748	738,227	91,434	145,521	R
Hawaii	137,845	205,286	21,623	67,441	D
Idaho	336,937	138,637	12,292	198,300	R
Montana	240,178	137,126	24,437	103,052	R
Nevada	301,575	279,978	15,008	21,597	R
New Mexico	286,417	286,783	21,251	366	D
Oregon	713,577	720,342	77,357	6,765	D
Utah	515,096	203,053	35,850	312,043	R
Washington	1,108,864	1,247,652	103,002	138,788	D
Wyoming	147,947	60,481	4,625	87,466	R
West Total	**10,188,663**	**10,643,113**	**899,978**	**454,450**	**D**
National Totals	**50,456,169**	**50,996,064**	**2,882,708**	**539,895**	**D**

SOURCE: *The Rhodes Cook Letter*, 1:6 (January 2001), pp. 9–10.

votes, scored a landslide margin of almost 1 million votes in Florida alone, and captured 53.4 percent of the national vote. Only in his home state of Texas and a dozen small, rural states, mainly in the Midwest and the Rockies, did the son secure a higher percentage of the vote than his father. By contrast, Al Gore actually outperformed President Clinton's 1996 reelection percentage in 13 states, including behemoths such as California, Florida, Illinois, New Jersey, New Mexico, New York, and Pennsylvania. Only New Hampshire and New Mexico, by tiny margins, deviated from the shading scheme.

The Florida photo finish overshadowed the two biggest surprises on the electoral map. First, as noted earlier, Gore failed to carry Tennessee, which both he and his father had represented for many years in both houses of Congress, thereby becoming the first major-party presidential nominee since George McGovern (D) in 1972 to lose his home state. Even more shockingly, Gore came up short in the heavily Democratic state of West Virginia, where his perceived liberal positions on the environment (anti-coal), gun control, gay rights, and abortion fell flat. Those same social issues may well explain a good part of the geographic divide. The culturally liberal coastal areas (Northeast-Atlantic, Midwest–Great Lakes, and Pacific Coast) were almost all Gore's. The culturally conservative South, farm Midwest, and Rocky Mountain states were almost all Bush's.

This "tolerant versus traditional" breakdown is becoming as important as race, gender, educational level, and income in explaining U.S. elections. Furthermore, although Bill Clinton's sex scandals did not create this split, they certainly aggravated it, to Al Gore's detriment. The current cultural division may be territorially stark, but fortunately it is not especially toxic—at least compared to the sectional split of the Civil War, the "rich versus poor" chasm of the Great Depression, and the generational gap of the Vietnam-driven 1960s. Still, it is fascinating to contemplate a nation whose elections are decided as much by cultural norms as party identification.

Of course, viewed another way, very little about the 2000 election was traditional. For example, both major-party camps were actively preparing for the possibility that Bush would win the popular vote and Gore the Electoral College. Many independent pundits believed this to be a credible, even slightly probable, scenario, and this analysis had adherents within the high commands of the Gore and Bush teams. On the Gore side, for example, elaborate plans were being constructed as

Figure 5-1.
The 2000 Electoral College Vote

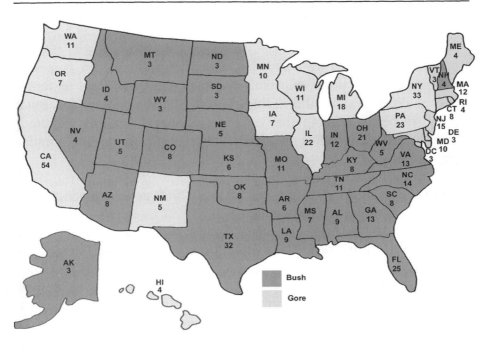

Design by Joshua Scott

late as the afternoon of Election Day to keep the Democratic electors from defecting to Bush on the basis of his expected popular vote plurality. One Gore campaign official, National Field Director Donnie Fowler—who was on-site at the Nashville national headquarters—told us that the Democratic "generals ... gathered information on each of Gore's electors in close states:"

> The Gore campaign believed that the Bush operatives would ask Gore electors with weaker loyalties to switch their allegiance, and thus swing the election, because the rightful president would be the one who won the most votes rather than the one who carved out a narrow Electoral College victory. Into the early

101

> afternoon of November 7, Gore's state political team
> ... made notes on who would reach out to each elector
> in key battleground states in case their operating
> assumption came true.[3]

Ironically, Election Day concluded with the candidates in precisely the opposite positions expected by many internal and external political observers. Politics being the art of the possible, the Bush strategists began arguing that only the Electoral College mattered, while the Gore advocates switched gears to contend that the popular vote was king.

One of the eyebrow-raising aspects of the 2000 general election was indeed Gore's upset in the popular vote. The Democrats appeared to be surprised by the degree of effectiveness of their own voter contact techniques. In retrospect, there is little question that the Democrats out-hustled the Republicans before and on Election Day. The Gore-Lieberman effort used national, state, and local figures to deliver targeted phone calls to potential voters. Bill Clinton and Jesse Jackson recorded messages to loyal Democrats reminding them to vote; Al Gore taped calls describing his stances on issues; Gore's Harvard roommate, the actor Tommy Lee Jones, supported his old friend with a taped recording about Gore's position on gun control; and Hollywood star Robert Redford delivered a pro-Gore environmental homily targeted to likely Nader supporters. Local and state officials pitched in with a generic get-out-the-vote reminder to turn out on November 7, noted Gore field director Fowler.[4]

Even the Republicans, perhaps especially the Republicans, acknowledged the Democrats' advances in the ground war. Ari Fleischer, Bush's campaign spokesperson and later the White House press secretary, attributed the extremely close election in part to Gore's unprecedentedly vigorous turnout program in key states such as Florida, Iowa, Oregon, Minnesota, New Mexico, and Wisconsin.[5] The Republican National Committee chairman agreed, and several senior Bush campaign operatives admitted that their underestimation of likely Democratic voter turnout was so substantial that they would need to overhaul their standard predictive turnout models.[6]

THE BUSH VS. GORE MAP IN POLITICAL PERSPECTIVE

Let's take one more look at the Bush versus Gore electoral map, but this time we can utilize political cartography. People vote, not rocks, trees, or territories. While the Electoral College helps small states to some degree, it is the population of the several states that matters most. This is the theory behind the political map of the United States (see figure 5-2).

This map is what politicians, their staffs, and political consultants actually see when they look at our nation. The political projection in figure 5-2 is based on the 2000 census, and it clearly shows that the smaller states in the country's midsection and the Rocky Mountain area are squeezed between the enormous growth on the West Coast, the still sizable Northeast, the expanding South, and the border states. Most readers will be surprised to see just how far the Northeast extends into the interior of the United States—essentially to the Mississippi River. The South sprawls to the Rocky Mountains, and it is of course dominated by two mega-states, Texas and Florida. The Midwest is the most mixed region, with large industrial states such as Michigan, Ohio, and Illinois mixing with smaller farm belt states such as the Dakotas, Kansas, and Nebraska. The West is dominated almost entirely by the super-state of California. Also, it should be noted that the areas of Hawaii and Alaska have been altered to reflect their respective shares in the U.S. population. Hawaii is close to real size, while geographically gargantuan Alaska appears smaller here than diminutive Rhode Island.

Larry J. Sabato

Figure 5-2.
Political Map of the United States, Divided by Regions

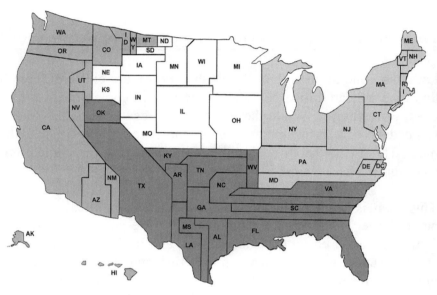

A final version of the political map puts the Bush-Gore race into perspective. Looking at a territorial map of the United States, it appears that George W. Bush won a sweeping majority (see again figure 5-1). That is a misrepresentation, however, because he carried most of the large, but lightly populated states throughout the country. The political map shows just how close the race really was, with Gore's political territory matching Bush's in proportionate size. (See figure 5-3.)

Given current census projections suggesting continued growth in the South and Pacific states, a similar political map of the United States drawn in 2011 will demonstrate these same trends to an even greater degree, giving politicians and their consultants alike an even more extreme picture to contemplate.

Figure 5-3.
Political Map of the United States, 2000: Bush vs. Gore

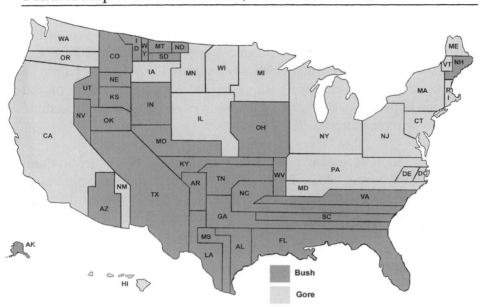

Copyright Larry J. Sabato, UVA Center for Governmental Studies, 2001
Design by Joshua J. Scott

EXIT POLLS: SLICING AND DICING THE VOTE

Naturally, the traditional demographic divisions of American politics were once again on display in 2000. The Voter News Service (VNS) exit poll, taken as voters left the balloting places, failed the networks on election night, but once adjusted for reality—that is, the actual vote totals—they give us an invaluable picture of the American electorate. (See table 5-2 for selected results.[7]) The fabled gender gap was again on display. Gore carried women by 11 percent, and Bush carried men by the same margin. Gore captured working women by 19 percent. Bush's main key to a razor-thin victory was the white male vote; he beat Gore in that category by 60 percent to 36 percent, even as white women split their vote almost evenly between Bush and Gore. Overall, the white vote went solidly for Bush (54% to 42%), and whites comprised more than eight out of every ten voters. All minorities were heavily for Gore, from 90 percent of African Americans, to 62 percent of Hispanics, to 55 percent of Asians. As has been widely noted since November 2000, the Hispanic proportion of the electorate grew slightly (from 5% in 1996 to 7% in 2000), and Bush's 35 percent of Hispanics greatly exceeded Bob Dole's paltry 21 percent four years earlier. Yet, given the rapid expansion of the Hispanic population, Bush may need to do even better with this ethnic group to win reelection in 2004.

Bush and Gore were nearly tied in all age groups, but education and income levels were clear dividing lines. Gore did best with voters who had the least and greatest education, as well as those with family incomes below $50,000. Bush's constituency had some college education, but not graduate school, and incomes over $50,000.

A dramatic difference emerged in marital status. The married population favored Bush by 9 percent, while those not currently married were in Gore's camp by fully 19 percent. Those with children under 18 were Bush's, but the childless or those with older children were Gore's.

Republicans were a bit more unified behind their candidate (Bush got 91% of them) than were Democrats (Gore carried 86%). Independents were about as split as the country between Bush (47%) and Gore (45%).

Gore easily carried the quarter of all U.S. households with a labor union member, 59 percent to 37 percent, but Bush won the larger non-union group by 52 percent to 44 percent. By varying margins, Gore secured majorities of liberals (80%), moderates (52%), first-time voters (52%), gays and lesbians (70%), and Clinton's 1996 voters (82%). Bush triumphed with conservatives (81%), Dole voters (91%), Ross Perot backers (64%), and gun-owner households (61%).

As expected, Protestants went heavily for Bush (56%) and Jews chose

106

the Gore-Lieberman ticket (79%). Catholics were somewhat of a surprise: normally Democratic, they split their votes in 2000, with only a narrow edge for Gore. (Clinton won Catholics by 16 percentage points in 1996.) The frequency of one's attendance at religious services was an excellent vote predictor in 2000. The most avid churchgoers went for Bush by 63 percent, and the "unchurched" were Gore's by 61 percent. Of course, white religious conservative voters, about 14 percent of the electorate, were Bush's by 80 percent. The abortion issue may have been a factor in the religious breakdown. Gore won 70 percent of those who wanted abortion to be always legal, while Bush secured three-quarters of those who preferred that abortion always be illegal.

While most of the demographic trends discussed here are standard in modern politics and expected,[8] one datum stands out as significantly changed. Republican Bob Dole captured a plurality of voters who decided for whom to cast a ballot in the last week of the 1996 campaign, yet Democrat Al Gore received a narrow nod from the late deciders in 2000. More than a quarter of the voters thought that Bush's DUI arrest was "somewhat" or "very" important, and over 76 percent of these people chose Gore. As discussed in Chapter 4 by Timothy Burger, Bush's driving-under-the-influence arrest revelation in early November may well have cost him a comfortable Election Day victory.

Other issues were also crucial, though the exit polls revealed little that could not be guessed after a long campaign. Voters who cared about taxes chose the tax-cut candidate, George W. Bush, and those worried about Social Security and health care picked the Democrat, who had stressed these concerns. Voters who wanted experience and a candidate who "cares about people" chose Gore, while those who were focused on honesty, likeability, and "strong leadership" qualities pulled Bush's lever.

Table 5-2.
2000 Presidential Election Exit Poll Results

Question	Horizontal % All	Gore	Bush	Question	Horizontal % All	Gore	Bush
Gender				**1996 Presidential Vote**			
Men	48	42	53	Clinton	46	82	15
Women	52	54	43	Dole	31	7	91
				Perot	6	27	64
Race by Sex				Other	2	26	52
White Males	48	36	60	Did Not Vote	13	44	52
White Females	52	48	49				
				Gun Owner?			
Vote by Race				Yes	48	36	61
White	81	42	54	No	52	58	39
African-Amer.	10	90	9				
Hispanic	7	62	35	**When Did You Decide To Vote?**			
Asian	2	55	41	In Last Week	17	48	45
Other	1	55	39	Before Then	82	48	50
Vote by Age				**Vote by Religion**			
18 – 29	17	48	46	Protestant	54	42	56
30 – 44	33	48	49	Catholic	26	50	47
45 – 49	28	48	49	Jewish	4	79	19
60 or older	22	51	47	Other	6	62	28
				None	9	61	30
Education							
No H.S. Degree	5	59	39	**Religious Services?**			
High School	21	48	49	More than Weekly	14	36	63
Some College	32	45	51	Weekly	28	40	57
College Grad	24	45	51	Monthly	14	51	46
Postgraduate	18	52	44	Seldom	28	54	42
				Never	14	61	32
Income							
Under $15,000	7	57	37	**White Religious Right?**			
$15–30,000	16	54	41	Yes	14	18	80
$30–50,000	24	49	48	No	83	54	42
$50–75,000	25	46	51				
$75–100,000	13	45	52	**Abortion should be ...**			
Over $100,000	15	43	54	Always Legal	23	70	25
				Mostly Legal	33	58	38
Married?				Mostly Illegal	27	29	69
Yes	65	44	53	Always Illegal	13	22	74
No	35	57	38				

Table 5-2.   (continued)

Question	Horizontal %			Question	Horizontal %		
	All	Gore	Bush		All	Gore	Bush
Children Under 18?				**First-Time Voter?**			
Yes	39	45	52	Yes	9	52	43
No	61	50	46	No	91	48	48
Which Mattered Most?				**Government Should Do …**			
World Affairs	12	40	54	More	43	74	23
Medicare/Rx Drugs	7	60	39	Less	53	25	71
Health Care	8	64	33				
Economy/Jobs	18	59	37	**Gay or Lesbian?**			
Taxes	14	17	80	Yes	4	70	25
Education	15	52	44	No	96	47	50
Social Security	14	58	40				
				Clinton Job Rating			
Party ID				Approve	57	77	20
Democrat	39	86	11	Disapprove	41	9	88
Republican	35	8	91				
Independent	27	45	47	**Clinton as a Person**			
				Favorable	36	83	13
Union Household?				Unfavorable	60	26	70
Yes	26	59	37				
No	74	44	52	**Country is On…**			
				Right Track	65	61	36
Vote by Ideology				Wrong Track	31	20	74
Liberal	20	80	13				
Moderate	50	52	44	**Moral Condition of United States**			
Conservative	29	17	81	Right Direction	39	70	27
				Wrong Track	57	33	62
Which Mattered Most?							
Understands Issues	13	75	19	**Bush's DUI**			
Honest/Trustworthy	24	15	80	Very Important	14	77	20
Cares About People	12	63	31	Somewhat Imp.	14	76	21
Has Experience	15	82	17	Not Too Imp.	20	56	40
Likeable	2	38	59	Not Imp. at All	48	29	67
Strong Leader	14	34	64				
Good Judgment	13	48	50	**Where Do You Live?**			
				Larger City	29	61	35
				Suburbs	43	47	49
				Rural Area	28	37	59

SOURCE: "Presidential   Exit   Poll   Results,"   CNN/Time   AllPolitics,   2000, http://www.cnn.com/ELECTIONS/2000/epolls/US/P000.html   (November   9,   2000).   The   VNS interviewed 13,130 voters across the United States to produce this exit poll.

Perhaps the most fundamental if simplistic philosophical determinant of the Bush-Gore contest was a voter's view about the size of government. By a 10-point margin, the voters wanted government to do less rather than more. Gore won 74 percent of the "more government" group, and Bush garnered 71 percent of the larger "less government" crowd.

Finally, even though Bill Clinton's name was not on the 2000 ballot, it might as well have been. Ever the polarizer, Clinton sharply split the electorate and defined both the Bush and Gore camps. Americans who approved of Clinton's job performance and liked him as a person were very likely to be Gore voters, and the reverse views practically identified the Bush constituency. Those who believed the nation to be on the "right track" generally supported Gore, but the citizens who perceived Clinton's America to be headed in the wrong direction—especially morally—usually joined Bush's parade. Interestingly, 36 percent of those who believed the nation was on the right track still voted Bush. That is a measure both of the "time for a change" theme that Clinton's scandals helped create and of the failure of Gore's campaign to capitalize fully on the six consecutive years of good economic times. This omission was the most puzzling shortcoming of Gore's effort, and indisputably fatal to his presidential hopes.

VOTER TURNOUT: NOTHING TO WRITE HOME ABOUT

A close, open-seat contest for the presidency ought to produce a decent turnout of voters. But it did not happen in 2000. Just 51.2 percent of the voting age population of nearly 206 million showed up at the polls (or cast a ballot by mail or absentee). Three of the last four presidential elections have seen about half the eligible citizens actually vote (50.3% in 1988, 48.9% in 1996, and 2000's 51.2%). The tumultuous election of 1992, which featured a popular independent candidate, Ross Perot, bumped up the participation rate slightly to 55.2 percent.

All in all, though, the country appears stuck in a dismal holding pattern: About half of American adults vote for president, and half do not. This is especially troubling since the federal government and most states have taken noteworthy steps since 1993 to streamline the voter registration process as well as make ballot access universal with early voting periods, simplified absentee ballot procedures, mail voting, and the like. Perhaps the extraordinary results in 2000 have driven home the lesson that every vote matters; yet one fears that the post-election passion play in Florida may have instead deepened public cynicism that not all votes count—so why bother. The turnout rates in upcoming elections will tell the tale, revealing which interpretation of the 2000 election has prevailed.

GREATEST MISSES: THE POLITICAL BLOOPERS OF 2000

No election analysis would be complete without a review of the most memorable bloopers that contributed to the 2000 election's chaotic place in American history. We all loved to focus on the candidates' microphone mistakes, such as Gore's loud sighing into the mike at the first TV debate on October 3, and Bush's term of non-endearment for a *New York Times* reporter ("a major league asshole") picked up inadvertently by the stage sound system in September, as Dick Cheney vigorously gave his assent ("big time"). But the exit pollsters, the television anchor/pundits, the quantitative political scientists, and, yes, the voting public all outdid the presidential nominees for bloopers in 2000.

Few will ever forget the election night theatrics on all five national networks. Misled by the stunningly inaccurate exit polling and encouraged by the traditional smugness and hubris of television celebrity, the anchors and their omniscient on-air analysts delivered embarrassing lines that will live forever in TV history. A brief sampling:

- CBS's Dan Rather, opening his network's coverage: "Let's get one thing straight right from the get-go. ... We would rather be last in reporting returns than to be wrong. ... If we say somebody has carried a state, you can pretty much take it to the bank. ..."

- ABC's George Stephanopolous: "[There are] three big battlegrounds: Pennsylvania, Michigan and Florida. ... Whoever wins two of the three of these states should be in the driver's seat tonight." [Note: Gore won Pennsylvania and Michigan ... and still lost.]

- All anchors, early in the evening, in seriatim: "Virginia, North Carolina, Georgia, Ohio are too close too call. ... Bad news for Bush." [Note: Bush won all four easily, the three Southern states in a landslide.]

- The TV anchors *before* 8 p.m. EST [when Florida Panhandle polls closed]: "We project that Al Gore will carry Florida."

- CNN: "A big call. ... [Florida is] a roadblock the size of a boulder to George W. Bush's path to the White House."

- Fox: "Disregard the raw vote percentages [that showed Bush ahead in Florida]."

- All networks within about an hour of the Florida miscall: "We are able to call Michigan ... and Pennsylvania for Al Gore." All TV analysts argue that these three states are, in effect, the election; the other 47 states and Washington, D.C., do not really matter. [Note: Every electoral vote mattered in 2000's squeaker.]

Now that Gore had carried the so-called trifecta, the television pundits prepared their audiences for Bush's demise:

- NBC's Tim Russert: "Gore closing in ..."

- CNN's Jeff Greenfield: "Bush has to run the table ..."

- ABC's Stephanopolous: "It's looking tough for Bush ..."

- NBC's Tom Brokaw: "It's beginning to look like [Gore has] the missile defense shield."

Suddenly, around 9:55 p.m.:

- CBS's Rather: "Bulletin: Florida pulled back into the undecided column. Computer and data problem."

- NBC's Brokaw: "What the networks giveth, the networks taketh away."

All networks yank Florida out of Gore's column. Then, at 2:20 a.m., Fox makes this stunning announcement:

- Brit Hume: "Fox News now projects that Bush will win Florida and thus ... the presidency of the United States." Graphics package of fireworks follows.

- CBS's Rather: "Bush wins. ... That's it. ... Sip it. Savor it. Cup it. Photostat it. Underline it in red. Put it in an album. Hang it on a wall. ..." All networks announce the Bush victory, complete with animated graphics.

Next, at about 3:27 a.m., NBC's Brokaw looks at the *real* Florida numbers that show a dead tie, and he explains why the network may pull back Florida for the second time in one evening: "Good grief ... that would be something if the networks managed to blow it twice in one night."

All the networks finally realize the voters have not cooperated with their projections, and they acquiesce in reality, leaving the election undecided at last—*where the contest actually has been all night.* NBC's Brokaw, preparing to sign off, makes the most honest comment of the evening: "We [the networks] don't just have egg on our face, we have omelet."

Live television is inherently dangerous and messy, but this car wreck had consequences. The early Florida call for Gore, combined with the networks' incessant chatter about the all-powerful "trifecta" of Florida, Michigan, and Pennsylvania along with the inaccurate characterizations about four solid Bush states as "too close to call," left a clear impression that Gore was very probably the winner. While it can never be convincingly proved, it is certainly possible that the media discouraged Bush voters from casting a ballot when polls were still open in the Sunshine State and throughout the nation. Theoretically, this situation could have helped produce the Florida cliffhanger and Gore's plurality in the national popular vote. On the other side of the ledger, the networks' premature declaration of a Bush presidency in the wee hours of November 8 made Gore appear to be a poor loser and bad sport for appealing a close election result after the winner had been crowned. In truth, there was no victor—and none should have been declared, thereby keeping the playing field even for the recount to come. Thus, the networks achieved something that the election could not: the uniting of the Bush and Gore camps in justifiable anger aimed at the TV anchors and seers.

The 2000 election night coverage was the video equivalent of the infamous 1948 *Chicago Tribune* headline, "Dewey Defeats Truman." The modern TV event deserves to be remembered just like the *Tribune*'s debacle, both as a desperately needed dose of humility for the networks and as a continuing warning to the public about television's transgressions.

Of course, the anchors were just the front men for the exit pollsters, of the Voter News Service, a consortium of most major news organizations.[9] Years ago, the networks conducted separate exit polls, thus allowing comparative study and cross-organizational checks on faulty election predictions. But primarily to save money, the bottom line–oriented, corporate-controlled networks, along with other news partners, joined forces and pooled resources to form VNS in 1990. The end of effective competition in exit polling created the possibility of a singular error producing a massive blunder on election night— exactly what happened on November 7, 2000.

Essentially, VNS's models of the likely electorate were off base in a number of states, creating a Democratic-leaning bias. In Florida the problem was compounded by a data-entry mistake double-counting some Bush votes; a more heavily GOP-weighted absentee vote than expected; and a dramatic underestimation of the remaining quantity of votes to be counted in some heavily pro-Gore counties late on election night.[10] The result is humiliating history. To its credit, VNS now understands its flaws, though as long as it has an effective monopoly on exit polling, the risk of disaster will continue. For now, VNS's directors are left pointing to its overall 99.8 percent success rate in election predictions—a claim that ignores many of its behind-the-scenes inaccuracies and inadequacies over the years.[11] In terms of the 2000 debacle, that boast is akin to telling Mrs. Lincoln that, other than the assassination, the play at Ford's Theatre was superb.

While we are passing out "Dewey Defeats Truman" raspberries, a loud rendition must also go to the gaggle of political scientists who design and publish election-prediction models.[12] Yes, these models have generally been accurate in recent years—with exceptions, and with great emphasis on the word "generally." But in 2000, the seven most cited academic models were well off the mark, having unanimously projected sizable Gore victories ranging all the way up to 60.3 percent of the two-party vote. The average political science forecast was a Gore win of 56 percent; Gore actually received 50.2 percent of the two-party vote, calculated when the votes for all third-party and independent candidates are excluded.

The political science models are based on a number of variables (including several economic indices and presidential popularity in the Gallup poll), and they employ refined statistical techniques, such as regression analysis, that have made the field opaque to all but certain academics. When asked to explain their miscalls, which were given wide pre-election publicity and credibility, especially by *The Washington Post,*[13] most political scientists were every bit as dodgy and defensive as the networks and the exit pollsters. They blamed the Nader vote, the long economic expansion that lulled voters into indifference about prosperity, and the Gore campaign's incompetence. (Said one modeler: "Gore didn't run a campaign consistent with the model," as though this were Gore's obligation.[14]) Still others actually insisted that their results were reasonably close and within an acceptable range of error—which, if true, makes the models fairly useless.

The more accurate assessment of what went wrong may well come down to two assertions. First, quantitative political scientists for a generation have given insufficient weight to the candidates' skills (or lack of them) and the quality of the campaigns run on their behalf. *Candidates and campaigns matter as much as the circumstances of the election year.* Second, political scientists are not seers, and they who live by the crystal ball often end up eating ground glass. The news media, especially *The Washington Post*, ought to remember that in future years.

One final group of 2000 election culprits rarely gets mentioned. Networks want viewers, newspapers want readers, and politicians want votes, so no one is inclined to cast aspersions upon the millions of citizens who threw away their franchise by means of careless voting. Granted, the half of the potential electorate that bothered to come to the polls is morally superior to the slacker half. But anyone who examines the ballots cannot help being appalled.

Take Florida, where a president won the White House for four years by a grand total of 537 votes. Uncounted were 111,261 overvotes, produced when a voter cast a ballot for two or more presidential tickets, and 64,826 undervotes by voters who had *no* recorded choice for president. As Tom Fiedler ably described in Chapter 1, even allowing for the punch-card machine problems and the infamous "butterfly ballot" in Palm Beach County,[15] tens of thousands of Floridians wasted their precious franchise. Incredibly, a study by *The Miami Herald, USA Today*, and Knight Ridder newspapers found that nearly 1,000 people voted for *all 10 presidential tickets;* more than 3,600 people voted for every candidate *except Bush;* more than 700 voted for every candidate *except Gore;* and many thousands voted for *both* Bush and Gore. While no one will ever know for sure, the spoilt, uncounted ballots probably made a decisive difference. One telling clue existed in the disqualified overvotes: 71,548 carried a Gore vote while only 25,082 had a Bush vote, potentially an extra 46,466 votes for Gore had these voters decided to play by the established rules of democratic elections.[16]

ELECTION OF THE CENTURY: THE PERFECT STORM

Analyzing a near-tied election like 2000 can be fruitful, but also frustrating. A million factors mattered, and all were decisive, with none dominating or uniquely determinative. In a Greco-Roman mosaic, which tiny painted stone is most critical? Even one well-placed, missing chip can be noticed by the eye and change perceptions of the whole, but only collectively do the stones make any real sense. So too with the election of 2000.

This chapter's examination of the election results has avoided many hard, unanswerable questions. Could the sullied Bill Clinton nonetheless have pulled out the election for Gore, had the vice president decided to put aside his personal animus toward the president and ask for more help? Surely, an energized Clinton stumping for weeks in Arkansas, West Virginia, and New Hampshire might have turned around at least one of those Bush states. On the other hand, Clinton's mediagenic presence each night on the national news might well have turned off enough voters to tip Wisconsin, Iowa, Oregon, and/or New Mexico from Gore to Bush. Who knows what the calculus might have been?

Similarly, did the vice presidential nominees matter? No one can point to a state Bush carried on account of Dick Cheney—a state the GOP nominee wouldn't have won anyway. Yet Cheney's deep and broad governmental experience reassured voters everywhere, making Bush seem less of a risk. Were there not 537 shaky Bush voters in Florida who embraced that rationale? Probably so. As for Joseph Leiberman, his Jewish religious affiliation may well have brought Gore to the brink of a victory in Florida, with its hundreds of thousands of Jewish citizens, as well as strengthened Gore's hold on the Northeast, Illinois, and California. But did Lieberman actually carry any state Gore would not otherwise have won? How interesting it might have been if Bush had chosen Pennsylvania Governor Tom Ridge and Gore had picked Indiana Senator Evan Bayh or Florida Senator Bob Graham. Would Bush have then won the Keystone State (23 electoral votes)? Would Gore have fared better with Hoosiers (12 electoral votes) or locked up Florida convincingly? Maybe. Who can ever say? But these vice presidential choices could easily have changed the outcome.

All things considered, it is remarkable that George W. Bush became the forty-third president. He was fighting the historically potent continuation of peace and a near-golden prosperity. His only major advantages were the Clinton scandals—generating the age-old "it's-time-for-a-change" mood—and an agreeable personality that contrasted sharply with Gore's amalgamated wood-and-plastic persona. The close 2000 decision is reminiscent of the 1960 Kennedy-Nixon contest. JFK also faced long odds and beat an incumbent vice president by a whisper, by means of the same two advantages of TV personality and change-agent image. Al Gore, of course, had hoped for a repeat of 1988, when a wooden two-term vice president capitalized on peace and prosperity to defeat an "ideologically extreme" governor. But Gore proved not to be Bush Sr., and Bush Jr.

refused to play his assigned role as a Republican Michael Dukakis.

At the same time, voters gave George W. Bush the presidency but no real mandate. How could a candidate who lost the popular vote by more than half a million votes and barely secured an Electoral College majority in a disputed state claim otherwise? Surprisingly, though, the tight results predict nothing about Bush's likely fate as president. Since popular elections essentially began in 1824, 4 in every 10 presidents have won less than a majority of the vote. These "minority presidents"[17] have included some of our best (Lincoln, Wilson, Polk, and Truman) and our worst (Buchanan, Taylor, and Nixon). Three presidents (Cleveland, Wilson, and Clinton) were twice elected with less than a majority. Fully nine of the minority presidents received a lower percentage of the vote than George W. Bush's 47.9 percent, including Lincoln in 1860 (39.8%), Wilson in 1912 (41.8%), and Clinton in 1992 (43%). As the country and George W. Bush are already learning anew, a presidential election—even one as stunning as 2000—is far more a beginning than an end, not an omen but merely an opening to history yet unmade and undetermined.

NOTES

[1] The even Senate split occurred for the first time since 1880, and the House breakdown of 222 Republicans to 212 Democrats was the closest division since 1952. In the Senate contests of November 7, 2000, Democrats gained a net four seats, while in the House Democrats captured just two seats, net. (The House totals for each party include one independent who caucuses with that party.) The even Senate split ended on May 24, 2001, when liberal Republican U.S. Senator James Jeffords of Vermont announced that because of the GOP's conservatism, he was leaving the party to become an Independent and would caucus with the Democrats.
[2] Theoretically, had Nader stayed on the ballot and the conservative candidates all been excluded, Bush *might* have won Iowa, Oregon, and especially Wisconsin. But only in New Mexico is this assumption a good bet worth a substantial wager.
[3] Written communication to the author, May 31, 2001.
[4] Ibid.

[5] Thomas B. Edsall, "Bush Lost 9 to 1 Among Blacks; Poll Findings and Fla. Fight Present Challenge to GOP Nominee," *The Washington Post*, December 12, 2000, p. A1.

[6] American Association of Political Consultants Forum, January 25, 2001, Washington, D.C. Thanks to Donnie Fowler.

[7] Gore officially received just 266 electoral votes, due to a "faithless elector" in the District of Columbia who cast a blank ballot to protest D.C.'s lack of voting representation in Congress.

[8] See the often-similar breakdowns for 1996 in Larry J. Sabato, *Toward the Millennium: The Elections of 1996* (Boston: Allyn and Bacon, 1997), pp. 148–154.

[9] VNS members include ABC, CBS, NBC, CNN, FOX, and the Associated Press.

[10] Joan Konner, James Risser and Ben Wattenberg, "A Report for CNN: Television performance on Election Night 2000", January 29, 2001.

[11] Associated Press story cited in *The Hotline*, May 18, 2001, item 4.

[12] See *PS: Political Science and Politics* 34:1 (March 2001), pp. 9–48. All major models are cited and described in six articles comprising a post-election symposium on predictive modeling.

[13] Robert Kaiser, "Is This Any Way to Pick a Winner?" *The Washington Post*, May 26, 2000, p. A1.; Kaiser, "Academics Say it's Elementary: Gore Wins," *The Washington Post,* August 31, 2000, p. A12; Kaiser, "We're Divided, And We'd Better Get Used to It," *The Washington Post,* November 12, 2000, p. B1.

[14] See D. W. Miller, "Election Results Leave Political Scientists Defensive Over Forecasting Models," *Chronicle of Higher Education*, November 17, 2000, p. A24.

[15] The "butterfly ballot" stretched out the 10 Florida presidential choices out over two pages, to increase print size for the elderly. But directions given to some voters suggested that a choice should be marked on every ballot page, leading many citizens to cast multiple votes for president—which spoiled their ballots.

[16] The results of this expensive and enlightening study were published in all participating newspapers on May 11, 2001. See also *The Hotline*, May 11, 2001, item 4.

[17] *The Rhodes Cook Newsletter,* 1:6 (January 2001), p. 5. As Cook notes, "minority" presidents are those elected with less than 50 percent of the total popular vote. Of the 45 presidential elections conducted by popular vote since 1824, 18 have produced a "minority" president.

Rank	Winner	Party	Election	Popular Vote	Electoral Vote
1	John Q. Adams	Federalist	1824	30.9 %	*32.2 %
2	Abraham Lincoln	R	1860	39.8 %	59.4 %
3	Woodrow Wilson	D	1912	41.8 %	81.9 %
4	Bill Clinton	D	1992	43.0 %	68.8 %
5	Richard M. Nixon	R	1968	43.4 %	55.9 %

6	James Buchanan	D	1856	45.3 %	58.8 %
7	Grover Cleveland	D	1892	46.1 %	62.4 %
8	Zachary Taylor	Whig	1848	47.3 %	56.2 %
9	Benjamin Harrison	R	1888	47.8 %	58.1 %
10	**George W. Bush**	**R**	**2000**	**47.9 %**	**50.4 %**
11	Rutherford B. Hayes	R	1876	48.0 %	50.1 %
12	James A. Garfield	R	1880	48.3 %	58.0 %
13	Grover Cleveland	D	1884	48.5 %	54.6 %
14	Woodrow Wilson	D	1916	49.2 %	52.2 %
15	Bill Clinton	D	1996	49.2 %	70.4 %
16	James K. Polk	D	1844	49.5 %	61.8 %
17	Harry S. Truman	D	1948	49.6 %	57.1 %
18	John F. Kennedy	D	1960	49.7 %	56.4 %

*Adams was elected by the House of Representatives.

CHAPTER 6

Media Mayhem:

Performance of the Press in Election 2000

Diana Owen
Georgetown University

> To err is human, but to really foul up requires a
> computer. ... If you're disgusted with us, frankly, I
> don't blame you.   *—Dan Rather, CBS News*
>
> Could you pass the crow.   *—Judy Woodruff, CNN*

"On Election Day 2000, television news organizations staged a collective drag race on the crowded highway of democracy, recklessly endangering the electoral process, the political life of the country, and their own credibility, all for reasons that may be conceptually flawed and commercially questionable."[1]

This passage, however melodramatic, captures the essence of an election that was pushed to near-crisis conditions by a reckless and self-interested mass media. That the passage opens a report commissioned by CNN in preparation for a congressional scolding is yet another twist in the bizarre story of an election night catastrophe, the gravity of which will not be fully understood for some time to come.

123

Diana Owen

The first presidential contest of the new century will go down as one of the most memorable events in American political history. The campaign itself was undistinguished and mostly followed established patterns of modern-day electioneering. The candidates' organizations primarily employed standard strategies for managing media and mobilizing voters. Candidates George W. Bush and Al Gore were not especially captivating to voters. Media coverage of the campaign diverged little from what citizens have come to expect. Reports focused heavily on the horse race aspect of the campaign, character issues, and conflicts between the candidates.

It is precisely because of press coverage as usual that the biggest election story of our lifetime began with a series of media blunders. The networks' collective election night errors in judgment, especially the events surrounding their reporting of the voting in Florida, put on public display the inadequacies of the current system of informing citizens about our society's most crucial decisions. Matthew Felling of the Center for Media and Public Affairs (CMPA) summed up the situation: "Campaign 2000 truly was the sinking tide that lowered all ships. The media gave the candidates low marks, the public gave the media low marks, and the Florida fallout diminished the image of our political system."[2]

Members of the press had plenty of warning that their Election Day reporting routines were problematic. Election postmortems have for decades included criticisms about the potentially dangerous flaws in a system where commercial imperatives compel news organizations to render snap judgments about election outcomes in order to earn bragging rights for being first. Academic studies have demonstrated the detrimental effects on voter interest, participation, and evaluations of the political process caused by poll-driven reporting and announcing election returns before balloting has ended.[3] Journalists themselves have pointed out the problems with ritual campaign reporting. Former *New York Times* and *Newsweek* reporter Robert Shogan warned that journalists should cover news, not predict it, especially given the limitations of polls.[4]

The story of election 2000 is largely about how media politics as usual resulted in the most unusual of political circumstances. As a result, this discussion, like the election itself, has a split personality. We begin with an overview of media politics as usual during the campaign phase of this electoral contest, focusing on press coverage of the campaign and candidate advertising. We then turn to an analysis of the role of the Internet in the election, which did surprisingly little to substantively change the usual course of events. "Campaign 1.0" was supposed to mark the advent of the Internet revolution in election coverage. Instead, the revolution did not even reach the level of a minor uprising.

The events of election night mark the turning point in our story line, as we explore the behavior, explanations, and implications of the news media's mistaken calls and the events that unfolded subsequently. We will look at exit polls as an election night reporting tool, review what went wrong on November 7, and examine the problems that plague the current system that is reliant on the Voter News Service (VNS) consortium. The post-election cliff-hanger proved to be a media bonanza, as the campaigns maneuvered, the courtroom dramas unfolded, and the public was spellbound. In the aftermath of the election, Congress held hearings, the press apologized, and the public was left wondering if things will be any different the next time around.

THE SAME OLD MEDIA STORY

At the very beginning of Campaign 2000, it appeared as though the press was making a serious attempt to break with set norms of election coverage. Issue coverage was more prevalent than usual, and the focus on strategy was downplayed somewhat. Both candidates seemed to be making a concerted effort to focus on issues that they hoped the press would cover. This interlude of more meaningful election coverage was, however, quite brief, as voters soon were treated to the same old election media story.

Media Coverage

Perhaps the most striking feature of news coverage during the 2000 presidential contest was the tremendous amount of information available from a wide range of sources. Voters had a great deal of choice about where they could go for election news. Cable news operations, such as CNN, MSNBC, CNBC, and C-SPAN, provided coverage of the campaign trail, punditry, and call-in programming. Morning talk programs and newsmagazines featured candidate interviews that the public tends to find useful when making voting decisions.[5] Entertainment talk programs, such as *Oprah!* and *The Late Show with David Letterman*, hosted appearances that allowed candidates the opportunity to counter traditional sound-bite coverage. Late-night programs also drew attention to the campaign through jokes and monologues that were popular with voters.[6] Online resources were plentiful and included not only candidate material but also technical information about voting. Extensive candidate biographies were made available in newspapers and newsmagazines, as well as on programs like the Arts and Entertainment Network's *Biography*. The amount of network campaign news, however, was not much greater than it was in 1996, when reporters lamented the dearth of newsworthy information generated by the campaign. Given that the audience for network news has been shrinking steadily over the past few years and that the availability of other sources had increased, the networks' limited campaign coverage hardly seemed to matter.[7]

Although information was plentiful, the quality and tone of coverage were largely in keeping with trends established in past campaigns. News reports were seriously lacking in information about governance, including the type of people the candidates would likely appoint to important positions and the candidates' ability to handle important policy realms, such as foreign affairs.[8] Although both candidates presented specific information about issues in their speeches and on

126

their web sites, the preponderance of news coverage focused on the worn-out themes of campaign strategy and the horse race. The number of network news stories assessing the candidates' relative standing in the campaign skyrocketed in 2000. CMPA data indicate that 71 percent of network news stories focused on the horse race, compared to 48 percent in 1996 and 58 percent in 1992. Far fewer media reports—40 percent—featured policy issues. A study by the Project for Excellence in Journalism (PEJ) found that stories in print, on TV, and on the web about the debates were more about performance (53%) and strategy (12%) than substance. Fewer than 10 percent of debate stories focused on issues, and few compared the policy positions of the candidates, which is a feature of news that voters find especially useful.[9] Internet news sites were similarly lacking in substance, as only 2 percent of campaign stories focused on the candidates' core beliefs and issues.[10]

In keeping with the rise in strategic and horse-race journalism, poll-driven reporting reached new heights. The use of polls as a reporting tool has increased exponentially in elections since the 1960s. An analysis by Stephen Hess, senior fellow at the Brookings Institution, revealed that two-thirds of the networks' general election stories were supported by polls, a figure that increased as the campaign got down to the wire.[11] The dominant news frame became the close election. In employing this frame, however, reporters focused on campaign tactics rather than the reasons underlying voter indecision. The closeness of the race between Bush and Gore was used by journalists to justify the overabundance of poll stories. Some journalists argued that poll stories in this campaign tended to energize the electorate, as they emphasized the competitiveness of the race.[12] Alternatively, poll stories in close races can alienate voters who become befuddled or annoyed by the barrage of data.

Polls gauging candidate preference and voter attitudes released during the campaign fluctuated a great deal, sometimes from day to day. One explanation for the vacillation in poll results was the fact that many voters did not make up their minds until late in the campaign.

Another, perhaps more compelling, reason lies in the quality of the polling procedures and methodologies employed. Added to the standard arsenal of polling information from news organizations, independent survey firms, think tanks, interest groups, and candidates were online polls, tracking polls, and quick polls. The wide variation in the type of polls made it difficult for news consumers to gauge the quality of information. Polls were being conducted in quick succession, and many did not use proper sampling techniques and question design. "Instant polls" conducted overnight to gauge people's reactions to dramatic events, such as the announcement of vice presidential candidates, proliferated. These polls, often fielded using auto-dialers with recorded messages, are notoriously inaccurate, as they average a 2 percent acceptance rate of homes dialed.[13] Further, online polls, which are quick and easy to field, yet highly unreliable,[14] abounded. News reports, especially on cable networks and online media, featured the results of Internet polls. Only occasionally did the reports include the feeble caveat that these polls are based on unrepresentative samples.

Campaign 2000 witnessed network news organizations showcasing pollsters leading focus groups of undecided voters. "Tabloid pollsters," such as Republican operative Frank Luntz, would put people in the studio and ask them to form opinions on air. "This stuff is rough and ready, and would hardly pass anyone's test of gauging a representative view of voters. I don't know what purpose it serves journalistically or in terms of research," observed Andrew Kohut, director of the Pew Research Center for the People and the Press.[15] The National Council on Public Polls censured NBC for portraying Luntz as someone who is objectively reporting on public opinion when in fact he has strong partisan leanings, especially as no Democratic counterpart was given air time.

Coverage of the campaign, like political news in general, was highly negative. Adverse character frames dominated media coverage of both candidates. Bush was taken to task for lacking intelligence. The press used Bush's regular abuse of the English language—for example, using "subliminable" to describe hidden messages in advertising—as evidence. Gore was labeled a serial exaggerator and even a liar. Media reports harped on an alleged misstatement he had made years earlier that he had invented the Internet. New gaffes, such as Gore's statement that he paid much less for arthritis medication for his dog than his mother-in-law had paid for the same prescription, provided corroboration of Gore's innate character flaw. Overall, the CMPA reports that Gore received 40 percent positive press compared to 37 percent for Bush. Campaign reports tended to be more even-handed earlier in the race and became increasingly harsh in the last month.[16] Press treatment of Gore became tougher after the first debate, countering the more favorable coverage he received in the first part of the campaign.[17] News about Gore tended to focus on strategic campaign politics, while reports about Bush were more likely to feature issue information.

Journalists' bashing of candidates for being the root cause of public disengagement has become another staple of campaigns. Political correspondents claimed that the lackluster candidates made the election as painful for them to cover as it was for voters to follow.[18] "The politicians provide us with a campaign that's superficial, deceptive, dishonest. It's hard for the reporters to change that," laments Robert Shogan. Veteran political journalist Jack Germond, who retired as a full-time reporter for *The Baltimore Sun* after the election, put his reaction to Election 2000 bluntly. "You couldn't find anybody who would walk through a wall for Al Gore. Bush was even more superficial. His candidacy was based primarily on the money he raised for his campaign. ... George Bush has a lack of knowledge of the world around him and Gore was too programmed. I find it very hard to describe why I was spending my dotage on these two people."[19]

Reporters stole the spotlight from candidates even more in 2000 than they have in prior elections. Since the 1980s, journalists have increasingly spoken for candidates, rather than allowing them to convey their messages in their own words. The average candidate sound bite on network news shrank to an all-time low of 7.8 seconds,[20] down from 10 seconds in 1988 and a little over 8 seconds in 1992 and 1996.[21] Since 1988, the length of candidate sound bites has decreased by 30 percent, while reporters' speaking time has increased markedly. Candidate speech constituted only 11 percent of network airtime, while reporters (74%) and other sources (11%), such as voters, campaign staffers, pundits, and experts, consumed the remainder.[22]

News organizations made an attempt to respond to some of the criticisms they have faced in recent elections. They provided more detailed biographical information on the candidates. The mainstream press also took a few cues from the "new media" formats, such as call-in programs and talk shows, made popular in the 1992 presidential contest. Traditional news programs included more average citizens in their election stories, soliciting their opinions and showcasing their involvement in the campaign. These improvements, however, were overshadowed, as reporters mainly fell back on stock routines of campaign coverage.

The public's evaluation of the press' performance in Election 2000 reflects dissatisfaction with the all-too-familiar campaign news offerings. Pew Research Center data indicates that citizens gave the press an average grade of "C" for media campaign work, with 6 percent giving the press an "A" and 20 percent an "F." Talk show hosts were ranked somewhat higher, improving their standing in the public eye from 1996.[23]

Media coverage of the campaign is important, as it stimulates voter involvement and aids decision making. The Vanishing Voter Project (VVP) discovered that public interest in and discussion of the campaign peaked when press coverage was high and diminished when it was low. Key campaign events, such as heated primary contests, conventions, and debates,[24] can drive up civic engagement.[25] Despite their dismal rating of the press, voters overwhelmingly believed that they received enough information to make an informed choice.

According to Pew Center data, 83 percent of the voters were satisfied with what they had learned from the campaign, compared to 75 percent in 1996. The candidates may deserve some credit, as 46 percent of voters felt there was more discussion of issues and an identical percentage believed that there was less mudslinging in Campaign 2000 than in the past.[26]

Candidate Advertising

The candidates adapted dynamic advertising strategies that changed with new campaign developments. Early in the process, both candidates strove to identify core themes and issues. As the campaign progressed, the ad wars became more reactive. Approximately half of the ads aired by the Bush campaign organization were comparative, as the candidate had committed himself to being a conciliator, not a fighter. The Bush campaign adopted a counterpunch strategy; advisers did not want to go negative until hit first.[27] The Gore campaign used a more common contemporary strategy of running comparative ads earlier and more frequently throughout the campaign.

Republican chief strategist Karl Rove started by laying out the ideal campaign, which was premised on using Bush's "compassionate conservative" agenda as a basis for his ads. The goal was to emphasize what Bush would do as a leader in particular areas, such as restoring dignity to the White House and revitalizing the military. The Republican strategy also emphasized traditional Democratic issues, like education, Social Security, and health care, in order to portray Bush as "a different type of Republican" who was less partisan. This initial strategy worked early in the campaign, but it became less successful as the Democrats attacked Bush on these issues and traditional Republican vulnerabilities surfaced, particularly for older voters. The ads were targeted broadly at voters over the age of 30.[28]

The Gore advertising effort was aimed more specifically at middle- and working-class voters. In early identification spots, Gore provided

131

a biographical sketch highlighting his independence, in an effort to distance himself from Bill Clinton. Other ads focused on Gore's commitment to family values and his status as a Vietnam War veteran. The Gore team worked to counter the effects of Republican ads that tread on Democratic turf. For example, a positive spot with Gore calling for a patients' bill of rights was aired in reaction to a negative Bush ad that attacked Gore's polices on health care, education, and taxes.[29] The Democratic National Committee ran issue-focused ads on health care and education that attempted to reclaim these issues for Gore.

Negative advertising is a standard feature of American national election campaigns. While negative ads are heavily criticized for debasing the electoral process and disillusioning voters,[30] there is evidence that going negative can be highly effective. Candidates go negative most often when they are trailing or when they fear they are losing ground. The most hard-hitting and graphic of the negative ads in 2000 were run in the last month of the campaign.

Negative ads can backfire dramatically. During the Republican primary, Arizona Senator John McCain, in an effort to attract independent voters, ran an ad that compared George W. Bush to Bill Clinton, stating that both stretched the truth. Focus group research indicated that this ad had crossed the line, as voters felt it was improper for a Republican to attack a member of his own party in this manner. While the McCain organization pulled the ad immediately, the resulting publicity and a Bush spot countering it worked to turn the tide of the primary election in Bush's favor.

It is interesting to note that while the press is quick to criticize campaigns for running negative ads, the media do much to publicize such ads. Journalists use attack ads as a mechanism for justifying their own negative coverage. During Campaign 2000, reporters would hound campaign officials on a daily basis asking if the candidates were planning to run any negative spots.

The Bush organization employed a two-tiered advertising strategy depending on whether funding came from the campaign or from the Republican National Committee (RNC). The RNC paid for and aired the contrast ads while the campaign organization focused more on positive spots. This distinction was picked up by the ad watches. The headline "RNC Gets *Really* Nasty" introduced an ad watch critique of a biting spot that questioned Al Gore's truthfulness by mocking his statement about inventing the Internet.[31] Another ad developed by the RNC that depicted Gore as untrustworthy, using dated clips of the vice president stating that neither he nor Bill Clinton had ever lied, was never aired because George W. Bush and his campaign would not approve it. Democratic Party organizations implemented some of the more negative advertising tactics employed on behalf of the Gore-Lieberman ticket. The Michigan Democratic Party used a recorded telephone message of a widow blaming Governor Bush for failing to improve standards in nursing homes that she claims resulted in her husband's death.

Some of the most inflammatory ads of the election were run by political groups not directly affiliated with the candidates' organizations. Aretino Industries, a nonprofit organization based in Texas, aired a remake of the infamous 1964 "Daisy" spot used by Lyndon Johnson against Barry Goldwater, this time targeting Gore. The Bush campaign denied having anything to do with the ad and called it "an anonymous attack."[32] The ad ran only four times, but it received substantial media coverage. While not officially coordinated with the Gore campaign, the AFL-CIO ran ads that assaulted Bush for his health care policies and his credibility. The NAACP Voter Fund produced a commercial that featured the daughter of James Byrd, who had been dragged to death in Texas, condemning Bush for his refusal to support hate-crime legislation.

Ad watches, in which journalists and academics fact-check candidate spots, once again were a fairly prominent part of the media campaign. While ad watches hold campaigns accountable for the accuracy of their claims, they have been criticized for being ineffective and inadvertently providing publicity for negative and faulty ads. Campaign organizations have come to appreciate ad watches. As Bush adman Rush Schriefer noted, "Ad watches are good. They kind of act as a referee. It prevents us from running ads that we can't back up, that we don't have the facts or documentation for, and it does it for the other side as well."[33] Campaigns have incorporated ad watches into their strategic decisions. Candidates use ad watches critical of the opponent to their advantage. They run reverse spots that ask voters whether they have seen the opponents' spot.

Candidates were moderately successful in reaching voters with their ads. Pew Research Center data reveals that by mid-October, 57 percent of the public reported having seen a Gore commercial and 61 percent had viewed Bush ads. Reaction to advertising for both candidates was not favorable.[34] Only 29 percent of the public considered the ads to be helpful in making decisions. The ads for both candidates received a better rating then press coverage, as they averaged in the "B" to "B–" range.[35]

THE CAMPAIGN ONLINE: STILL AWAITING THE REVOLUTION

Expectations that the Internet would be established as a powerful force in electoral politics were not met during the 2000 campaign. Candidates, parties, news organizations, interest groups, nonpartisan civic groups, individual citizens, and even schoolchildren contributed to the proliferation of political web sites. The amount of election information available on the Internet was extraordinary. The audience for the online campaign, however, was just not there.

The Internet presence in the 1996 and 1998 elections provided a preview of the potential for the medium to transform the political process. Candidates and political parties could use the Internet to circumvent traditional media gatekeepers and get their message out on their own terms. The public could participate in unfiltered interactive discussions with politicians, journalists, and average citizens. The press could use the Internet as a quick information source and to track the competition's breaking stories.[36] The fact that public demand for online election results caused some news organizations' servers to crash was seen as a sign of the online political revolution to come.

At its best, the online campaign acts as a countervailing force to the mass media campaign as usual. Reliable voter information, the full text of candidate documents, in-depth analyses, and diverse ideological commentary are readily available. At its worst, the Internet facilitates, and even exacerbates, the problems that plague the media election. Rumors are passed off as news at lightning speed, while parody candidate web sites confuse—even as they amuse— voters. Defamatory messages are hosted in online chat rooms, which this election included anti-Semitic comments against Democratic vice presidential candidate Joseph Lieberman.[37] Further, the commercial incentives of the online news business interfere with democratic goals. As Chris Hunter, an analyst with the Annenberg Public Policy Center, observed about Net Campaign 2000, "It was all very disappointing ... lots of dot-coms weren't there to promote democracy, but to get another round of venture capital."[38] As Internet journalists adopt the bad habits of the mainstream press, and acquire some new ones of their own, the public's faith in the media system continues to be undermined.

Campaign Web Sites

Voters who accessed candidate sites during earlier campaigns complained that they were basic and did not exploit the web's technological possibilities. Further, citizens were disappointed by their inability to interact online with candidates who sought to maintain control over the flow of information. By the 2000 election, Internet technology had become more sophisticated and could accommodate highly innovative types of campaign communication.

Users are drawn to political web sites for their convenience, search features, and multimedia capabilities.[39] The presidential candidate web sites had these features and contained much of the content desired by users. Both the Bush and Gore web sites supplied voters with news updates, speeches, position papers, local campaign information, and Spanish content. The sites allowed visitors to view ads and video streams of special events, such as stump speeches and interviews with journalists. The candidates solicited donations, signed up volunteers, and sold campaign paraphernalia online. Information about campaign contributors and online voter registration was available on the Bush site. While both campaigns regularly sent correspondence to e-mail lists, the Gore site hosted interactive conversations with "netizens."

Negative campaigning was not the primary focus of either candidate's web site, and the sites contained little comparative information. Negative content was introduced through the inclusion of news releases from outside sources or links to other sites. In the final days of the campaign, the Bush site "News Releases" section sported the following headlines accompanied by selectively edited article excerpts: "Gore Campaign Struggling: Independent Pollster: Lack of Enthusiasm for Gore Should Scare Democrats to Death" (*The New York Times*); "Tennesseans Don't trust Al Gore ..." (*Knoxville News–Sentinel*); and "Voters Feel They Are Being Taken for Granted ..." (*Boston Globe*).

Early enthusiasm for the Net campaign was driven in part by mass media coverage of political sites, especially during the primaries and through the nominating conventions. Much was made of online firsts, such as candidate chats and web-based fund-raising efforts. Reporters celebrated the innovative techniques employed by political portals, such as the now-defunct Voter.com,[40] to engage participants in the process. There was great anticipation that the Internet would come of political age during the national nominating conventions just as television had 52 years earlier. "Internet Alley," an amalgamation of 35 dot-com companies which covered the Republican National

Convention from four tents outside the Philadelphia Convention Center, was as much a story as the happenings inside the hall.[41] The Democrats offered similar web coverage of their national convention in Los Angeles, including "video webcapting" that allowed blind and deaf users to follow the events. Online convention coverage featured such novel offerings as publicly available press releases, instant polls, and live online chats with speakers just after leaving the podium.[42] However, technical glitches and ho-hum coverage caused users to become disenchanted. Further, some of the sites were difficult to locate.

The Internet campaign was in many ways like throwing a party and having nobody come. Political web sites offered much quality information and many new ways for citizens to take part in the political game. Yet, despite that fact that the Internet audience had grown substantially in the period between elections to include more than half of the population,[43] only a small proportion of voters tuned into the campaign online. Less than 20 percent of the public went to the web for election news.[44] In fact, web traffic during the national conventions actually dropped for some news sites. MSNBC.com's site traffic decreased by 27 percent of its normal rate, while CNN.com lost 18 percent of its audience.[45] The highly touted GOPConvention.com site received only 106,000 visitors during the Republican National Convention.[46] Estimates suggest that fewer than 10 percent of voters accessed a candidate's web site and that the average stay lasted less than three minutes.[47] Candidates were able to recruit only a very small number of volunteers using online appeals. Fund-raising efforts were far less successful than the media hype that surrounded them, as is illustrated by the exaggerated reports of web-generated contributions to John McCain's primary campaign war chest.[48]

Campaign organizations realized that web sites were an ancillary, and not an integral, part of the election strategy, especially during the general election. That few people were driven to candidate sites mitigated their usefulness as a tool for recruiting and reinforcing supporters. In addition, web sites were far less effective than traditional advertising media in disseminating the campaign's unfiltered messages. According to Republican strategist Rush Schriefer, "Candidates were never able to bypass the traditional media or traditional processes through the web."[49] The sites served to a large extent as a resource for journalists, loyal supporters, and political junkies.

Online News Coverage

The scope, quantity, and novelty of online campaign coverage increased drastically during the 2000 presidential contest. News organizations' web sites had much to offer audience members in terms of rich content and innovative ways of receiving information. Users' capacity to quickly download audio and video clips was perhaps the most significant new development.[50] Voters were able to engage in online political discussions with commentators and witness live online interviews with print reporters who in the past would have remained faceless bylines. Media organizations' web sites also contained their fair share of gimmicks of questionable value. Quick polls and instant analysis were common site features.[51] Sites even featured surveys that would tell participants for whom they should vote. Still, 25 percent of all political news site front pages contained stories recycled from other sources with no additional reporting, and one-quarter contained no interactive features. Contrary to popular belief, lead stories were well sourced and accurate.[52]

Reporters, even those who use the Internet, are skeptical about the significance of the online campaign. A survey of Washington, D.C.-based journalists who covered the election revealed that the press had come to conclusions about the Internet election that were similar to those of campaign strategists. While journalists generally consulted news and political web sites several times a day, they felt that Internet coverage was doing little to transform election reporting. The reporters surveyed believed that television and newspapers would be the media mainstays of presidential campaigns in the foreseeable future. Interestingly, print reporters had the most negative evaluations of the quality of online journalism, perhaps reflecting their fear of competition from a medium that has been dubbed the "electronic newspaper."[53]

It may well be the case that the growth in online political offerings has contributed to the mainstream media's ability to maintain the status quo in election coverage. Media scholar Lawrence Grossman has observed that the Internet is becoming the ghetto for quality political information. Television coverage, which is still by far the main source of campaign information for most voters, differed little in Campaign 2000 from that of the past. "Go to our web site for more information" has become an excuse for news organizations to continue televised political coverage as usual, or even reduce it.

Technology and Campaign Strategy

Electoral strategies in recent years have incorporated new technologies to facilitate internal communications among campaign operatives and external relationships with the media and voters. Not too long ago, fax machines and cell phones, technologies that we now take for granted—modernized the way that campaigns designed their strategies and journalists filed stories. Computer technologies are responsible for some new innovations in campaign media strategies. The two presidential campaigns in 2000 employed computer technologies to somewhat different extents.

Al Gore's fascination with technology was put into practice with the implementation of a computer-assisted methodology for informing the campaign's media tactics. A computer program used for the first time in a presidential campaign produced a map of the United States color-coded for the extent of media coverage in particular locales. Data input into the program included weighted scores for a visit by members of the candidate entourage. A visit by Al Gore might be worth four points, compared to a campaign stop by Joe Lieberman's

139

wife Hadassa, who rated a single point. The type of press opportunity, a stump speech or a quick pass-through, also was taken into account. Media coverage of the visit was rated using a point system, with high scores going to national television news and print sources while local news would rank lower. Each day, a revised map would be circulated among the various branches of the campaign. Programmers emphasized the fact that the map was a rough indication of the extent of media coverage, especially as the coding scheme was highly subjective. Still, campaign officials frequently would treat the map as definitive information and would use it to direct media strategies. Gore might be sent into a particular state because the color of the map indicated that a media push was in order.[54]

The Bush campaign predominantly used tried-and-true methods of targeting their media efforts, relying mostly on focus groups. The campaign did make use of digital cameras and the Internet to expedite internal communications. Media advisers were able to send prospective ads to the candidate on the road via the Internet. Bush would pull down the ads and comment on them prior to their airing.[55]

ELECTION NIGHT FIASCO: THE TURNING POINT

The major television networks initiated their election night coverage with remarks that would soon become understatements, observing that it would be a long and unusually interesting evening. At 7:40 p.m., the Voter News Service, the consortium that pools the resources of ABC, CBS, NBC, CNN, Fox, and the Associated Press, released exit poll data indicating that Al Gore had won the state of Florida. By 8 p.m., all six VNS member organizations officially placed Florida's 25 electoral votes in Gore's column, sparking much media speculation that Gore might be headed to the White House. The networks began to rescind this call at 10:48 p.m. when conflicting data from exit polls and precinct returns placed the initial call in doubt. With Florida once again up for grabs and the primary focus of media attention, the networks scrambled to make their next move. Fox News called Florida for Bush at 2:16 a.m., once again setting the stage for the network pack to fall in lockstep. A decisive Bernard Shaw of CNN proclaimed, "George Bush, Governor of Texas, will become the forty-third president of the United States."

The media's pronouncement of Bush as the winner prompted Gore to depart from his hotel in Nashville to make his concession speech. While Gore was en route, Democratic campaign manager William Daley urgently contacted the candidate and instructed him not to concede. Daley had telephoned the networks, which now had doubts about the vote count in Florida. Bush's victory lasted about 90 minutes, until the networks backpedaled once again and proclaimed the election too close to call. Speaking to the crowd in Nashville, Daley stated, "I've been in politics a long time. But there's never been a night like this one. Just an hour or so ago, the TV networks called this race for Governor Bush. It now appears their call was premature."[56]

The networks' mistaken call of Florida was not the only faux pas of the evening. News organizations called New Mexico for Gore too soon, only to issue a retraction hours later. Although the state eventually went to Gore by a narrow margin, the outcome was clearly too close to predict on election night.[57] In addition, the networks erroneously characterized Virginia, North Carolina, Georgia, and Ohio as being too close to call, when in fact they went easily to Bush. These incorrect calculations resulted in charges of anti-Bush bias in reporting being leveled by prominent Republicans.

Newspapers did not fare any better than television news in their rush to report a winner. The *New York Post*'s bold red headline proclaimed, "Bush Wins!" while "Bush Triumphs" graced the front page of the *Charleston Gazette*. The *Miami Herald, San Francisco Chronicle, Des Moines Register, Forth Worth Star–Post, Atlanta Journal–Constitution*, and many other papers followed suit. The *New York Times* released 100,000 newspapers stating that Bush "appears to have won" before rolling back the presses. At 3 a.m., the *Times* web site made the announcement "Bush Captures the White House," only to retract the statement an hour later.[58] *The Washington Post* was able to kill a front page with the headline "Bush Appears Victorious," minutes before it was scheduled to go to press.[59]

Early Calls

Scholars, political observers, and journalists themselves have argued for decades about the potentially harmful effects of news organizations' obsession with being the first to call election campaigns. Most debates focus on the influence of reports of exit polls and early election returns on voters in districts where ballots are still being cast. This issue was first brought to public attention in 1964, when CBS News named Barry Goldwater the winner in the California primary before the polls had closed statewide.[60] The 1980 presidential contest again brought this issue to the forefront, as the networks called the election for Ronald Reagan early in the evening. Critics argued that early calls depressed turnout on the West Coast, possibly affecting the outcomes of non-presidential races. In the early 1980s, the networks, in an effort to avoid formal congressional action, agreed to police themselves by avoiding early calls in states where the majority of polls were still open. Since there is no formal enforcement mechanism in place, even networks with the best of intentions can be pressured into calling states prematurely because a competitor has done so.[61]

The 1980 campaign sparked a spate of academic studies on the effect of early calls on voter behavior and election outcomes. The evidence is somewhat mixed.[62] Some argue that there is no effect, or that turnout can be stimulated by early calls as voters realize that their vote could matter, especially in tight races. This is the research that is selectively used by the networks to justify continuing their practice of early calls. However, there is enough empirical support for the contention that the networks' early calls adversely affect turnout and

142

disenfranchise voters to be a cause for concern.[63] In addition, the majority of voters find early calls objectionable even when they are correct.[64]

Exit Polls

Exit polls are face-to-face interviews conducted as voters are leaving their polling places on Election Day. Voters complete a short survey that includes their vote choice, demographic information, and questions about issues and candidates. Exit polls are fielded in a small number of voting precincts with the goal of acquiring representative data. These polls not only are used by media organizations in their election night coverage, but also are employed by scholars conducting research on the campaign.

Until 1992, each network had its own exit polling operation. In an attempt to cut costs, the Voter News Service was formed in 1989 to serve as a single source of exit poll data. VNS now serves five major television networks, the AP, and more than 100 newspapers, radio, and television stations on election night. News organizations generally employ experts to work with the data from VNS and make decisions about calling races. In the case of the networks, this information is passed on to the "talent" who make the on-air announcements. VNS performs two functions on Election Day. It conducts a national exit poll as well as more detailed exit polls in some individual states. In addition, VNS collects and tabulates unofficial election night voting results based on information gathered from county election officials across the country.

Because they are conducted quickly on a single day using a methodology that relies heavily on the skill of interviewers, exit polls have a history of problems. These difficulties were magnified with the institution of VNS. According to pollster Andrew Kohut, the breakdown in Florida was in the sample precincts, not the exit polls. Because of a desire to keep costs low, VNS did not use a large enough number of sample precincts to be able to detect aberrations in the data. VNS interviewed 1,818 randomly selected voters in 45 precincts in Florida.[65] The VNS sample included a precinct in the Tampa area that overrepresented the Democratic vote, prompting the initial Florida call for Gore. Bias can occur in a sample for any number of reasons, including interviewer effects, the timing of interviews, the selection of respondents, and the willingness of subjects to participate. Ideally, three precincts should be polled to represent a single locale, allowing for a comparison check of the results.[66]

The facilities and methodologies employed by VNS played a role in the election night miscalculations. The equipment and software used by VNS are not state-of-the-art. The statistical models employed by VNS to analyze exit poll data were designed in the 1970s by pollster Warren Mitofsky, and they have not been updated to fit the current context. These models do not include sufficient statistical checks to ensure quality control and verification of the data.[67] The current procedures are insufficient for estimating the impact on election outcomes of absentee voters and outstanding votes from unreported precincts in close races. The models are most effective in dealing with situations in which there are thousands of votes separating the candidates, and not hundreds or fewer.[68]

Not all of the blame for the bad election night calls lies with VNS. The networks, in fact, called Florida before VNS had rendered its decision on the state. News organizations' internal analysts make the final calls based on their assessment of exit polls, voting returns from closed precincts, the number of absentee ballots in a state, and a variety of state-based historical factors, such as the normal partisan vote and how quickly the state has turned in its vote counts in the past. Different criteria and information are employed by particular news organizations, and some are more careful than others.

Even when news organization have access to sufficient data to carefully weigh their decisions to call a state, pressures to beat the competition come into play. In their post-election debriefings, the networks were quick to defend against the charges that the incorrect calls were the result of professional rivalries driven by business imperatives. But the facts suggest otherwise. CBS was the third network to call Florida for Gore 20 minutes after Fox's initial announcement, which followed NBC by less than 2 minutes. Before moving Florida into the Bush column, the CBS News Decision Desk "took [only] another 30 seconds to finish their data check" after Fox (followed immediately by NBC) made the call.[69]

The problems with the exit polls in the general election were foreshadowed by polling data during the primary campaign. On the eve of the New Hampshire primary, the *CBS Evening News* reported that the Republican primary was "too close to call" and on the Democratic side that Al Gore "had a comfortable lead" over Bill Bradley. McCain won formidably in New Hampshire, while Gore defeated Bradley with difficulty. Similar mistakes were made by news organizations predicting primary outcomes in South Carolina and Michigan.[70]

A system of determining election night calls that relies solely on exit poll data from VNS lacks the checks and controls that would exist if there were alternative operations in place. Professional norms dictate that journalists consult multiple sources when fact-checking a story. The same standards should apply when making decisions that have serious consequences for voters and leaders.

POST-ELECTION FERVOR: A MEDIA BONANZA

In an ironic twist, the press benefited greatly from the overtime election. The candidates' public relations machines were in overdrive as they attempted to set the agenda and sway public opinion. Journalists used the opportunity of covering the momentous post-election events to restore their sullied reputations. Citizens were transfixed by the spectacle of sparring lawyers and ballot counting. They followed every step of the complex political and legal battle with an intense interest that has long been absent from American politics.

The Media Regroups

The excitement generated by the history-making election without an outcome was a boon to the press. The post-campaign drama boosted television news ratings, rekindled participation in call-in shows, and propelled Internet use. There was far more news coverage of the recount period than of the general election. The networks devoted over 21 hours to news reports in the five weeks following the election compared to 13 hours and 21 minutes during the nine-week general election, which represented a 60 percent increase in coverage.[71] In the first week of the deadlock, the networks provided more coverage of the election than they had of any of the major stories of the decade, including the Clinton-Lewinsky scandal and the deaths of Princess Diana and John F. Kennedy, Jr.[72] Cable news stations featured "all election, all the time," with continuous live coverage of ballot counts, courtroom battles, and press conferences. Call-in television and radio programs require regular shots of adrenaline in the form of new scandals and crises to invigorate ratings. The post-election drama provided much fuel to drive up audience shares as hosts lambasted the mainstream press for endangering democracy by their irresponsible behavior.

Internet use the day after the election was the heaviest in the history of the medium. News and information sites saw their traffic increase by between 130 percent and 500 percent. ABCNews.com received 27.1 million page views, substantially breaking its previous record of 10 million page views with the release of the Starr report. MSNBC.com doubled its record-breaking traffic of 3 million visitors that it received in the wake of major disasters, such as the crash of the Air France Concorde. Even Internet-only sites that generally have lower audience shares than those with mainstream media counterparts had a banner day. Salon.com received 1.7 million page views.[73] The boom in web site traffic persisted along with the recount as users sought to get the latest bits of new information.

It is no surprise that the strategic frame emphasized by the media during the primaries and general election became the primary focus of post-election coverage. The maneuvering of the candidates, their operatives, and their media-friendly legal teams became a major focus of press attention. The Democratic team was portrayed as using moral arguments based on the fact that Gore had won the popular vote to bolster its public appeals. The implication was that the Republicans were attempting to steal the election from the voters. This approach intensified as Bush made preparations for the transition to the White House. The Republican camp was seen as depicting the opposition as desperate and petty while working to make Bush appear as if he was above the fray and ready to assume a position of leadership.

Star journalists sought to recover from their election night blunders by attempting to handle the momentous developments with an air of formality. Journalists in the star system's bullpen were elated by the opportunities the overtime election afforded to make them major players. In a *People* magazine interview, MSNBC reporter Ashley Banfield, a Canadian who admitted she had no stake in the election, stated that the post-campaign cliff-hanger was the career break for which she had been waiting. Banfield's frequent on-air appearances allowed her to market her trademark dark-rimmed glasses as she read copy from a notepad to give the impression that the monotonous recounts were really late-breaking developments.

The Public Engages

Public involvement in and monitoring of the campaign via mass media surged in the period following election night. Citizen interest peaked radically in the first week after Election Day. According to

VVP data, 46 percent of the public claimed to be paying "a lot to a fair amount" of attention to the campaign in the final week before going to the polls; this figure soared to 77 percent in the following week.[74] Levels of interest vacillated as the saga dragged on, with interest peaking at critical junctures, such as the announcement of the most recent court decision, but always remaining higher than during the general election campaign itself. Even young people, who are notoriously disengaged from the political process, paid close attention to the campaign's aftermath.

The election-on-hold had some positive civic consequences. The events stimulated discussion about politics and the political process. The VVP discovered that 80 percent of citizens discussed the election with someone in the first week of the post-campaign. The situation highlighted aspects of the political process that are not often on average citizens' radar screen, prompting them to seek information about their rights and obligations as well as how the system operates.[75]

The post-campaign period also created frustration among voters. The VVP found that citizens became more disheartened about the situation as time went on. Seventy percent of the public reported being discouraged by the post-campaign events, and 50 percent claimed that the election was unfair to voters. Further, citizens' sense of political efficacy, their belief that they have an influence on government and politics, diminished significantly. VVP data indicate that the proportion of people reporting that they have no effect on government increased from 10 percent to 25 percent in a two-week period beginning just prior to Election Day.

THE AFTERMATH

In the immediate aftermath of the protracted election, there was much posturing by politicians, political observers, and journalists about the need to reform the media's election night procedures. There was a flurry of activity by members of Congress to introduce greater oversight and propriety into the electoral process. Legislation was introduced to form a bipartisan commission on election integrity, the Government Accounting Office was asked to examine state election practices for rules on fraud and irregularities, and a study to ensure the speedy and accurate reporting of election results was commissioned.

The House Energy and Commerce Committee held hearings to investigate television news organizations' flawed election night coverage. Top executives from the major television networks and the Associated Press as well as experts from academia and think tanks appeared before the committee. Some news organization officials, including Louis Boccardi, president of the AP, and Roger Ailes of Fox News Network, objected to being called before the committee, and they expressed their concerns that congressional intervention might lead to violations of the First Amendment freedom of the press. The results of an independent review commissioned by CNN and internal reviews conducted by ABC, CBS, and Fox[76] identified problems with the system of election night reporting and presented a series of reform proposals. A highlight of the hearing was the airing of a videotape of clips that graphically illustrated the networks' shifting reports on the status of Florida.

In many ways, the hearings let the individual networks off the hook by placing the heaviest blame on the VNS. The committee concluded that the VNS was in need of a serious overhaul and that exit polling was getting worse over time rather than better. According to Representative Billy Tauzin (R–LA), chair of the committee, "If you combine the bad sampling at VNS and bad modeling, you consistently get an overabundance of Democratic votes and an underabundance of Republican votes."[77] While Tauzin concluded that there was no intentional bias on the part of news organizations, the fact that all the major networks rely on a single source for exit polling data is a major defect in the system.

The testimony and reports generated a range of reform proposals for improving data collection, the rules for predicting races, the timing of election night calls, and reporting election results. The networks agreed that there was a need for more data and that multiple sources should be used for ascertaining vote counts. However, recommendations differed on specific issues, including whether there should be more exit polling in close races and more precincts sampled. CNN advocated the toughest standards for calling races and pledged not to use exit polls in close races or where there is less than a one-point margin of victory for a candidate. All of the networks agreed that their reporters need to disclose the process of calling races to the public and to make it clear that the calls are only projections and not actual vote tallies.[78]

In a preemptive strike, media organizations pledged to implement their own reforms without congressional intervention. The networks are committed to holding off on calling states for candidates until all, and not just most, of the polls in a state are closed. Despite the problems, all six member news organizations decided in June 2001 to sustain the VNS. The operation will be revamped to update the computer system, improve the statistical models used to estimate vote projections, and deal better with mail-in ballots and early day returns.[79] After reviewing the reports and testimony, the committee considered options for reform. A uniform national poll closing time was one suggestion, although not all media organizations accept the utility of this idea. The frenzy over reforming the system of election night media coverage faded quickly after the hearings. The issue currently appears to be far on the back burner of congressional concern.[80]

CONCLUSION

News organizations have been quick to point out that major errors in reporting presidential election outcomes are nothing new to the American scene. Dating back to 1812, when *Paulsen's American Daily Advertiser* incorrectly reported that De Witt Clinton had defeated James Madison, newspapers have made premature calls. The poll-supported error in 2000 conjured up memories of the infamous "Dewey Defeats Truman" banner headline on the front page of *The Chicago Tribune* in 1948 and early prediction by CBS television news of Richard Nixon over John F. Kennedy in 1960.[81]

Election 2000, however, has no parallels. It served as a referendum not only on the performance of the press but on the political process itself. As Larry J. Sabato, Mark Stencel, and Robert Lichter have aptly observed, "The press is on trial with readers and viewers."[82] The emphasis on scandals and negative politics has been taking its toll on journalists' credibility. Prior to the election, it was evident that the decline in public trust in the press has resulted in political disinterest and disengagement. The events of Election 2000 may have done even more harm to the democratic system by causing citizens to question the legitimacy of the very process by which they choose their leaders.

*Author's Note: I am indebted to Jeffrey S. Owen for his outstanding research efforts.

NOTES

[1] James Risser, Joan Konner, and Ben Wattenberg, "Television's Performance on Election Night 2000: A Report for CNN," January 29, 2001, p. 1.
[2] Personal interview with Matthew T. Felling, analyst, Center for Media and Public Affairs, May 28, 2001.
[3] Diana Owen, *Media Messages in American Presidential Elections* (Westport, CT: Greenwood Press), 1992.

[4] Robert Shogan, *Bad News: Where the Press Goes Wrong in the Making of the President* (New York: Ivan R. Dee), 2001.

[5] Marion R. Just, Ann N. Crigler, Dean E. Alger, Timothy Cook, and Montague Kern, *Crosstalk: Citizens, Candidates, and the Media in a Presidential Campaign* (Chicago: University of Chicago Press), 1996.

[6] "2000 Year in Review: TV's Leading News Topics, Reporters and Political Jokes," *Media Monitor* (Washington, D.C.: Center for Media and Public Affairs), January/February 2001.

[7] The Center for Media and Public Affairs (CMPA) analyzed coverage from Labor Day to Election Day and found that network newscasts spent a total of 805 minutes reporting campaign news, up slightly from 788 minutes in 1996. The *Hess Report* examined similar data for the same period and concluded that the evening network news devoted the lowest number of minutes in history to the campaign, down 12% from 1996, until the last week, when coverage increased dramatically. See "Campaign 2000 Final: How TV News Covered the General Election Campaign," *Media Monitor* (Washington, D.C.: Center for Media and Public Affairs), November/December 2000; Stephen Hess, "Dwindling TV Coverage Fell to New Low," *Hess Report on Campaign Coverage in Nightly Network News*, November 7, 2000; "Election 2000: Network News Coverage of Election Lowest in History," CNN.com, November 7, 2000.

[8] Stephen Hess, "Critical Information Not Covered by Media," *The Hess Report on Campaign Coverage in Nightly Network News*, September 25, 2000.

[9] "The Last Lap: How the Press Covered the Final Stages of the Presidential Campaign," *Election Coverage 2000* (Washington, D.C.: The Project for Excellence in Journalism), December 2000.

[10] "ePolitics: A Study of the 2000 Presidential Campaign on the Internet," *Election Coverage 2000* (Washington, D.C.: The Project for Excellence in Journalism), November 2000.

[11] Stephen Hess, "Poll Stories Are Often Wrong," *The Hess Report on Campaign Coverage in Nightly Network News*, October 29, 2000.

[12] "Perplexing Polls," *Online NewsHour*, http://www.pbs.org/newshour, October 31, 2000.

[13] "Errors Associated with 'Instant' and Overnight Polls," Statement by the National Council on Public Polls' Polling Review Board, http://www.ncpp.org/instant.htm.

[14] Mick P. Couper, "Review: Web Surveys," *Public Opinion Quarterly* (Winter 2000): 464–494.

[15] Personal interview with Andrew Kohut, May 30, 2001.

[16] In the last two months of the campaign, Gore received 13 percent positive coverage and 56 percent negative coverage. Bush fared slightly better, receiving 24 percent positive coverage and 49 percent negative coverage. See "The Last Lap: How the Press Covered the Final Stages of the Presidential Campaign."

[17] "Campaign 2000 Final: How TV News Covered the General Election Campaign," *Media Monitor*, November/December 2001.

[18] Dana G. Williams, "Covering Campaign 2000 Was a Real Drag, Reporters Say," *The Freedom Forum Online*, http://www.freedomforum.org, January 17, 2001.

[19] Abbie VanSickle, "Veteran of Political Journalism Criticizes America's 'Bloodless' Presidential Contest," *The Daily Northwestern*, January 30, 2001.

[20] Al Gore's sound bites averaged one second longer than those of George W. Bush.

[21] Thomas E. Patterson, *Out of Order* (New York: Knopf), 1994.

[22] "Journalists Monopolize TV Election News," Center for Media and Public Affairs, http://www.cmpa.com/pressrel/electpr10.htm, October 20, 2000.

[23] "Media Seen as Fair, But Tilting to Gore," news release, Pew Research Center for the People and the Press, October 15, 2000.

[24] The audience for presidential debates, while still sizable, has been diminishing. Fewer than 30 percent of respondents claimed they tuned into the first debate in 2000 in its entirety. See "Election 2000: How Viewers 'See' a Presidential Debate," *The Vanishing Voter* (Cambridge, MA: The Joan Shorenstein Center on the Press, Politics, and Public Policy), October 3, 2000.

[25] "News Coverage Propels Election Interest," *The Vanishing Voter* (Cambridge, MA: The Joan Shorenstein Center on the Press, Politics and Public Policy), September 20, 2000.

[26] *2000* (Washington, D.C.: The Pew Research Center for the People and the Press), 2001.

[27] Republican advertising strategists were not opposed to going negative; they realized that negative ads are effective and that people learn from them. Personal interview with Rush Schriefer, media consultant to the Bush campaign (Stevens and Schriefer).

[28] Personal interview with Rich Bond, former chair, Republican National Committee, May 28, 2001.

[29] One of the spots decrying Gore's plan for expanding Medicare contained a split-second image of the word "RATS," causing an uproar over the use of subliminal advertising.

[30] Stephen Ansolabehere and Shanto Iyengar, *Going Negative: How Political Advertisements Shrink and Polarize the Electorate* (New York: Simon and Schuster), 1997; Darrell West, *Air Wars* (Washington, D.C.: CQ Press), 1997.

[31] "Campaign 2000 Ad Watch," *CBS News*, http://www.cbsnews.com, August 31, 2000.

[32] John Berman, Mark Halperin, Dana Hill, Aditya Raval, and Katy Textor, "Down and Dirty," *ABC News*, http://www.abcnews.com, October 28, 2000.

[33] Personal interview with Rush Schriefer, May 25, 2001.

[34] "Campaign 2000 Highly Rated," news release (Washington, D.C.: The Pew Research Center for the People and the Press), November 16, 2000.

[35] "Media Seen as Fair, But Tilting to Gore."

[36] Richard Davis and Diana Owen, *New Media in American Politics* (New York: Oxford University Press), 1998; Richard Davis, *The Web of Politics* (New York: Oxford University Press), 1999.

[37] Lisa Guernsey, "Choice of Jewish Candidate Is Noted in Slurs on Internet," *The New York Times*, August 9, 2000.

[38] Comments of Chris Hunter, Annenberg Public Policy Center and election analyst for NetElection.org during Campaign 2000, August 18, 2000.

[39] Steven M. Schneider, "Congressional Candidate Web Sites in Campaign 2000: What Web Enthusiasts Wanted and What Candidates Provided" (Philadelphia: Annenberg Public Policy Center of the University of Pennsylvania), January 2000.

[40] Shortly after the campaign, Voter.com, a site that was regularly consulted by campaign insiders, particularly Republicans, closed down due to lack of funds.

[41] Lisa Napoli, "Covering the Convention, Net-style," MSNBC.com, July 31, 2000.

[42] Lisa Napoli, "Parties Take News into Own Hands," MSNBC.com., August 16, 2000.

[43] The Gallup Poll, http://www.gallup.org, February 2000.

[44] "Internet Election News Audience Seeks Convenience, Familiar Names" (Washington, D.C.: Pew Research Center for the People and the Press), December 3, 2000.

[45] Leslie Wayne, "Online Coverage Fell Short of the Hype," *The New York Times*, August 19, 2000.

[46] Napoli, August 16, 2000.

[47] The Wisconsin Continuous Monitoring Survey (WISCON) data indicate that 7 percent of the population has looked at a candidate's web site. The Vanishing Voter Project found that 8 percent of the general public had looked up candidate information online. The February 2000 Gallup poll reports that 11 percent of online users had visited a candidate's web site. Similarly, the February 29, 2000, Kaiser Family Foundation Study of Internet use reported that 10 percent of those online are "very likely" to use the Internet to find out candidate information or ballot issues.

[48] Funds raised using telephone solicitations were logged into the McCain campaign's web site, elevating the total Internet figure. See Rebecca Fairley Raney, "Volunteers' Actions Lead Skeptics to Question McCain's Online Donations," *The New York Times Online*, February 12, 2000.

[49] Personal interview with Rush Schriefer, May 25, 2001.

[50] Observations by Mark Stencel, managing editor, washingonpost.com, and Doug Bailey, president, FreedomChannel.com, at a panel titled "Has the Net Transformed Politics?" sponsored by the Freedom Forum, October 9, 2000.

[51] Josephine Ferrigno-Stack, "Public Opinion on the Web: Confusion, Chaos, and Fabulous Pie Charts," http://netelection.org, November 22, 2000.

[52] "ePolitics: A Study of the 2000 Presidential Campaign," November 2000.

[53] Survey of journalists' perceptions of online election coverage conducted by Diana Owen and Joe Cutbirth, Georgetown University, February 2001.

154

[54] Personal interview with John M. Fohr, computer media strategist, Gore campaign, April 19, 2001.

[55] Personal interview with Rush Schriefer, May 25, 2001.

[56] "Remarks by Chairman Bill Daley Election Night, Nashville, Tennessee," Official Gore-Lieberman Campaign Web Site, November 8, 2000.

[57] "Election Night: A Media Watch Special Report," *Online NewsHour*, http://www.pbs.org/newshour, November 12, 2000; Linda Mason, Kathleen Frankovic, and Kathleen Hall Jamieson, "CBS News Coverage of Election Night 2000: Investigation, Analysis, Recommendations," CBS News, January 2001.

[58] "Florida Election Returns Prove Achilles' Heel for News Media," Associated Press, November 8, 2000.

[59] Steve Luxenberg, "Is TV to Blame? Well, Let's Go to the Videotape," *The Washington Post*, November 12, 2000, p. B5.

[60] Mason, Frankovic, and Jamieson, January 2001, p. 52.

[61] The author was an election poll analyst for NBC News during the 1988 presidential campaign, prior to the establishment of VNS. Tom Brokaw made it clear that he did not want to call any state prior to poll closings. As election night wore on, producers monitored other networks. If an early call was made, NBC followed suit almost immediately.

[62] Harold Mendelson, "Election Day Broadcasts and Terminal Voting Decisions," *Public Opinion Quarterly* (1966): 212–225; Laurily K. Epstein and Gerald Strom, "Election Night Projections and West Coast Turnout," *American Politics Quarterly* (1981): 470–492. Epstein headed the NBC election night polling division in the 1980s.

[63] Michael X. Delli Carpini, "Scooping the Voters? The Consequences of the Networks' Early Call of the 1980 Presidential Race," *Journal of Politics* (1984): 866–885; Philip L. Dubois, "Election Night Projections and Voter Turnout in the West: A Note on the Hazards of Aggregate Data Analysis," *American Politics Quarterly* (1983): 349–364; Raymond Wolfinger and Peter Linquiti, "Tuning In and Turning Out," *Public Opinion Quarterly* (1981): 65–70.

[64] Michael W. Traugott and Paul J. Lavrakas, *The Voter's Guide to Election Polls*, 2nd edition (New York: Chatham House), 2000.

[65] Richard Morin and Claudia Deane, "Why the Florida Exit Polls Were Wrong," *The Washington Post*, November 8, 2000.

[66] Personal interview with Andrew Kohut, May 30, 2001.

[67] "Bad Calls," *Online NewsHour*, November 8, 2000.

[68] Kathleen A. Frankovic, "Lessons from Election Night 2000: Lessons for the News Media," paper presented at the Annual Meeting of the American Association for Public Opinion Research, May 17, 2000.

[69] Mason, Frankovich, and Jamieson, January 2001, p. 15.

[70] Stephen Hess, November 29, 2000.

[71] "Florida Trouble Triples TV Attention," press release (Washington, D.C.: The Center for Media and Public Affairs), December 20, 2000.

[72] "Media Feeding Frenzy in Florida," press release (Washington, D.C.: The Center for Media and Public Affairs), November 22, 2000.

[73] Farhad Manjoo, "Net Traffic at All-Time High," *Wired News*, http://www.wirednews.org, November 8, 2000.

[74] "Interested But Discouraged: Americans' View of the Election Drama," *The Vanishing Voter* (Cambridge, MA: The Joan Shorenstein Center on the Press, Politics, and Public Policy), November 21, 2000.

[75] Citizens' questions to experts in online question and answer discussions that became popular during this period were sophisticated and indicated a desire to learn about such issues as constitutional provisions regarding the Electoral College and the technical requirements of voting. Personal experience as an online election analyst for AOL on election night and during the post-election period.

[76] NBC did not submit its review at the time of the hearings, presenting instead a three-page summary to the House Energy and Commerce Committee.

[77] Ian Christopher McCaleb, "House Lawmakers May Suggest Uniform Poll Closing Time," CNN.com, February 2001.

[78] Frankovic, May 17, 2001.

[79] "Voter News Service Opts to Carry On, But Revamp," *The Washington Post*, June 1, 2001.

[80] Telephone calls to the office of Rep. Billy Tauzin and the House Committee on Energy and Commerce revealed that election night reforms are not on the congressional agenda, and interest in the issue has all but disappeared.

[81] Eric Newton, "Tight Races, Egged Faces," *Freedom Forum Online*, November 10, 2000.

[82] Larry J. Sabato, Mark Stencel, and S. Robert Lichter, *Peepshow: Media and Politics in an Age of Scandal* (Lanham, MD: Rowman & Littlefield, 2000).

CHAPTER 7

The Labor of Sisyphus:
The Gore Recount Perspective

Ronald A. Klain and Jeremy B. Bash
Gore-Lieberman Legal Advisers

I also commend Vice President Gore, for persevering
in the labor of Sisyphus; each time he attempted to
comply with the Code, he was forced to begin anew.
—*Gore v. Harris,* 773 So. 2d 524, 530
(Fla. 2000) (Shaw, J., concurring)

The only thing worse than being thwarted in a just pursuit is *believing*
that you have made progress in that pursuit, only to find out that you
in fact have made very little progress, in the end.

That was the feeling we had on December 13, 2000—the day we left
Tallahassee after the partial recount of the presidential ballots in
Florida. It was a partial recount, of course, because some of the votes
cast for president on November 7 were never counted, not even once.
Despite 23 court proceedings, two appeals to the Florida Supreme
Court, and two arguments before the United States Supreme Court,
some voters in Florida never had their ballots counted. Just as quickly
as vote counts were ordered, they were disrupted, halted, and

ultimately shut down. Each time we thought that vote counting would continue, another person—a canvassing board member, a GOP attorney, a state official—stood in the way. Each time we made a bit of progress, that progress was reversed.

While it was going on, the right metaphor for the experience never came to mind. But after it was over—when the Florida Supreme Court issued a little-read, after-the-fact opinion just before Christmas Eve—a fitting description was finally offered. It came, ironically enough, from Justice Leander Shaw—one of the three Justices on the Florida Supreme Court who had voted against our appeal there. Justice Shaw compared our efforts to the labor of Sisyphus, the Greek mythological character, who, when tasked with pushing a bolder up a mountain, found himself slipping back down the mountain just as the summit seemed within reach.[1] Such was our experience in Florida: Each time it seemed that we were on the verge of getting the vote count completed, some setback would push us back to the starting line. Like Sisyphus, our task was never completed—though we never stopped trying, until the bitter end.

For the two of us, who spent five weeks striving for what seemed like a simple enough objective—a full, fair, and timely tally of the votes in Florida—the premature termination of that effort will always be a story of professional and personal frustration. And though media recounts conducted under differing and debatable rules have all yielded conflicting results, two underlying facts have not changed since December 13 and are not seriously disputed now: More people left the polls in Florida on Election Day believing they had voted for Al Gore than for George Bush; and nonetheless, Florida's 25 electors were awarded to Bush, who as a result, won the presidency. The reality of the first of these two facts did not change the reality of the second, because of a combination of avoidable voter mistakes, ruthlessly partisan tactics by Florida election officials, and, ultimately, an inability and unwillingness of the courts to rectify those wrongs.

THE FIRST FEW HOURS SET A PATTERN

When we left for Florida early on the morning of November 8, we did not know whether Al Gore or George Bush had gotten more votes in that state. But within the first 24 hours, the two overriding facts that would shape the next 36 days became clear.

First, it quickly became clear that more Floridians had left the polls on Election Day believing they had voted for Al Gore than had voted for George Bush. Though it took a few days for the precise extent of this to be quantified, the scope and scale of the electoral problems were overwhelming. Due to the confusing (if not illegal) "butterfly ballot," almost 10,000 voters in Palm Beach County had their ballots counted as votes for Pat Buchanan (or thrown out as "overvotes" because the voters had punched both Buchanan and Gore)—in a heavily black, heavily Jewish county where Buchanan would have been lucky to crack 1,000 votes. In Miami-Dade County, almost 1,000 votes were thrown out because voters punched a hole next to Joe Lieberman's name, not Al Gore's—the product of how punch-card ballots misaligned when pulled from the machine. In predominantly African-American Gadsden County, which Gore carried by a 2 to 1 margin, about 1 in 8 votes were thrown out as "invalid"; next door, in predominantly white Leon County, the discard rate was just 1 in 680.[2] The list went on and on and on. The exact numbers could be debated, but the conclusion could not (and still, to this day, has not been): Florida's voters had meant to choose Gore.

At the same time, another unfortunate development also became clear, very quickly: Florida's election officials were not about to let the reality of which candidate the voters preferred stand in the way of their efforts to crown the candidate those officials preferred: George Bush. We arrived in Florida to find that Jeb Bush was everywhere—literally. When our airplane landed in Tallahassee on Wednesday, November 8, the Governor's plane pulled up beside ours on the tarmac. It was an appropriate metaphor for the next five weeks. Republican-controlled canvassing boards across the state commenced

159

the mandatory machine recount—but they were doing so on their own terms and without any semblance of participation from Democratic observers. (In fact, some Gore-Lieberman staffers who had flown to Florida on November 8 to "observe the recount" were told by CNN that the recount was already "complete" in many places, even as those staffers stood in line at the rental car counter at the airport.) On June 1, 2001, *The Washington Post* reported that 18 of Florida's 67 counties (totaling more than 1.58 million votes) never actually recounted their votes—they simply checked their original results.[3] Perhaps most importantly, within hours, Florida's Secretary of State—Katherine Harris, George W. Bush's campaign co-chair in Florida—issued the first of five legal opinions that sought to stop the counting of votes. Each of the five—every one—was ultimately found to be legally erroneous by the Florida courts.[4] But the delays and obstruction caused by her partisan efforts on behalf of President Bush were diversions at best, and probably fatal in the end.

THE CHALLENGE: COULD THE COURTS SORT OUT THE MESS?

Though it was the Bush campaign that went to court first (with a frivolous federal lawsuit designed to stop the ballot counting), we quickly understood that with the political system so heavily stacked against us, we would have to turn to the courts for justice. The challenge was obvious: Did the courts have the time, the tools, and the tenacity to right the wrong? Or would the pressure of the ticking clock, the looming Florida legislature, and the unfortunate gaps in Florida law make such a result impossible?

We faced four main challenges when we arrived in Florida. First, we were behind among the ballots that had been tabulated, and that meant two things: We were the ones who had to "overturn" the "status quo"; and the public believed that because Bush was in the lead, he had probably won.

160

Second, the mechanisms for tabulating votes were in the hands of our opponents. Even where canvassing boards had "neutral" judges, some, including judges Charles Burton and Robert W. Lee, were in fact appointed by Jeb Bush. The state's chief election official was the Bush campaign co-chair. And the governor was our opponent's brother.

Third, we had to operate within the confines of Florida's somewhat clumsy election laws, which had no procedures for a dispute or recount of a statewide election. Although we did the best we could with the statutes we had, any process for resolving this matter was going to have to be cobbled together from imperfectly applicable statutes and remedies. When you are contesting a presidential election, it is never reassuring to hear that the procedures you are seeking to invoke have not been used in a statewide election in this century—or in most cases, in any election more significant than county sheriff.

Finally, time was our enemy. In the electronic communications era, the nation had never gone past noon Wednesday without knowing who its president would be. Indeed, in the 40 years since the Kennedy-Nixon race, most Americans had become accustomed to victory and concession speeches before bedtime on election night. We did not know how long the public was prepared to wait to learn the identity of its next president, whether world events might make the delay seem dangerous, or whether support among leading Democrats—never that strong for Vice President Gore—might collapse.

In retrospect, the last factor—which is easily discounted now that December is long over—cannot be underestimated. It too was a lesson learned painfully, early on: When on the Friday night after the election (November 10) one of us (Ron Klain) went on CNN and rather offhandedly noted that there was plenty of time for a full and fair counting of the people's votes, given that the electoral votes were not scheduled to be counted until December 18, the next morning's

161

Washington Post reported, on page 1, a building revolt of party leaders over those made-for-cable comments.[5] Time was not on our side.

CRAFTING A LEGAL STRATEGY

Our legal strategy was guided by one simple premise: Since more people left the polls believing they had voted for Al Gore than for George Bush, all we were seeking was a legal ratification of the will of the voters.[6] If legal remedies that discerned the true "will of the voters" could be won, Vice President Gore would win the recount. Our client's interest, and democracy's first principle, were aligned.

More immediately, we believed that our legal strategy was firmly based in Florida law. For while that state's statues lacked clarity and completeness when it came to recount procedures, there was no ambiguity as to their ultimate aim: that the will of the voters, not technicalities or mechanics, should prevail. As the Florida Supreme Court *unanimously* wrote: "Th[e] essential principle, that the outcome of elections be determined by the will of the voters, forms the foundation of the election code enacted by the Florida Legislature."[7]

The legal strategy we developed had four prongs for overcoming the four challenges outlined above.[8] First, we were behind in the tally, so our goal was to seek a more complete tally of *all* of the votes. Within the time constraints we faced, we wanted the greatest share of the 150,000 overvotes and undervotes that had not yet been tallied, to be tallied. We knew that any count of those votes would inevitably be incomplete and—at least in some respects—arbitrary. But we firmly believed that a count that left out *all* of those votes (as did the tally that Secretary of State Harris wanted to certify, before she was stopped by a 7–0 decision of the Florida Supreme Court) was even *more* incomplete and even *more* arbitrary. Put another way: We knew that any remedy imposed in this period would be attacked as unfair—

but it was hard to see how the status quo in Florida on November 8 could be thought to be more fair.[9]

Second, since our opponents controlled the political means for recording tabulations, we needed to discipline their political excesses with the rule of law. That meant seeking rulings from the Florida courts to set aside the arbitrary and baseless "orders" from Secretary of State Harris directing the Boards of Canvassing to stop their recounts; to reverse the lawless decision of one board to stop a half-completed count; and to try to win the time for the counts to be completed before the overly eager election certifiers declared the result final, no matter what the tally showed.

Third, because the state lacked adequate procedures for dealing with a statewide recount, we sought to invoke analogous procedures found in Florida statutes and cases, borrowing from county recount procedures to "create" a fair and just process. That meant looking at rulings from the era of paper ballots to determine what should be done in the era of paper punch cards—often with mixed success.

Fourth, because time was not on our side, we supported getting the recount done quickly—and sometimes, sacrificing completeness for speed. That meant supporting a count of four counties, when it seemed like counting more would take forever; it meant accepting deadlines, like the December 12 date, even if in doing so, we would risk losing some flexibility in the end; it meant accepting partial counts such as an "undervote only" recount in Miami-Dade County, when the only choices available were to support that count— or see no count at all.

The strategy was far from perfect. But we had the law on our side, the facts on our side, and an outstanding legal team in state and federal court. It should have worked ... but obviously, it did not.

163

Ronald A. Klain and Jeremy B. Bash

WHY DIDN'T IT WORK?

Given what we had on our side, why did we not win? First, it is worth noting how close the strategy did in fact come to working. In ruling that the two-hour-late recounted votes from Palm Beach County and the partial counts from Miami-Dade County should have been added to the vote totals, the Florida Supreme Court's December 8 decision left Al Gore just 136 votes behind George Bush, with thousands of votes ordered to be counted. The margin one month before, on Wednesday, November 8, had been nearly 1,600 votes. A month of recounts, of hand counts, and of fighting for those counts had wiped out 90 percent of the gap. But, of course, if there were ever a case in which the old adage about "close only counts in horseshoes" had applicability, it certainly would be this one.

Second, we think it is too easy, too simplistic, and just plain wrong to take the entire proceeding and reduce the explanation of our defeat to a single sentence: "We were robbed by the U.S. Supreme Court." We know that many of our colleagues and fellow partisans feel that way. But such a one-dimensional analysis ignores all the other events and actions that created the circumstances, that made the Supreme Court's stay and ultimate ruling decisive: the obstruction by Secretary of State Harris; the deliberate application of an incorrect tabulation standard in Palm Beach County[10]; the illegal abandonment of the recount in Miami-Dade County; the persistent effort by the Bush campaign to block any counting of any votes; and so on. The U.S. Supreme Court's decision was final, and it was the end—but if countless other things had gone differently prior to that Saturday, the Court would have faced a very different case (if any case at all).

So if the cause was not the U.S. Supreme Court (well, at least not entirely), what accounted for the failure of our legal strategy? The answer is best seen if we review what happened to our four-pronged legal strategy, point by point.

With regard to the first objective—to seek the most complete vote count possible—we were undone by an endless series of obstacles thrown in our way to stop most of the vote counting even before it started. Counting was blocked for several days in Palm Beach County due to an erroneous legal opinion issued by Katherine Harris. Counting was blocked in Miami-Dade County by lawsuits filed by Republican leaders—one a day—to squander precious hours. Republicans lawyers in Broward County subpoenaed vote counters so that they had to spend their days in court testifying rather than at tables, counting. The GOP lawyers even had a name for the tactic: "mudballing."[11]

Our efforts to advance vote counts were also frustrated by fatigue. All over the state, we found that election officials and election workers were exhausted and anxious to put the entire chapter behind them. Some officials had post-election vacation plans: in Broward County; for example, procedures and processes were thrown in doubt because a member of the Board of Canvassing resigned to go on a cruise. The human dimension of the process led to letdowns that were understandable, but frustrating just the same.

The fact of the matter was that while we had only one way to win—getting more votes counted—our opponents had countless means to stymie us. In 36 days in Florida there were only 3 days when vote counting went on in more than two counties.

On point number two—trying to temper politics with law—we were clearly at a disadvantage, compounded by the shortness of time. While we were busy seeking relief in the courts to compel the counting of votes, our Republican colleagues were busy trying to prevent those actions from moving forward, and then asking those same courts to stop the vote counting altogether. Moreover, the legitimacy of judicial rulings in our favor was undermined by heated rhetoric from the Bush camp, calling into doubt the fairness and the impartiality of the courts. GOP leaders attacked the courts directly, saying that the Florida courts were "changing the election laws of Florida by judicial fiat." By incessantly questioning the legitimacy of the Florida judiciary, our opponents limited that institution's ability to effectuate justice in Florida.

And, of course, our ability to temper politics with law was itself tempered by the narrow 5-to-4 decision of the U.S. Supreme Court, whose ruling ending the recount included an interpretation of Florida law that, as we have seen above, even one Florida Supreme Court dissenter thought was dubious.

The third element of our legal strategy—borrowing from county recount procedures to fill the vacuum left in Florida law concerning a statewide recount—ran into two obstacles. First, it is difficult—if not impossible—to develop "neutral rules" in such a politically charged environment.[12] No matter what rule of decision was developed by either side, it was immediately susceptible to the charge that it was designed to tally more votes for Bush or Gore. The two camps would even flip-flop positions as the facts shifted: Early in the post-election period, when rumors of a large trove of pro-Gore overseas ballots abounded, Bush surrogate (and former Florida Secretary of State) Jim Smith released a position on the tabulation of overseas ballots that was highly restrictive. Later, when the geography of the received but not-yet-tabulated overseas absentee votes suggested a likely pro-Bush outcome, efforts to enforce Smith's own rules were called "unpatriotic" by GOP spokespeople.

In addition, the challenge of filling in gaps in Florida election law was confounded by the whipsaw created by an overinterpretation of the federal election law safe harbor provision (3 U.S.C. §5). This law, which insulated from attack state election contest results based on procedures established before Election Day, was deftly twisted by the Bush team into a federal injunction against "changing the rules in the middle of the game." As a result, whenever we proposed specific practices and procedures for resolving disputed issues in Florida—or whenever a court (like the Florida Supreme Court) sought to impose such order on the process—the charge came that such procedures were "new rules" in "violation" of the safe harbor provision. But, conversely, whenever we suggested that the count go forward without such rules, we were accused of advancing a count that was "arbitrary" and "standardless." Lacking an ability to announce new rules, or to proceed without such rules, the Florida judicial process sputtered when attempting to shape a mechanism for conducting a fast and fair statewide recount during the final weekend of the contest.

Finally, with regard to the fourth prong of our legal strategy—to still the loud ticking of the clock—our support for expedition was an approach that sometimes came back to haunt us. For example, when, on November 20, before the Florida Supreme Court, we accepted December 12 as a deadline, that position seemed safe enough: The recount was 12 days old; public patience was already wearing thin; we needed just a few days of counting to get the job done; and a deadline that was 22 days away seemed like no real deadline at all. While this concession on our part was *not* the basis for the U.S. Supreme Court's ruling that Florida law set December 12 as the deadline, the example is illustrative of how the "need for speed" caused complex problems.

In the end, it is not clear to us that if we had employed a different approach, we could have achieved a different result in Florida. A determined and ruthless opposition, a weary electoral system, a judicial system put to the test by an incomplete and inadequate statutory scheme, withering attacks on the courts, control over the tabulation and certification process in partisan hands, and a divided U.S. Supreme Court were a difficult set of obstacles to overcome. Our approach got close—very close—to succeeding. And in retrospect, the more amazing thing may be not that we lost, but that we got as close as we did.

PUTTING SOME WHAT IF'S TO REST

That said, it is only natural and appropriate that when one side loses the most important legal dispute in a generation, questions about the choices that team made will be asked, and asked, and asked. There are things we could have—and should have—done differently. (Whether they would have made a difference or not remains doubtful to us.) But two of the most persistent questions about our approach reflect, in our view, a misguided understanding of what happened in Florida, and why. We address each of them here.

First, should Al Gore have asked for a statewide recount in Florida, instead of just a recount of four counties where he was sure to do well?

This is a constant theme of the post hoc analysis: If the Bush camp was wrong to resist recounts, the Gore camp was equally bankrupt in asking for counts only in "strongly Democratic" counties. Thus, according to these critics, we "deserved" the injustice of having those voters' votes left uncounted. As twisted as this criticism is in the abstract—it seems odd to conclude that because not all the voters will have their votes counted, a large share of them should be denied that right—it is simply wrong on the facts.

First, Al Gore *did* ask for a recount of all the ballots in the state. He proposed it to Governor Bush on national television, just five days after the first hand counts were requested:

> I am also prepared, if Governor Bush prefers, to include in [any] recount all the counties in the entire state of Florida. ... I would be willing to abide by that result and agree not to take any legal action to challenge that result.

Simply put, the reason that there was no statewide recount in Florida was not because Gore did not ask for one—it was that Governor Bush rejected the suggestion out of hand.

Some critics acknowledge this but then wonder why Gore did not, on his own, unilaterally seek such a recount through the state procedures. Again, the answer in part is that we did: Our counsel informed the Florida Supreme Court during its first oral argument in this matter that we would accept such a statewide recount (and again, the Bush team opposed this);[13] before the U.S. Supreme Court, we defended the closest thing to a statewide recount ordered in the proceeding—the statewide undervote recount—and the Bush team opposed it.

But more fundamentally, our problem was that there was no mechanism under Florida law for a uniform, comprehensive, statewide recount in response to a single candidate's request. Absent a mechanism for a statewide recount, our only approximate alternative would have been to apply to each of the 67 counties *individually* and asked for a county-by-county recount. But many (the ones under GOP control, presumably) would have said no. It is ironic that the same people who fought us so hard for seeking recounts in four counties now lambaste us for not making the same request in 63 more counties.

Moreover, some counties would have been well within their rights not to conduct manual recounts. The law required an "error in vote tabulation" *in that county* for a recount to be required *in that county*. Thus, had we asked for a recount in many counties, we would have been told no, and properly so.

In the end, we decided to ask for hand recounts in just four counties, and we did so for two reasons. First, we were trying to keep the entire recount—and the subsequent election contest—as narrow as possible. We were not on a "fishing expedition," but a search for the most accurate possible result in the shortest possible time. The American people wanted a quick resolution to the matter, and 67 recounts would have surely eroded public support for the recount. Second, we asked for hand recounts in places where there were clear "errors in vote tabulation." In Volusia County, 9,000 votes appeared for the Socialist Workers Party in the initial vote tabulation—yet the actual total was under 400. In Broward and Dade counties, there were record numbers of undervotes. And in Palm Beach, the evidence of an "error in vote tabulation" was beyond dispute.

Had George Bush accepted Al Gore's proposal for a statewide recount—had the two sides jointly petitioned all 67 counties for such a count—presumably it would have happened, and much of the debate and division that has surrounded the post-election period would have been rendered moot. Those who are frustrated that this did not happen should not blame the candidate who was working to get the most egregious errors in tabulation corrected; rather, they should vent at the candidate who opposed any additional tabulations whatsoever.

Would it not have been better to end the "protest" phase and begin the "contest" phase earlier? Would that have given you the time you needed to count the votes?

Monday-morning quarterbacks have taken us to task for delaying the contest phase of the recount and extending the protest phase instead. Would we have been better off getting to the contest sooner?

Frankly, "no" is the answer, for a variety of reasons. First, the "delay" in question was relatively minor, even in the each-day-is-a-lifetime world in which we were living. Had we not sought to prolong the protest, Secretary of State Harris would have certified the result on November 18 instead of November 26, when certification finally took place. Thus, our contest could have been filed on Monday, November 20, instead of Monday, November 27, when it was ultimately lodged. The bottom line: Without the "delay," we would have gotten to the courtroom of Judge N. Sanders Sauls seven days faster. Would those extra seven days have helped?

Probably not. One of the seven days was Thanksgiving, and another was a Sunday—meaning that only five court days were lost in the end. And the odds are that those five days would have been eaten up by slightly slower proceedings before Judge Sauls, a slightly longer proceeding in the Florida Supreme Court, and a slightly longer proceeding in the U.S. Supreme Court—and not left for an additional vote-counting window at the end. Put another way, there is little reason to think that if we had gotten to Judge Sauls' court with five extra days, we would have gotten out of the U.S. Supreme Court and back to the counting tables any faster than we did.

By contrast, those five days were worth their weight in gold during the protest proceeding. Had we gone to court as our critics suggest on Monday, November 20, we would have been 1,300 votes behind (not the 537 that were later certified); we would have had to demand the counting of approximately 600,000 unrecounted votes in Broward County (a count that was not completed until Saturday, November 25); we would have had to demand the counting of approximately 600,000 unrecounted votes in Palm Beach County (a count that was not even commenced until Friday, November 17); and we would have had to demand the counting of approximately 600,000 unrecounted votes in Miami-Dade County, which, again, had scarcely been started by November 20.

On November 27, we went to a trial court trailing by 537 votes—with Broward finished, the dispute in Palm Beach limited to 3,000 ballots, and the Miami-Dade votes sorted to 10,000 undervotes—and asking only a modest thing: that 13,000 ballots be reviewed and tabulated. Had we gone to court on November 20, we would have been more than 1,300 votes behind, seeking the tabulation of 1.8 million ballots. Given that the Bush campaign was able to thwart our much more modest request, by arguing in part that we had been unable to show that the chance of changing the outcome merited the small effort of counting 13,000 ballots, what would the result have been if we were twice as far behind, and asking that 1.8 million ballots be counted?

In the end, three or four days of uninterrupted, unhassled counting could have gotten the job done. The fact that that did not happen during the 36 days of the post-election period is due much more to the GOP efforts to block the counts than to any "delaying" on our part.

171

Ronald A. Klain and Jeremy B. Bash

THE LABOR OF SISYPHUS: WAS ANYTHING GAINED?

In mythology, the story of Sisyphus is a parable about futility. Sisyphus never achieved his end. Indeed, Sisyphus never achieved much of anything at all.

The Florida recount was not quite so futile. Yes, our ultimate goal—a full, fair, and timely count of the votes—was not achieved. The person for whom more voters believed they had voted was not awarded that state's electoral votes. Most starkly, the wrong candidate became president. As lawyers, our efforts were a failure. As partisans, our candidate was defeated. As participants, we left Florida deflated and disappointed.

But in time, it has become clear that our work in Florida was not totally for naught. Florida has enacted a sweeping electoral reform package that will result in thousands of Floridians—mostly lower-income, mostly minority—having their votes more completely and fairly tabulated in the next election.[14] Around the country, similar efforts are under way; indeed, Congress appears likely to move on a national electoral reform package.[15] TV networks have pledged new restraint in making election night projections or otherwise letting the race to be first obscure the need to be right.[16] Abusive efforts to deny the franchise to voters with a legal right to vote have been put in the spotlight and may be abolished or restrained. A wide variety of groups have pledged renewed efforts to ensure that voters are well informed and well educated in marking their ballots.

On another front, even as it was being twisted to thwart democracy, the law may have been left in a stronger position to help the disadvantaged in future cases. For in concluding that the relatively minor unevenness in the hand recount violated the Constitution's Equal Protection Clause, the U.S. Supreme Court may have opened the door to new challenges to other electoral processes and procedures that produce even greater voter inequities.[17]

On a more personal level, those of us who labored for Al Gore and Joe Lieberman in Florida were changed forever. Even as we failed to win the result we wanted, our resolve to fight for our causes in the future was redoubled. Even more importantly, as we talk to scores of political activists and young lawyers about Florida, we see a new commitment to civic involvement and legal advocacy born from frustration over an injustice that was not remedied, a wrong that was not set right. And most importantly of all, a new generation of Americans has been reminded that their willingness to participate in the process can make a difference—registering, educating, and bringing to the polls even a handful of voters can make *the* difference in a close election.

We would like to be able to say that Florida taught America that every vote counts. But when not all the votes are counted, that is a hard message to sell.

Florida taught America that every voter, every activist, every citizen, can make a difference. This is the sort of success that Sisyphus never achieved—and the true victory that Al Gore won in Florida, no matter the electoral votes tallied in January 2001—or whether he seeks a "recount" in January 2005.

NOTES

[1] More ironic than Justice Shaw providing this metaphor, however, was the fact that his post hoc opinion stated that the U.S. Supreme Court had been wrong in concluding that December 12 was the absolute deadline for vote counting under Florida law, in *Bush v. Gore*, 773 So. 2d 524, 528-29 (Fla. 2000) (Shaw, J., concurring). That Justice Shaw, who dissented from the Florida Supreme Court's ruling for Vice President Gore's contest, reached this conclusion is highly suggestive that it might well have been a majority view on that court.
[2] Both counties, by the way, used optical-scan ballots, not the infamous punch cards.

---

[3] John Mintz and Peter Slevin, "Human Factor Was at Core of Vote Fiasco," *The Washington Post,* June 1, 2001, p. A1.

[4] First, Katherine Harris ruled that counties could not extend the deadline for hand count. That was rejected by the Florida Supreme Court. Second, she ruled that the county's excuses for taking more than seven days was invalid. (This ruling was prompted by Judge Lewis's ruling that she had to be "reasonable" in her rejection.) This was rejected by the Florida Supreme Court. Third, Harris petitioned the Florida Supreme Court to vacate all the lower court decisions in Gore's favor. This was rejected by the Court on the Friday that they granted a stay preventing her from certifying the election. Fourth, Harris ruled, in an advisory opinion, that there could not be hand counts unless there was an error in the vote tabulation. The Florida Supreme Court rejected this. Finally, Harris ruled that Palm Beach County's votes could not be counted because they came in after her deadline. The Florida Supreme Court also rejected this ruling. See *Palm Beach County Canvassing Board v. Katherine Harris, et al.*, 772 So.2d 1220 (Fla. 2000); *Albert Gore, Jr., and Joseph I. Lieberman v. Harris*, 772 So.2d 1243 (Fla. 2000); *Gore v. Harris*, 772 So.2d 1273 (Fla. 2000); *Gore v. Harris*, 773 So.2d 524 (Fla. 2000).

[5] David S. Broder, "Democrats Urge Gore Not to Push It Too Far," *The Washington Post,* November 11, 2000, p. A1.

[6] Vice President Gore was fortunate to have an incredible group of lawyers—mostly volunteers—willing to work on his behalf in this effort. The legal strategies outlined here were developed by this team as a group. Its members deserve tremendous credit for their hard work, intellectual power, and individual determination. As members of that team, the authors are especially grateful to our leaders, Bill Daley and Warren Christopher, as well as the legal "all-stars" who served on the team: Laurence Tribe, David Boies, Dexter Douglass, Mitchell Berger, Theresa Roseboro, Kendall Coffey, Ben Khuene, Joe Sandler, Bob Bauer, John Hardin Young, Jack Corrigan, Andrew Pincus, Jeffrey Robinson, Steve Zack, Lisa Brown, Rich Cordray, Dennis Newman, John Newton, Mark Steinberg, and countless others. The legal team also could not have done its work without attorneys Richard Lucas, Dan Feldman, Mark Messenbaugh, Andrew Shapiro, and Irwin Raij. While these outstanding individuals—and many, many more—deserve credit for the legal theories we discuss in this article, we alone are responsible for the views presented here.

[7] *Gore v. Harris*, 772 So. 2d 1243, 1253 (Fla. 2000).

[8] Actually, we had a fifth prong to our strategy: Pray for a miracle. But the various "miracles" that the voracious Florida rumor mill spawned never materialized. A much-ballyhooed lost ballot box in Broward County was ultimately found—empty. A sack of 2,000 overseas absentee ballots that was supposedly on its way from Israel never reached U.S. shores—if it ever existed. Proof of a number of alleged scandals of GOP manipulation of domestic and overseas absentee ballots never coalesced—if they were true.

And court victories for long-shot cases in which some observers placed great stock (i.e., the Seminole and Martin County absentee ballot cases) never came—and perhaps were never merited. In the end, all we had to work with were the votes cast on Election Day—and yet, properly and fairly counted, that would have been enough to win.

[9] The Bush campaign did create a theory under which the partial count was "more fair" than a complete count: a sharp denunciation of hand tabulation of ballots as less accurate than machine counts. Their success is in persuading the American public of this "fact" during the recount period speaks to the adeptness and skill of their communications team. In reality, we do not know a single person who would be prepared to accept a machine accounting of their bank account, credit card bill, or payment records as "final" in lieu of a human review of any alleged errors in such a machine accounting, notwithstanding the tendencies of humans to be "arbitrary" or "biased." Closer to the subject in question, as we attempted to point out countless times during the recount period, the law of President Bush's home state—Texas—specifically states that hand counts are considered to be more accurate than machine counts. Ultimately, this same conclusion was reached by leaders of both parties in Florida: The recently passed Florida electoral reforms make hand counts the final arbiter of election results when the tally is particularly close (such as the 2000 presidential election). But, like so many ironies around this matter, this Florida statute—which would have mandated the hand tabulation that we fought so hard to achieve in November and December—was passed too late to help Al Gore.

[10] It was always our view that the law requires "intent of the voter" to be the standard. The Canvassing Board repeatedly stated that it was using a rigorous chad standard, which in our view did not comport with the "intent of the voter" standard mandated by Florida law. Thus, we believe the board deliberately used the wrong standard.

[11] See Jake Tapper, *Down and Dirty: The Plot to Steal the Presidency* (New York: Little, Brown, 2001).

[12] This point was amusingly illustrated by the following phenomenon: Virtually every day we were in Florida, we would get an e-mail message from someone with a Ph.D. in political science or statistics, suggesting that from a scientific perspective, the election was a tie, and the electors should be split evenly. Usually, the e-mail would include an invective against us "silly" lawyers for not understanding this fact. In the abstract, such a rule (stating that when the candidates were separated by less than 0.1% of the vote, the result would be considered a tie for Electoral College purposes) might make very good sense. Both Bush and Gore might even have accepted it if someone had thought to propose it *before* Election Day. But by November 8, with Gore at 267 electoral votes and Bush at 246, any "neutral" approach that would have split Florida's 25 electors 12 (for Gore) to 13 (for Bush) did not seem particularly viable.

---

[13] Oral Argument of David Boies, *Palm Beach v. Harris,* November 20, 2000.

[14] See Michael Peltier, "Florida Lawmakers Reform Patchwork Voting System," Reuters, May 4, 2001.

[15] See Thomas Ferraro, "Bipartisan Drive to Revive Election Reform," Reuters, May 15, 2001.

[16] See, for example, "CNN Announces Election Night Coverage Change, Following 'Debacle,'" CNN web site, posted February 2, 2001.

[17] See Ronald A. Klain, "How Democrats Can Use Bush v. Gore," *The Washington Post,* March 22, 2001, p. A29.

CHAPTER 8

A Campout for Lawyers:

The Bush Recount Perspective

George J. Terwilliger, III
Bush Legal Counsel

Election Day 2000 found me in Tampa, Florida, at a final settlement conference in a case with the government that had dragged on for over two years. I had voted two days prior to the election under a special procedure permitted in Virginia for persons who would be unexpectedly out of the jurisdiction on Election Day. My meeting ended in the late afternoon, and I boarded the plane bound for Washington, D.C., anticipating an evening of watching election returns in a close, but nonetheless victorious, race for George W. Bush.

My first acquaintance with the Bush family began rather serendipitously in the back of a firehouse. It was 1988 and the elder George Bush was in the thick of campaigning in the state of Vermont. While it probably wasn't his most glamorous stop, I was honored to meet him after he spoke to the crowd in the station. When the senior Bush became President, I was privileged in 1991 to join his administration as the number two official at the U.S. Department of Justice.

A decade later, I literally bumped into his son, then Governor Bush of Texas, in the ballroom of the Willard Hotel in Washington, D.C., while attending a fund-raiser for his reelection in Texas. The cavernous room was overflowing, and as I worked my way through the crowd to get to the side of the room before the speeches began, I bumped into someone's shoulder and turned to excuse myself. With his hand extended and a warm smile on his face, he simply said, "Hi, I'm George Bush." After making apologies for the jostle, I told him that I had been a part of his father's administration and that I sensed great excitement about his potential should he ever decide to run for president. I told him that it seemed that Americans of all political walks were expressing a deep desire to see a person of character and commitment occupy the Oval Office. We talked baseball for a few minutes, and then I noticed a long line of less than pleased faces waiting for a moment and a handshake from the Governor. I excused myself and moved on.

Two years later, I was 30,000 feet above the state that was about to become the epicenter of an election earthquake. If someone had told me that within 24 hours I would be representing the Governor of Texas in one of the most engrossing legal cases of my career, I would have called the prediction sheer fantasy.

I nodded off to sleep on election night about 2:45 a.m., feeling relatively secure in the outcome since the networks had reversed themselves and called Florida for Bush. An hour or so later, awakened by a jangling telephone, I was greeted by the incredulous tones of my son, Zach, a student at the University of Virginia, expressing shock and disbelief that Florida had now been taken out of Bush's column and was being called "too close to decide." I switched on the television and caught up with the news. It was, indeed, an astounding situation. The nation would awaken to the shock that it did not yet know who would be its next president.

At about 6:30 a.m., I was on the telephone with my law firm partner at White and Case, Tim Flanagan, now deputy counsel to the president of the United States. We discussed the situation from a legal point of view and decided that we ought to locate the person in charge of the legal issues with the Florida election and offer to help as needed. After a few calls, we both concluded that no one was yet "in charge," but that an election law team would be formed at Republican Party headquarters in Tallahassee. One of our other law partners in the Miami office, Mark Jimenez, was the brother of Frank Jimenez, the acting counsel to Governor Jeb Bush. Mark suggested that we come down because it appeared that litigation was almost a certainty; it appeared that there would be a few days of legal wrangling over recount procedures and the like.

Tim Flanagan and I agreed that he and Bob Bittman, an experienced litigator, together with Laura Flippen, a bright young lawyer in the firm, would go to Tallahassee on the next available flight. They would call later in that day and advise me on whether I should join them or stay in Washington to do some backroom work.

At my office in Washington, I had several telephone conversations with fellow lawyers concerning what were shaping up as issues in the Florida election. I had previously litigated several voting and election cases and had served as outside counsel to the Senate Rules Committee when it investigated vote fraud in a Louisiana senate election.[1] By ten o'clock in the morning, Fox News was asking if I could come over to the studio around midday and provide some commentary on the Florida election situation.

I was sitting on the Fox set, about to go on the air, when the cell phone in my breast pocket rang. Initially, I was embarrassed that I had neglected the fundamental precaution of turning it off. My secretary was on the phone informing me that Bush-Cheney Campaign Chairman Don Evans was calling from Austin. I had never met Don but obviously knew who he was.

During the campaign, I had done some work on criminal justice issues and had spoken in favor of Governor Bush's candidacy to a couple of

179

law enforcement groups. I asked my secretary to tell Mr. Evans that I would call him back in a few minutes, just as soon as I finished the interview.

I connected with Mr. Evans during a cab ride from the Fox studio near Union Station back to my office in downtown Washington. Don asked me what I thought of the situation in Florida. I said I thought it was shaping up to be a mess, but, assuming that there was no fraud or other massive irregularity in the election, a recount would more likely than not still show Governor George Bush as the winner, although the margin might change. I also told him that if the matter went into court, experience told me that Florida would be a difficult forum in which to litigate election issues.

I had been involved in some Florida cases before, including a nasty fight in which I represented John Walsh, host of *America's Most Wanted*, in a disagreement with newspapers over access to the contents of the homicide investigation file concerning the murder of John and Reve Walsh's son, Adam. At the time, both John and I were incredulous that the Florida courts would use the "open access" law to put the interests of a newspaper ahead of the needs of law enforcement officers trying to find the person who had kidnapped and murdered Adam.

Other Florida matters in which I had been involved had left similar impressions. I told Mr. Evans that very early in law school I had learned a legal rule of thumb: "Tell me the judge and I'll tell you the ruling." I added, somewhat offhandedly, that if there was going to be a court fight over the election, we needed to think about getting into federal court sooner rather than later. This was not any brilliant legal insight or analysis on my part, but rather a basic gut instinct born of experience in the courts.

After the taxi had traveled a few blocks and our conversation had gone on for five minutes or so, Don Evans asked me if I might be able to go to Florida and help out with whatever legal challenges ensued. I said that I would be pleased to try to help and asked him when he wanted me to get down there. He politely, but urgently, asked if I could be there that evening, which was November 8. Indeed, I didn't pause long to think this one over. I said I'd be there as quickly as possible.

With the help of the great young lawyers and paralegals at White and Case, I quickly pulled together some election law materials, went home to Virginia, and reluctantly told my wife, Carol, and youngest daughter, Virginia, that I was going back to Florida. As I boarded the plane at Dulles Airport, I was tired but also experiencing the first surge of the adrenaline that would become so dominant over the next month.

On the plane, I read some of the materials I had gathered and made some preliminary notes. Those notes were very sketchy, but among them were three lines that said: "Federal Court: How? For What? And When?" Meanwhile, as I was flying, the organized effort among lawyers to deal with the aftermath of the election on the Republican side began to take shape. There was a conference call that evening led by Ben Ginsberg, the campaign's experienced counsel. Unfortunately, the call was so oversubscribed that the telephone bridge went down. As might be expected, the conference call raised more questions than answers.

Tim Flanagan and Bob Bitman met me at the airport around eleven o'clock that night and told me what the team knew so far. It wasn't much, but it was pretty clear that there was going to be some kind of recount and that the Gore campaign was already looking at taking the election controversies into the courtroom. Questions regarding the clarity and use of Palm Beach County's infamous "butterfly ballots" were already emerging.

I dropped my bags at a hotel and was in the office in Tallahassee by midnight. Another two and a half or three hours of conversations and discussions ensued among the few lawyers who were present at that point, including Ben Ginsberg.

As I left the meeting in the wee hours of the morning, I had a certain sense of foreboding that took me back to national events in March of 1981. I was working as a young Assistant U.S. Attorney in Washington, D.C., when I learned of the assassination attempt against then-President Reagan at the Hilton Hotel on Connecticut Avenue. Carol was in Columbia Hospital for Women in Washington, having just given birth to our second child the day before. I had hoped to have a quiet afternoon, taking care of a few necessary things in the office and then leaving. Instead I became one of a team of prosecutors who spent all that afternoon and evening working on the legal procedures necessary to charge John Hinckley with various crimes and to search the hotel room where he had stayed in Washington.

I remember quite vividly feeling as if I had dropped through a trap door into a maelstrom, but at the same time feeling a great sense of responsibility and professional challenge to make sure everything was done right, given that the subject matter involved an armed assault on the president of the United States. Almost 20 years later, it seemed that we were all about to become players in yet another national drama, played out live on television, in the first case ever where someone sued to become president.

GETTING ORGANIZED: THE TEAMS AND THE PLAYERS

I must confess that once the games began in earnest, many events became blurred, blending into one another as a series of rapid-fire, overlapping and intense occurrences—which is what they really were. By the end of the first week, former Secretary of State James Baker was on the job in Tallahassee, bringing a small but very capable staff with him. Ben Ginsberg was there, and Barry Richard, a Florida lawyer, had been hired to be the most visible attorney in the courtroom.

Initially, there was no great clarity on which lawyers and staff were responsible for which legal and political issues. It became clear, however, that there would be a senior team of lawyers and campaign officials who would consult with each other and make recommendations concerning the actions to take, mostly through Secretary Baker. While the press reported that Secretary Baker's role was really as an elder statesman or spokesperson, he quickly emerged as the leader-in-fact of the senior team. Over the next few weeks, as I worked more closely with him, I was greatly impressed by his skills as a lawyer and his quick grasp of and insight on legal issues. Along with Bob Zoellick and Margaret Tutwiler, Secretary Baker took the helm of the Tallahassee end of the operation, but the group operated very much through a process of consultation and consensus. It was a modus operandi that all of us who had been in government before found very familiar and comfortable.

As one of the team members with a finger in most of the pies, I greatly enjoyed working with so many extremely capable attorneys. Many of these were people with whom I had worked before, but others, particularly some of the younger people, were new to me. One of those, a bright young former Supreme Court clerk named Noel Francisco, came up with a wonderful Lewis Carroll quotation that was very appropriate to our position in the contest litigation. The quotation was from *Alice's Adventures in Wonderland*. The King suggested a trial but got this response: "No, no!" said the Queen. "Sentence first—verdict afterwards."

This quotation was originally included in one of our briefs to the Florida Supreme Court, but it had been taken out in the editing process. I appropriated it for use as the opening to the brief argument I made before Judge Saunders Saul in the contest trial. Perhaps because we were involved in very serious business, we appreciated both humor and irony in the day-to-day work. I especially enjoyed that quotation, because it captured an essential aspect of our position in the trial, to the effect that the remedy of counting votes should not be made available until a legal entitlement to a recount was

183

established.

Already, we faced legal maneuvering in five counties where Gore supporters had initiated court proceedings. In addition, the local county Canvassing Boards were assessing administrative complaints by voters on the election's ballots and recount protocols. It appeared that we were at war on a number of legal fronts and confronting a relentless level of media attention. All of us felt that one of the greatest risks was that permanent doubt could be cast on the validity and integrity of the election results.

One of my highest and most immediate priorities was to understand the Florida election code, particularly the procedures for conducting recounts and contesting election results. One local lawyer who had been involved in Florida election law cases had some helpful ideas, but it quickly became clear that nothing like this situation had ever occurred before.

I obtained a copy of the election code and we began to study it in earnest. In coming days, as attorneys found out that I had one bound, easy-to-read compilation of the code, it kept disappearing from my office. We managed to send someone over to a state office to get additional copies. I put my name in big black letters on the cover of one copy and asked that it remain in the small conference room we used as our makeshift office. In a very short while, the outstanding support staff from the Florida party office would have us set up and humming like a real law office, complete with a local computer network and three square meals a day. However, in those first few days, our headquarters felt like a campout for lawyers.

As we reviewed Florida's election laws, it quickly became apparent that there were substantial uncertainties and ambiguities in the language. The more one tried to look ahead and chart factual scenarios of what could develop, the more difficult it became to analyze the law. It was unclear exactly what the procedures would be and what the standards were for those proceedings.

But one crucial factor was crystal clear in the Florida code: A timetable and deadlines existed for local and state officials in tabulating votes and certifying the outcome of the election. The law provided that the results of the election, as tabulated by the machine ballot readers, must be certified within seven days of the election; then a tally of overseas absentee ballots would be added to that; and— within ten days—the matter would be closed. This was not to be.

On Thursday, November 9, the Gore camp called for a hand recount of ballots in four counties, in effect requiring more time before election results would be final. Meanwhile, on Friday, the votes coming in showed that Governor Bush was leading by 960 votes with 66 of the 67 counties counted. Manual recounts quickly ensued of so-called sample precincts in the four counties where the Gore team seemed poised to contest the election results: Palm Beach, Broward, Volusia, and Miami-Dade.

Our review of the Florida election code made it clear that there would be wrangling over recount procedures. Both sides would need lawyers and extremely sensitive observers on the scene. We believed this precaution necessary to properly represent our clients' interests and to do as much as possible to ensure that the process was fair and honest.

In addition, in those first few days, we recognized that not only was litigation going to occur, it was likely to be prolonged. As a result, a few of us began telephoning lawyers whom we knew and trusted. These were practitioners for whom we had a high professional regard, and we believed they could assist us in what was to come.

Crisis need not be chaos. A crisis is in essence a series of interlocking issues or problems. As lawyers, we are taught that all questions and answers can be broken down to their constituent parts. In a crisis, separating the parts is the first step in organizing a response.

We separated the legal issues of the election recount into categories and set out to address each one. Because of the number of cases and legal issues we faced, we organized teams to deal with these separate parts. Each team had de facto leadership, and the "big team"—our whole group—had a leadership team. By assigning people to discrete parts of the effort, we had the advantage of getting ahead of many of the developments and were able to concentrate some considerable legal talent on relatively particularized issues.

People began to arrive in Tallahassee over the first five days in significant numbers. While many of us were senior lawyers, there was a remarkable degree of respect for an ad hoc but discernible chain of command. We quickly achieved a working cohesiveness due, in large part, to this varied group of lawyers' willingness to lay aside ego and pursue assigned tasks with dedication and determination. We found ourselves immersed in the basics of researching and writing pleadings, rather than our usual roles of reviewing and editing of briefs created by junior attorneys. If the truth were known, I think some of us enjoyed feeling like young lawyers again, doing the kinds of hands-on work that makes the law such a rewarding profession.

One of the first anticipated challenges concerned the so-called butterfly ballot in Palm Beach County. The media was rife with commentary about how people had mistakenly voted for the wrong candidate, voted for multiple candidates, or engaged in some other error in the process of marking their punch-card ballots. The result, according to some commentators, was an election so irregular that new elections might have to be held.

At first blush, the idea of redoing an election because of a ballot design that supposedly resulted in widespread voter confusion and error might seem to have merit. But it did not take long to recognize that no makeup election would be permitted in Palm Beach County in the presidential election of 2000. The Constitution of the United States and the attending federal law make it clear that there is only one day upon which a presidential election will be held every four years. That election is it, warts and all. As I remarked to Secretary Baker, there are simply no "do-overs" in a presidential election.

Whatever problems may have existed with the Palm Beach County ballot design, that issue was not going to invalidate the presidential election. After a lot of noise and commentary, a judge concluded just that by dismissing the lawsuits brought challenging the election results based on the ballot design.

However, it took several weeks to get there.

THE FEDERAL CASE: DEFINING THE ISSUE

Of much greater immediacy was our desire to move the legal action from the often conflicting and overlapping claims made in state court lawsuits to a federal venue. By doing so, we believed that we could affirmatively defend the interests of the Bush-Cheney campaign. I shared the belief that one case, in federal court, provided an avenue by which the federal interests raised in the election dispute could be adjudicated directly. In addition, it seemed clear, albeit remote, that if this election were to be decided by court proceedings, it would not be finally decided until the U.S. Supreme Court had ruled. Part of my thinking, shared by many others, was that if we were going to eventually wind up in the Supreme Court of the United States, then we ought to exert some control over what issues would be framed in that case.

However, there was no groundswell of enthusiasm in our camp for the federal filing. Many of our lawyers, philosophically conservative, did not believe that federal court was where state election disputes should be resolved. Rather, out of respect for the sovereignty of the states and their preeminent place in our federalist system, states should resolve disputes on their elections in their courts. Nonetheless, this election was different. It was an election for president and vice president of the United States, the only election in which the American people, through the Electoral College system, vote for candidates on a nationwide basis. In addition, a presidential election is

187

different because the Constitution itself provides for that election and is rather precise in describing how the election is to be conducted. Most particularly, the Constitution gives plenary authority to state legislatures to choose the method for selecting the electors who will vote in the Electoral College to determine who shall be president and vice president. It is the legislatures' sole prerogative to prescribe a method for choosing those electors. All states have now chosen to use the popular vote as the means to choose electors. But that does not at all mean that, as a constitutional matter, a presidential election is like every other election in which there is a popular vote.

Nonetheless, we all recognized that Governor George Bush would be subject to substantial criticism for initiating a lawsuit when he had been, through spokespersons, already decrying the number of lawsuits that had been filed by or on behalf of his opponent. Secretary Baker stated in his remarks on Saturday, November 11, concerning the filing of our lawsuit, that we would drop this case if the Gore camp and its confederates would drop all of the many cases that they had already filed in the state courts of Florida. However, nobody seemed ready to drop anything at that point.

DEADLINES AND DIMPLES

It was apparent within just a few days after the election that the Gore team was going to push to extend the statutory deadlines for certifying the results of the election. It was absolutely clear under Florida law, passed by the state legislature, that the election returns would be certified on a statewide basis seven days after the election, that is, November 14, and would be finalized with the inclusion of the overseas ballots by Saturday, November 18. It was quite apparent to all that the election returns that would be certified on November 14 would result in Governor Bush being declared the winner, and while the overseas ballots might affect that tally, they would not change the result.

It also was quite apparent that the Gore team had other ideas about the finality of the election results. It became quite clear that they were going to press the argument that there was a great deal of hand recounting of punch-card ballots that needed to be done. But the only way that could realistically occur would be if the deadlines for certifying the results of the presidential election of 2000 in Florida were extended. It was also quite evident that the only way this was likely to happen was if a court rewrote the legislature's law and overrode the state officials, including Secretary of State Katherine Harris, who had a responsibility under the law to meet those statutory deadlines for certifying the election results.

As that issue became joined in the first few days of the first week following the election, the nation had already been treated to some of the methodology of recounting by hand punch-card ballots in Florida. The nation had scenes of election officials holding ballots up above their heads and then calling out the result of that ballot as to a selection for president, or not, as the case might be. What these officials were doing, as we all now know so well, was looking for pinholes of light that might have been made by a stylus indicating that a voter had attempted to vote for a particular officeholder as reflected on the punch card, but which had not been read to be a vote by the machine optical reader.

To me, this scene was reminiscent of an old Johnny Carson *Tonight Show* routine in which Carson, portraying Carnac the Magnificent, a seer, holds a sealed envelope above his head and states an "answer." Carson's longtime sidekick and straight man, Ed MacMahon, opens the envelope, and *voila!* The question (usually humorous) turns out to have been foreseen by Carnac. Some of the election officials interpreting what they saw on the ballot looked like "Carnac the Canvasser." Of course, this is not meant to ridicule the generally hardworking election officials, but rather to capture the subjectivity of a process in which human beings were using varied and rather undefined standards to identify what voters meant to communicate on a ballot. This is what was at the heart of the election dispute in Florida in Presidential Election 2000.

In order to give the election officials time to hand-count all the ballots on which the machine indicated that no preference for president had been given, the Gore camp moved to extend the deadlines. This approach was most significant. Federal law states that contests in presidential elections should be decided under law in effect on Election Day. The Gore camp was now asking the Florida state courts to rewrite that law.

An undercurrent of another issue quickly emerged in the Gore camp's claims. It was apparent that the team believed that if so-called dimpled ballots were counted, their candidate's vote total might increase. They argued, for a variety of reasons, that some voters may have attempted to punch out (with the pointed stylus) a selection on the punch card, but the selection was not sufficiently punched to dislodge the little perforated square (the chad). If so, their argument went, then under Florida law that ballot should be counted anyway based on the results of a hand examination that showed a dimple in the chad. Counting dimples took time, so deadlines became the first big issue in the case.

I took to saying that the case was all about "deadlines and dimples." While the Gore team focused its legal efforts initially on deadlines, the case was really about dimples. I believed that the more subjective the hand-counting process became, the more at risk our interests in a fair election process grew. I cannot say whether dimples should count as votes or not. But I knew then, and believe now, that whatever counts as a vote ought to be decided *before* the election is held, not after.

RULES, FAIRNESS, AND EQUAL PROTECTION UNDER THE LAW

The real heart of our case, and the argument that I believe carried the day as a matter of justice, is the notion that there is an importance to adhering to rules. We do not adhere to rules in our society just for the sake of doing so. We are a free, liberty-minded people who would just as soon not have rules where we do not need them. However, we recognize that rules are essential to fairness. This is particularly so in human endeavors where competition is great. Obviously, that describes elections. Thus, rules are also important to the process of resolving difficult and complex election questions or contests. The process of electing public officeholders is so basic to democracy that we cannot afford to allow it to become subject to the push and pull of partisan politics after the election has been held. Rules governing how elections have been held, how votes are tabulated, and how election contests are resolved are designed to accomplish the goals of (1) assuring citizens and candidates alike that elections are fair and honest and (2) that their finality deserves citizen support. Election contests should not be yet another opportunity for candidates, with a strongly personal and partisan interest, to try to manipulate a process to bring about a certain result.

Under Florida law, as established by its Supreme Court in 1976, reflecting the will of the people is identified as the supreme interest in resolving election contests. It is not hard to ascribe to that notion; of course an election result should reflect the will of the people. Equally important, the people should perceive that the election result reflects their will. One of the surest ways to accomplish both of those goals is to have rules for the election, and any contests or controversies arising from it, that are perceived to be clear, fair, and as free as they possibly can be from manipulation by election officials, or judges, who may have or appear to have partisan interests.

Thus, making rules before an election and enforcing them in election contests after the votes have been cast seems to me to be something of paramount importance. Conversely, changing the rules after an election is held is unfair, not merely to one candidate or the other, but to the citizens, their voting system, and, indeed, their democracy. It is to them that we have a responsibility to make rules and stick to them. The Gore camp did get the rules changed in Florida after the votes were cast. Over our strong objections, the Florida Supreme Court rewrote the Florida election code and extended the time for certifying the election results.[2] The court did so even after a lower court judge ruled that the counties must meet the deadlines, unless Secretary Harris, in her discretion, extended them if necessary. As importantly, the real issue in the case emerged for the public during this initial recounting process. Millions of Americans were exposed to the vagaries of the hand-counting procedures and the questions, ultimately unanswerable questions, about what ballots count as votes.

This occurred, over a period of several hours, in the context of Palm Beach County's own internal disputes among its Canvassing Board members about what standards should be applied to decide whether a punch-card ballot contained a valid, and thus countable, vote. The board members argued among themselves, and ultimately a court became involved in addressing the issue. But regardless of the merits of the various points of view, what the nation saw was a system wherein the rules were anything but clear, and in fact seemed to be being created as the process went along. It was easy for many people to see that this was unfair. Articulating that unfairness as a legal claim was the lawyers' job.

Under the Constitution all persons enjoy the "equal protection" of the law. This venerable constitutional protection has been applied in a variety of contexts, but is always used for the same fundamental purpose: to assure that all persons in our society are seen as equal in the eyes of the law. Rich or poor, urban or rural, or any one of the other myriad factors that make people different and of different stations, equal protection ensures that under the law they will all be treated the same. In the context of voting, it is well established under federal law that this equality is reflected in two important principles.

First, every person gets one vote, and, second, every vote has to count the same. That is, residents of the poorest counties in the country have the same weight as voters and the same representation in elected bodies as do residents of the wealthiest. In the tabulation or counting of votes, all votes have to be given equal weight and an equal chance to count in the result.

But it quickly became apparent that there was an emerging and very serious issue with the methods being used to identify votes to be counted in the four counties in Florida where the Gore team was contesting the election results. Each of those counties appeared to be using different standards or factors in deciding what ballots contained valid votes. To accurately present this picture, one must consider for a moment the punch-card ballots themselves and how they are used.

To vote using a punch-card ballot, a citizen is given a so-called blank ballot with all of its perforated squares, or chads, intact. To vote, the ballot is placed in a device, which is not really a machine but simply a device to hold the ballot in place. On this ballot are written the names of the candidates for office, and to the side of those names, circles are marked. In the middle of each circle there is a hole. A stylus, a kind of pointed pin-like device, can be inserted through the hole in the paper ballot, which is held in place by clear, rigid plastic with a corresponding hole.

In inserting the punch-card ballot into the paper ballot device, the voter must fix the ballot properly so that these tiny 1/16-inch squares match up to the holes in the ballot next to the names of the candidates. A voter who pushes the ballot in too far is likely to wrinkle it, perhaps loosening chads. Too little, and the voter may wind up punching chads not for the candidate of choice, but for another candidate whose chad happens to be beneath the hole corresponding to the circle on the ballot. Sometimes, there is no candidate where a misplaced chad is punched, and the machine will later read this as no vote at all.

In the next step, the ballot cards are removed and, according to many experts, should be inspected and "cleaned" by the voter. That is, any loose or hanging chad should be removed so there is no chance that the ballot will be misread in the next phase. Later, in the Florida system, the ballots are taken to a central location where they are put through an optical reader that utilizes light shined through the card to determine which holes have been punched. The ballots move through the machine, that is, through the optical reading device, by means of air or pneumatic pressure. This means, again according to experts, that any chad that is, say, swinging by two corners may be blown shut in the process. In fact, there is a 50-50 chance that it will be blown open or shut any time that it is put through the machine. If the chad is blown open, then the ballot is counted as a vote for the candidate to whom that chad corresponded on the paper ballot. If it is blown shut, no vote at all for that office is recorded.

The manual recount of ballots in the 2000 Florida presidential election involved taking those in which no vote was recorded and examining the ballot to see if, in fact, it did contain a vote. Obviously, if a hole is punched, then the ballot ought to have been counted and some machine failure resulted in it not being counted in the first place. But if the chad is not punched through completely, then there are differing theories as to what should be counted and what should not. And it was differences over those theories that led to the testimony about the punch-card ballots in the Gore election contest trial in Florida, and in the discussion of those issues in various appellate courts.

Suffice it to say that there is no universal answer as a matter of law as to what constitutes a validly cast ballot that can be counted. More importantly, in the Florida election, there clearly was no universal rule in effect before the election as to what ballots should be counted. Thus, if one were to establish a rule that, say, counted all dimples, then that rule would have been one established after the election, arguably in contravention to a federal law.

It also became clear that not only did the standards differ within Palm

Beach County, but also among the four counties that were counting ballots. This meant that a voter who merely dimpled a ballot in one county might not have his vote counted while a voter in another county who punched the ballot sufficiently to remove one corner of a chad might indeed have her vote counted. This circumstance raised serious equal protection problems.

The Florida Supreme Court tried to solve those problems by simply stating that any ballot would be counted where, from examination of the ballot, the intent of the voter could be divined.

As of November 20, deadlines had been extended and ballots previously found as not containing a vote had been included in the count. The Florida Supreme Court had overridden the deadlines originally established by the Florida legislature and those established by the executive official, Secretary of State Harris, empowered to carry out the law. Despite all of this, on November 20, 2000, the responsible state election officials declared George Bush and Dick Cheney the winners of the election and appointed presidential electors accordingly. The communication of the appointment of those electors was dispatched directly to Washington, as required by federal law.

It is simply a fact of life that every election is flawed to one degree or another. This one was no different. Election flaws become matters of great public attention only when elections are close. If a candidate wins an election handily by, say, a million votes, whether it was 1.1 million or 1.2 million really does not matter to the public too much. But when an election result is razor-thin, minor variations in the tally of votes take on great significance. However, election systems have inherent flaws and cannot deliver perfection.

It is also a fact of election life that flaws must not merely be recognized but accepted. To suggest otherwise is, in my humble judgment, to suggest that every close election should have two phases: first the campaign and the initial tally, and then what could be an endless battle over the implication of flaws in the voting or tabulating process. Because of these factors, and the fact that the Gore camp had really gotten what it had asked for in extending the deadlines, I never really thought after November 20 that George Bush would lose the election. However, the contest was not over yet.

The Case: Bush v. Gore

When our complaint was filed in the U.S. District Court in Miami, the Supreme Court in Washington, D.C., seemed very far away. In reality, though, what happened in Miami foreshadowed the decision in Washington. The federal case we filed and the arguments we made had a considerable, if not determinative, effect on the outcome of the entire election controversy. It was not so much the procedural device of filing a case in federal court, but rather the focused effort of the Bush legal team to identify federal issues, or in the parlance of the law, "federal questions," that was to prove extremely important.

One of the fundamental features of our constitutional system is that there is a decided separation of jurisdiction between state and federal courts. The state courts have broad and plenary authority over most legal disputes. It is the state courts that have the jurisdiction and authority to apply the common law that traces its roots to the ancestral courts of the English Middle Ages. The federal courts, established by Congress as inferior courts to the United States Supreme Court, have much more limited jurisdiction. The federal courts have jurisdiction over a limited range of so-called federal questions. These are legal issues and controversies that arise under the U.S. Constitution, under laws enacted by Congress or, sometimes, in regard to treaties with foreign nations.[3]

There are, for example, a broad range of cases in which federal courts have jurisdiction where the dispute involves citizens of different states and the amount in controversy is larger than a particular monetary threshold. Federal cases also arise from specific federal statutes that run the range of matters in which the federal government has asserted a regulatory or other legal interest. In addition, cases that present constitutional questions are matters in which there is federal court jurisdiction. In particular, even if a federal constitutional question is raised first in state court proceedings and later ruled upon by the highest of all state courts, that opinion is still subject to review by the U.S. Supreme Court if the Court chooses to undertake that review.

Elections and the electoral process are matters established and addressed under state statutes. State governments establish election procedures, and local governments administer elections through the voting process and the tabulation of votes. States have statewide election codes that both establish procedures which election officials and candidates must follow and serve as guides for the exercise of discretionary actions by state election officials. Most states also have an official of statewide jurisdiction who is the ultimate "election official" in a state. This is often the secretary of state.

Because elections are state law matters, disputes concerning elections under those laws are matters for the jurisdiction of state courts. Most election codes establish procedures to be utilized when it is necessary to take a dispute or election under state election law into court. Federal courts, as a general matter, defer to state courts on state election law matters. There are, of course, significant exceptions. Congress passed the Voting Rights Act in order to provide federal law enforcement authorities and federal courts with jurisdiction to address the vestiges of voting discrimination in a number of states, mainly in the South.[4] In addition to this statutory authority, federal courts have long recognized that fundamental guarantees of the U.S. Constitution establish certain minimum standards that apply to state election procedures. The Equal Protection Clause of the Constitution, for example, requires that every person's vote should count the same. An example of this principle applied is the Supreme Court's ruling that all congressional districts must be relatively the same size, that is, have the same voting population so that the representation of all citizens in Congress is equal.

In sum, the law at the time the 2000 presidential election controversy erupted in Florida provided that as a general matter, state courts were responsible for disputes regarding elections, but with a significant carve-out for certain matters of federal interests, particularly where constitutional principles were implicated. Of course, onto this state of affairs must be grafted the undeniable fact that a presidential election is unique among all elections held in the country for several reasons. First, the election of the president and the basic method for conducting it is a matter expressly spelled out in the Constitution.[5] Second, federal courts, particularly since the Voting Rights Act, have not been reluctant to step in to state election law matters where constitutional issues are raised. Third, as a practical matter, because the election of the president is a matter striking the delicate balance combining state and federal interests, it would be absurd to view a presidential election as a matter completely outside the purview of federal courts. Lastly, it is realistic to assume that once a presidential election dispute is taken into the courts, the citizenry would not consider the dispute finally resolved until the U.S. Supreme Court, the highest court of the land, had dealt with the issues involved.

It must also be acknowledged that all of the legal maneuverings and wrangling, particularly on the federal level, were novel exercises. There had never before been a lawsuit the outcome of which could determine who would be president of the United States. The closest the nation had experienced before was the 1876 presidential contest, Samuel Tilden versus Rutherford B. Hayes. Hayes emerged victorious and became the president of the United States after a dispute concerning the election results. That dispute was resolved by the action of a commission specially appointed by Congress, rather than as the result of litigation in courts. Interestingly enough, though, the Chief Justice of the United States presiding at that time was appointed to chair that commission. Then, as now, there was a perception that the imprimatur of the highest court in the land was an important component of assuring both integrity of the process and the finality of the result in deciding a presidential election contest.

The argument to be made on behalf of candidates Bush and Cheney in the Supreme Court in December was grounded in the originally crafted federal complaint we filed in Miami a month before the

Supreme Court's final decision. Ironically, it was not a decision in that case by the Supreme Court which brought finality to the matter. Rather, it was an appeal to the U.S. Supreme Court of a Florida Supreme Court ruling. The state Supreme Court had overturned the Florida trial court's verdict that Vice President Gore had failed to meet his burden in the election contest trial he initiated. The Florida Supreme Court had virtually ignored the trial court's findings and ordered on its own that hand recounts should commence. While what we appealed to the U.S. Supreme Court was that decision, our position turned on the very arguments that had been made on behalf of the Bush-Cheney ticket in the federal case we filed in Miami four days following the election.

Shorn of its procedural and theoretical complexities, the Bush argument was as follows: First, a vote, as reflected in an election ballot, is a form of communication that is meant to convey the choice of a voter. As a form of communication, what was communicated ought to be determined by objective criteria. In a secret ballot system such as the one we use, if the vote is unclear on the ballot, the voter cannot tell us what his or her intent was. Thus, under normal circumstances, if a voter marks no vote for a particular office on a ballot or if a voter marks two choices for a particular office on a ballot, that vote simply will not be included in the tabulation. This is true even if the voter intended to do otherwise. Florida law, however, provides some elasticity in the principles governing which ballots count as valid votes. Florida law, as interpreted by the Florida Supreme Court, instructs that the ballot should be examined and should be included in the tabulation if the examiner can determine the intent of the voter. This leaves a lot to the judgment of individual examiners, without much in the way of rules to guide them. Some would argue that this rule leaves so much discretion that it might allow substitution of the intent of the examiner for the intent of the voter.

If you imagine an old-fashioned paper-style ballot on which the voter puts an "X" in the box next to the name of the candidate of his or her choice, then you can easily imagine that the dispute in Florida was really about this: How much of an "X" does there have to be in the box for a ballot to be a vote? Is it necessary that it be a full "X"? Will one diagonal line do? Or will simply a stray pencil mark anywhere in the box count? Boiled down to its essence, that is what the dispute in Florida was about, except that instead of being fought over paper ballots marked with an "X," it was fought over punch-card ballots marked by punching out what we all now know as chads.

The Bush argument continued with the point that since a ballot was a form of communication that could be judged objectively, then there should be consistent criteria for judging which ballots do count as votes and should be included in the vote tabulation. Most importantly, the criteria need to be uniform among precincts and counties throughout a state in order to satisfy the Constitution's equal protection standard. Just the opposite was true in Florida. There were no standard criteria for which ballots counted as valid votes in regard to punch-card ballots where the chad was less than completely removed. Even in Palm Beach County, the three members of the Canvassing Board could not agree among themselves on a single standard, changed their minds several times, and finally asked a court to tell them what the standard should be. It was evident to the entire nation, watching the recount process on television, that there were no rules for which ballots should count and that there was the potential for real mischief in making those rules up as the process went along.

As a consequence, the Bush team argued that the failure to have standard criteria which these officials could use to perform a hand recount resulted in a violation of the requirements of the Equal Protection Clause of the Constitution which holds that all votes should count the same. If different criteria were used in different counties to count the punch-card ballots, then not all votes would count the same. This would be a constitutional violation.

However, in addition to that, there was another common-sense requirement of federal law that became extremely important to the

Bush argument and the eventual decision of the Supreme Court. The federal law passed by Congress after the Tilden/Hayes dispute requires that in order for a presidential election contest to be considered valid, it has to be fought and decided on the basis of law in effect before the election is held. The results cannot be based on rules or laws made afterward. Simply put, since there were no standard criteria in Florida for what was a valid ballot before the election was held, then making one up afterward, after the ballots had been cast, would violate this provision of federal law. Making up new rules would, at the least, render the result of any recount undertaken pursuant to the election contest of little or no value in ultimately resolving the election dispute.

The final U.S. Supreme Court case involved hearing arguments on both points: that is, whether the Florida Supreme Court was using new rules in the election contest and whether the recount procedures it adopted violated the equal protection clause. In its decision, though, the Court framed the question it decided as follows:

> The question before us, however, is whether the recount procedures the Florida Supreme Court has adopted are consistent with its obligation to avoid arbitrary and disparate treatment of the members of its electorate.[6]

In answering this question the Supreme Court specifically found that the process of examining a ballot to determine the intent of the voter (Florida's legal standard) was capable of determination by objective criteria. The Court said, "The search for intent can be confined by specific rules designed to insure uniform treatment."[7] The Court then went on to find that this objective standard had essentially been conceded, as it must, and that the standards for determining what ballots would count as valid votes and therefore be included in the tabulation varied not only from county to county, but within a county between one recount team and another. The Supreme Court then found that the Florida Supreme Court's decision endorsed this

201

unequal treatment. As a result, the Court found that the procedures endorsed by the Florida Supreme Court violated the equal protection clause of the Constitution. The Supreme Court also found that in order to comply with federal law, a recount would have to be completed by December 12, which was, in fact, the date of the Supreme Court's decision and just a day following the submission of the case after oral argument. As a result, it was clear that there was insufficient time to perform a recount that would meet the minimal constitutional requirements. The decision of the Florida Supreme Court was therefore reversed. No more deadlines were to be extended, and there would be no more debate about dimples. The election was over. George W. Bush would be the next president.

AFTER THE ACTION

The full impact of the historical case in which I had been involved did not strike me until January 20, 2001, when on a very cold and rainy afternoon, I sat with one of my daughters a short distance from the West Front of the U.S. Capitol and watched George W. Bush and Dick Cheney take their oaths of office. I will never forget how the Capitol and the flags atop it looked to me that day. They were outlined starkly against a gray and desolate sky that to me seemed full of promise, hope, and yes, indeed, justice.

I think that the lawyers on both sides of this question, reflecting the views of their clients, were careful not to overplay their hands in the case. While both sides showed dedication, determination, and zealous effort to win, it was not an effort to win at any cost. I believed that our clients had made clear that we would press such claims as we believed credible and well advised, but that there clearly were boundaries to what we would argue and how long we would argue it. We never defined what those were, but we also made certain to stay well inside the lines.

In addition, no chapter on the contest would be complete without noting the laudable conduct of Vice President Gore when the fight was finally over. He behaved magnanimously and did much to heal any wound that had been opened by the bitterness of partisans surrounding the contest. He demonstrated a keen insight as to what the country needed at that particular moment and did all that he could to provide it. For this, all citizens should be grateful.

LOOKING AHEAD

In concurring in the stay decision granted by the Supreme Court on December 9, 2000, Justice Antonin Scalia wrote:

> Count first, and rule upon legality afterwards, is not a
> recipe for producing election results that have the
> public acceptance democratic stability requires.[8]

There is great insight in that short quotation concerning the symbiotic relationship between elections and election contest procedures and the maintenance of a stable democracy. If it were to appear to the public that elections and election results could be manipulated by one candidate, an interest group, or anyone else having a stake in the outcome, then the fragile sharp edge of democracy is dulled. This, in turn, portends a loss of epic proportions. It puts at risk very fundamental characteristics of our social system grounded in order through law. These are things that prior generations literally fought and died to maintain. Courts are supposed to be above and outside the political fray. Sometimes, though, courts are the only referees available who can whistle to stop political games that have gotten out of hand. Florida did not reach that point—but it was close.

It is true that elections and the election process are essentially political acts, thus suggesting that judicial restraint and a limited role for courts is appropriate. But courts do have a role to assure that constitutional rights in the election process are maintained. In addition, it is within the traditional province of courts to address frauds and other irregularities that may affect the fairness and the outcome of an election. But courts, in my judgment, should not be looked upon as a vehicle to fix all of the numerable irregularities that are—unfortunately—a part of our electoral process.

Rather, it is important for state legislatures and election officials to constantly reform and renew the process in order to smooth out the imperfections. In Florida, this type of reform has already been undertaken. It is being talked about as of this writing in other states, though one fears that the momentum for change may be lost with the passage of time and the emergence of new issues in the public consciousness. But there needs to be an ongoing commitment to make this very fundamental element of the democratic process as fair as it can possibly be. The more legislatures move to reform and improve the process, the less chance there will be that elections will be decided by judges instead of voters.

There is no doubt that there will be renewed talk of eliminating or fundamentally changing the Electoral College process. This is unnecessary, in my view. First, the Electoral College was not really an issue in the 2000 election dispute. Rather, it functioned as designed and limited the impact of a very close election to one disputed jurisdiction. This illustrates a second point, that the Electoral College has proved over the last two hundred years to be amazingly resilient, adaptable, and a good mechanism to administer presidential elections in our federalist system, the only nationwide elections we hold for public office.

In fact, the Electoral College, in yet another testimonial to the wisdom of the Framers, continues to secure the same interests that it was intended to when created: to provide freedom from corrupt political processes in the selection of the president, balance federalism issues, and address the competing values of popular election and the power of the states as sovereign entities.

However, the procedures spelled out by a nineteenth-century Congress to implement the Electoral College system, codified in Title 3 of the United States Code, do present some issues that deserve attention. Given the availability of modern communications and information processing, these include speeding up the dispute resolution process of the Electoral College, particularly as it concerns the Congress. I doubt that the country could stand postponing knowledge of who would be the next president and the beginning of the transition process until January, when the electoral votes are counted in Congress. In addition, clarifying the standards and procedures that apply to congressional review of a contested state's electoral votes is another issue that bears examination. However, with this and other tinkering with the Electoral College procedures, enough can be done to modernize the Electoral College to suit the conditions in our society today. It would be a mistake to throw the baby out with the bath water.

As with all matters of this historical value, only time can truly judge how all performed and how the system worked in the contested 2000 presidential election in the state of Florida.

It is true that the Bush team prevailed in a legal case. But I truly believe that was because we had the better part of the legal argument. More importantly, notwithstanding commentary to the contrary, more of the votes that should have been counted went to Bush than to Gore.

The real question was not about what votes should be counted, but rather what ballots count as votes. Florida law provided no definitive answer, and that was really the ultimate undoing of the Gore legal argument. But whatever lessons about the legal system, election law, and principles of federalism one might choose to draw from the Florida election, there is a much greater lesson learned.

Nine fellow human beings with pen and paper carried the day in a battle that in many other times and places might have been decided by a mob or an army. No riots took place. No tanks were in the streets. No troops surrounded the Capitol or the Executive Mansion. The country's love and respect for the rule of law was reinforced. There are some who disagree with the Supreme Court's decision as a matter of law. Still others disagree because they do not care for the outcome. That is, of course, all understandable. But most importantly, the American people accepted the result of this legal tumult. They respected the process. The American people recognized that a candidate had to win, and, somehow, that winner had to be determined. They trusted their courts to resolve the competing claims. This is the essential characteristic of the successful rule of law. We can be proud of our system, of our society, and, most of all, of our people.

Let us be thankful for our country, for the wisdom of those who designed this lasting system, and for the dedication of those who keep it well today. I have always felt privileged to be an American and all the more so for this experience.

NOTES

[1] The case involved defeated state Representative Louis "Woody" Jenkins, the Republican candidate, alleging that more than 10,000 illegally cast ballots helped his Democratic opponent, state Treasurer Mary Landrieu, win the 1996 Louisiana senate election by 5,788 votes. The Senate Rules Committee spent the majority of 1997 investigating these allegations while Landrieu began her first term in office, and eventually the allegations were dismissed.

[2] See Opinions of the Supreme Court of Florida, SC00-2431 *Albert Gore, Jr. v. Katherine Harris.*

[3] See *The Federalist Papers*, where Alexander Hamilton in Numbers 80-83 delineates the proper balance federal and state courts should hold in presiding over judicial questions.

[4] The Voting Rights Act was initially adopted in 1965 and further revised in 1970, 1975, and 1982. It is considered the most successful piece of civil rights legislation

adopted by the U.S. Congress in that it strengthens the Fifteenth Amendment to the Constitution to ensure that no American citizen is denied the right to vote because of race or color.

[5] See Article II, Section 1 of the U.S. Constitution.

[6] *George W. Bush, et al., v. Albert Gore, Jr., et al.*, 531 U.S. 527, 530 (2000) (Per curiam).

[7] Ibid.

[8] Supreme Court's stay decision in *Bush v. Gore*, 121 S. Ct. 512 (2000) (Scalia, J., conc.).

CHAPTER 9

Down and Dirty, Revisited

A Postscript on Florida and the News Media

Jake Tapper
CNN and salon.com

A mere matter of hours after George W. Bush accepted the presidency, I was on a plane from Washington, D.C., to Fort Lauderdale to begin research for my book on the recount, *Down and Dirty: The Plot to Steal the Presidency*. I must confess, I wondered if there was much new that I would be able to learn and write about. After all, the recount had received 24-hour-a-day saturation coverage. But before long, I was both excited and somewhat dismayed at how much there was that I didn't know. Excited for myself, for purely selfish reasons, for the book. Dismayed for you, for the American people, for what that said about the media.

One of the problems—and perks—that comes with being a reporter is that every day or so a new subject is thrust your way, a new expertise to feign. But this time, as the new information came at me like rabbit punches, I was stunned. This particular subject was a story I had been working on for 36 days. It was a story that the entire media universe had been working on for 36 days. That is why my ignorance of the subject matter was so stunning to me. Here I was, back in Palm Beach County, interviewing the major players—judges and elections officials and lawyers and politicians and voters—and I was learning tons. Waaaaaay too much. It was unnerving how much I did not know, because my lack of information reflected how much the world did not know.

On one level the reticence of the involved parties was not that big a surprise. During the recount fracas, which ran from November 7 until December 13, few of the players were talking—too much was at stake. Who knew what tumble of dominoes could be set in motion because of one ill-timed disclosure?

And yet, this fact was troubling: I—just some punk kid, a 31-year-old reporter for a struggling Internet magazine—was quickly becoming vastly more knowledgeable about this crucial chapter in our political history than network news anchors and newspaper bureau chiefs. It meant that a lot of us had not really done our jobs during the recount.

Even worse for the country—but again, good for me and my book—the media had already moved on to the next subject, the impending Bush presidency. So while I ran all over the state bugging the players for interviews, I had almost no competition. With a handful of exceptions, the media at large showed almost no interest at all in getting to the bottom of what happened in Florida.

Which was—and still is—no small charge. We *should* know: How the hell did everything get so screwed up? How did so many voters not get to properly exercise our hard-fought right to choose our leaders? What was motivating the various players? What was going on behind the scenes? How did Bush's and Gore's respective teams wage war—and what did that say about them, and us? And underneath it all lay the fundamental question of whether Bush was really the rightful heir to the throne.

The unsettling matter of how on earth I came to be an expert on this subject, especially when there were dozens of reporters, editors, and producers out there with far more means who should have theoretically been far better informed, would never go away. In fact, it would only get worse.

FLORIDA'S TIPPING POINT

One week into the recount, an editor at the New York City publishing house Little, Brown & Co. had phoned me. He was interested in having me write an examination of the recount. This was the second week of November. We all thought it would be over by Thanksgiving at the latest. I signed the contract.

By the time the cranberry sauce hit my plate, it still had not ended, of course. And so it wasn't until December 15, barely two days after Al Gore finally conceded—and George W. Bush accepted—the presidency, that I flew into Fort Lauderdale to find out what was going on in the minds of all these people who had held their tongues for 36 days. I spent December, January, and February hopping around Tallahassee, Fort Lauderdale, Miami, West Palm Beach, and Washington, D.C., interviewing about 200 people, trying to find out what *really* happened.

One of the first sit-downs I pursued was with Judge Charles Burton, chairman of the Palm Beach County canvassing board. Burton was beloved by the media for his easygoing manner, but he was a controversial figure among the politicos. Democrats, in particular, came to think of him as the enemy, whispering that Burton had sold out his Democratic roots, constantly ruling against a lenient ballot standard so as to get into Governor Jeb Bush's good graces. Such unfounded conspiracy theories did not hold much water with me, but I was interested in why Burton behaved the way he did during the recount.

Led by Burton, the canvassing board changed its ballot standards several times. For most of the recount, Palm Beach County elections supervisor Theresa LePore—shell-shocked from the nasty backlash against her because of her horrible "butterfly ballot" design —followed Burton's lead on such decisions. In the end, Gore lawyers thought that the board's reluctance to count every dimple as a vote cost them maybe a thousand votes, in other words, the election.

Malcolm Gladwell's fantastic book *The Tipping Point*[1] illustrates the way in which one man, on one night, because of one relatively small turn of events, can indeed change history, despite our basic inclination to see history as large and uncontrollable weather fronts storming into our neighborhoods. Burton was a tipping point. Why was that?

Soon enough, Burton and I sat and chatted. A Jewish Democrat from Newton, Massachusetts, the judge had voted for Gore, and all things being equal he would have liked Gore to have won. But he saw his job as judge, not to mention as canvassing board chairman, as putting impartiality above all else. Bearing this desire in mind, we can see how two vectors collided in the canvassing boardroom—and specifically in Burton—affecting everything from there.

One attack was delivered with a smile by Kerey Carpenter, a demure, attractive strawberry blond lawyer from the office of Secretary of State Katherine Harris. During those early days, Harris and Carpenter were feigning neutrality. As the county conducted its 1 percent sample hand recount of the county's ballots on November 11, Burton—new as a judge, confused as a canvassing board member—was not sure whether a full county recount was in order. All day, and during cigarette breaks, Carpenter kept telling Burton that he should seek an advisory opinion from Harris as to whether or not he should do the 1 percent recount. Not once did she tell him that if he did make such a request, the decision from Harris's office would be legally binding.

The other vector came from the Gore lawyers. Unlike Carpenter's crafty (and duplicitous) way, the Gore lawyers were abrasive and aggressive. Working with the third member of the canvassing board, County Commissioner Carol Roberts, the Democrats chased Burton off the Democratic reservation, to the point that he told me he was considering changing his voting status from Democrat to No Party. That night, as the 1 percent hand recount concluded, Roberts, in Burton's view, ran roughshod over what should have been a calm and balanced procedure. LePore, for her part, was being told what to do, Svengali-style, by a local Democratic attorney. *Down and Dirty* goes into this scene in detail: suffice it to say that that night changed Burton's mind-set, and that change changed history. [2]

There were many other tales. There had been no shortage of reporters in Florida during the recount, including me, and yet with every passing hour in my research I learned something new. Almost every new interviewee allowed me to wave away expertly crafted obfuscations like so much smoke. Burton's story was just the beginning.

There were the Bush political operatives who held a conference call on November 11. Soldiers voting by absentee ballot had until November 17 to get their ballots in, though they were supposed to have been already cast and mailed by Election Day, November 7. No matter, the Bush political operatives said. They could get the voting records from the counties, determine which soldiers were white Republicans, and have political operatives in the field and abroad chase them down. Did they do so? It is still impossible to know for sure, but while there were only around 450 ballots that had arrived in Florida on November 13, a suspicious-looking 3,300 or so more had flooded in by the November 17 deadline. And in these ballots lay Bush's official margin of victory.

More and more tidbits of news emerged as I shuttled between a Tallahassee Motel 6 and a pal's pad in South Beach. Some of it was just interesting: Gore chairman Bill Daley, infuriated by the GOP campaign to impugn the Gore recount effort by constantly referencing the alleged vote frauds of his long-dead father, referred to Bob Dole as a "limp-dicked motherfucker."

Some of it was bizarre: Katherine Harris, so deluded and odd and completely in the tank for Bush, told folks about a dream she had in which she galloped into the Florida State-University of Florida football game with the FSU flag in one hand and the vote certification for Bush in the other. Equally strange, Gore seemed to lose it at times behind closed doors, pitching weird conspiracy theories to television news producers.

Some of the news was disturbing: the Republicans, forgoing the candidate's cry to make the GOP more inclusive, tried to get one judge recused specifically because she was a black woman—a reason that so offended Bush attorney Barry Richard that he refused to sign the recusal motion.

More significant was the inescapable conclusion that both Bush and Gore had led inherently corrupt, and morally bereft, recount efforts. There were approximately 175,000 undervotes and overvotes throughout the state that machines didn't read, ballots that represented Floridians, people, Americans. Quite significantly, as I continued with my research I learned how Gore's team never made any effort to "count every vote"—how, in fact, the team repeatedly *blocked* efforts to have the undervotes and overvotes analyzed if they weren't from the four carefully selected Democratic-leaning counties.

Bush's team was no better; they did everything in their power to stop *any* counting of the 175,000, except where it benefited them, as in the heretofore unheard-of Jackson County.[3] Dick Cheney referred to the 175,000 unread ballots as "no votes," as if these ballots merely represented voters who didn't like any of the ten listed tickets. But this was not the case—there were clearly discernible votes on thousands of these ballots. By not caring about these 175,000 voters, and instead focusing just on their own selfish power-mad scrambles for the presidency, both Bush and Gore proved themselves unworthy of the honor.

The first draft of *Down and Dirty* was finished on February 5, 2001. Edits were completed by early March. The book hit the stores on April 5. It wasn't just a *Deadlock*[4] (the name of the *Washington Post* book). It wasn't just a matter of *36 Days*[5] (the name of the *New York Times* book). No, this was a grim struggle in a mud pit. It was *Down and Dirty*. It was *The Plot to Steal the Presidency*—a massive plot, on every side, by politicians of every stripe, to steal the presidency. From us.

WHO REALLY LOST?

It is impossible to write about the reaction to my book in a way that would seem anything but self-serving. I was lucky; *Down and Dirty* got a decent amount of attention. Lots of authors are not so lucky. One friend of mine spent years working on a biography of Al Gore that painted his life in vivid detail, revealing why the man was the way he was, what his flaws and his strengths were and how they emerged. His book, published during the campaign, did not get nearly enough attention. None of this should be news: TV glosses over substance; reporters are always chasing the next story, seldom looking back; journalism is a highly competitive field in which less lofty human and organizational characteristics can deprive viewers and readers of knowledge about what others have reported. In this world, *Down and Dirty* has received its share of attention. But what happened in Florida has not.

Whenever I am at a book signing and I tell folks some of the above stories, they gasp. They gasp again when I share the details that illustrate just how hollow Gore's "count every vote" rhetoric was. Over and over they gasp when I share any of the new materials that fell in my lap during research for my book largely because I had merely bothered to show up and express a modicum of curiosity.

Far more troubling than those media that did not make use of the news scoops I managed to find is the general lack of interest the media have shown about Florida since December 13, 2000. Where are the investigations? Where are the explorations of what went on, how everything got so horribly screwed up? Where are the revelations about individuals in the Bush and Gore camps who let us down? With the exception of media in Florida—*The Miami Herald* and *The Palm Beach Post*, most notably—none of the press has seemed to care, devoting its resources to other topics, such as further probing into the death of JonBenet Ramsey.

Writing *Down and Dirty* was a wonderful experience for me as an author and as a journalist. But the experience has left me with some misgivings. I know in vivid detail the many ways in which the Gorebies and Bushies, some of whom have contributed other chapters in this book, have failed you, as an American. I could go into their chapters with a red pen and underline the things they have written that are not true, matters that do not hold up to scrutiny. The problem is that very few of us have been willing to hold them to such vigorous scrutiny. Apparently very few of us in journalism want to find out what really happened in Florida. One critique of *Down and Dirty* that never ceases to amaze me is that my outrage is somehow rooted in naïveté—that I should expect and, I suppose, accept—lying and cheating from our political leaders. I may be personally and professionally better off thanks to *Down and Dirty,* but the book has also caused me to have much graver doubts about the foundation on which this democracy's political system stands.

NOTES

[1] Malcolm Gladwell, *The Tipping Point: How Little Things Can Make a Big Difference* (New York: Little, Brown, 2000).

[2] Jake Tapper, *Down and Dirty: The Plot to Steal the Presidency* (New York: Little, Brown, 2001), pp. 113–131.

[3] With no media attention or fanfare at all, on Election Night 2000, the Jackson County elections supervisor reviewed all the 1,400 undervotes and overvotes in the GOP-leaning Opti-Scan county. Where the "intent of the voter" could be ascertained, she adjusted the ballot accordingly. For instance, if a vote had filled in the oval next to Bush's name and had also filled in the oval next to "Write in" and written in the name of either Bush or Cheney, that second, superfluous oval was covered over with a white sticker so the machine would read the overvote as a vote. This was done to approximately 300 ballots in a county that Bush won 9,138 to Gore's 6,868 (*Down and Dirty*, pp. 428–429).

[4] Political Staff of The Washington Post, *Deadlock: The Inside Story of America's Closest Election* (New York: Public Affairs, 2001).

[5] Correspondents of the New York Times, *36 Days: The Complete Chronicle of the 2000 Presidential Election Crisis* (New York: Holt, 2001).

CHAPTER 10

Stalemate

The 'Great' Election of 2000

Rhodes Cook
The Rhodes Cook Letter[1]

There have been a lot of words used to describe the election of 2000, but one rarely heard is the word "great." Yet roughly once every 30 years or so—reappearing much like *Brigadoon*—there have been "great" elections that have defined the political landscape for the next generation. They have been watershed elections, like that of 1860, which first ushered the Republicans into national power; that of 1896, which cemented the ascendancy of urban over rural America; that of 1932, which launched the Democrats' activist "New Deal"; and that of 1968, which formally saw the arrival of a Republican South.

Calendar-wise, it was about time for another "great" election. Election 2000 turned out to be great for a much different reason than those of the past. Rather than providing a sharp partisan redirection, this election will be remembered for the opposite reason, its very closeness—not just for president, but for the Senate and the House of Representatives as well.

It is an election that may have propelled us into a political era unseen

---

[1] As originally published in the January/February 2001 issue of *Public Perspective.* This piece has been updated wherever appropriate.

219

for more than a century, in which neither party has more than a tenuous grip on either end of Pennsylvania Avenue.

But dramatic as it is, there has been a dispiriting tone thus far to this era. Nearly two centuries ago, there was a brief period in American history known as the "Era of Good Feelings," largely because there was only one political party. What we have now is quite the opposite, an "Era of Ill Feelings" if you will, in which razor-thin margins have heightened partisan anxiety and bitterness.

It is an era that did not arrive overnight. This is the third straight presidential election that has been won without a majority of the popular vote, and this was the third straight election in which neither party has won a majority of the votes cast for the House of Representatives.

Whether this will be the state of national politics for the foreseeable future remains to be seen. The upcoming round of congressional redistricting could decisively tip the partisan balance in the House. The health of aging members of the Senate could have a pivotal impact on which party controls the nation's upper chamber in the immediate future. And the recent candidacies of Ross Perot and Ralph Nader have shown the ability of third parties to dramatically affect the outcome of presidential elections.

CLOSE, CLOSE, CLOSE

There is no doubt that the election of 2000 has become an instant classic because of its almost impossible-to-resolve closeness. The popular vote for president is the closest since 1968, when Richard M. Nixon defeated Hubert H. Humphrey by a margin of barely 500,000 votes out of more than 73 million cast.

The electoral vote for president is the closest since 1876, when

Rutherford B. Hayes defeated Samuel J. Tilden by a margin of just 1 electoral vote. This time, President George W. Bush won by 5 votes, 271 to 266 (with one Democratic elector in the District of Columbia leaving her ballot blank rather than vote for Gore). There is little doubt at this point that Bush's Electoral College victory flies in the face of a popular vote win for Vice President Al Gore, the first time there would be different popular and electoral vote winners in a presidential election since 1888.

The bizarre closeness of the results is equally evident at the other end of Pennsylvania Avenue. The Senate breakdown of 50-50 was the first partisan tie in the Senate since the election of 1880. (Editor's note: The even Senate split ended on May 24, 2001, when liberal Republican U.S. Senator James Jeffords of Vermont announced that because of the GOP's conservatism, he was leaving the party to become an Independent who caucuses with the Democrats.) The post-election House breakdown of 221-212 (with two Independents) is the closest disparity in Republican and Democratic ranks since the election of 1952.

Why were the results so close? At the presidential level, there were strongly conflicting tides that, at the end, virtually canceled each other out. Gore was boosted by the nation's prosperity and by high performance ratings for the Clinton administration, of which he was a part, factors borne out in presidential election models that were virtually unanimous in predicting a comfortable Gore victory.

Propelling Bush were Clinton's low personal ratings, a sentiment for change that often begins to work against the incumbent party at the eight-year mark, and a liberal third-party candidate in Ralph Nader, who posed a much greater problem for Gore than conservative Patrick J. Buchanan did for Bush.

The presidential race also pitted two conflicting political eras against each other—a short-term Democratic period that twice elected Clinton in the 1990s, and a longer-term Republican era that gave the

GOP victory in five of the six previous presidential elections. In the House, Democrats had been inching back to a position of near-parity since their loss of congressional control in 1994. And much of the closeness in this year's House voting was due to the lack of competition, which kept partisan change to a minimum.

While 435 seats were at stake, the playing field was really barely one-tenth that size. Well-heeled incumbents and the lack of galvanizing issues or presidential coattails all proved to be powerful forces promoting the status quo and deterring significant competition in most districts.

In short, barring an unexpected turn of events, neither party was going to win by much. And in the end, only 18 House seats changed party hands—10 going to the Democrats, 8 to the Republicans—for a net Democratic gain of 2. Most of the switches came in the open seats, as only six incumbents were beaten, producing an incumbent reelection rate that approached 98 percent.

In the Senate, Republicans had more seats to defend (19, vs. 15 Democratic), and that fact was reflected in the final results. The Democrats registered a net gain of 4 seats, picking off some of the more vulnerable members of the large GOP class of 1994—Rod Grams of Minnesota, Spencer Abraham of Michigan, and John Ashcroft of Missouri, who, in one of the more bizarre results of a bizarre election, lost to the state's late governor, Mel Carnahan.

Each party lost at least one veteran incumbent: the Democrats, Virginia's Charles S. Robb; the Republicans, Delaware's William V. Roth, Jr., and Washington's Slade Gorton. The parties traded open seats: Democrats gained one in Florida; the Republicans picked up one in Nevada. (Even with a 50-50 tie, though, Republicans were guaranteed control of the Senate after January 20 because Bush's vice president, Richard B. Cheney, is entitled to cast the chamber's tie-breaking vote.)

A TALE OF TWO NATIONS: INSIDE
AND OUTSIDE THE "L"

When the chad from the ballots had finally settled, the national vote was razor-close but highly fractured. Exit polls showed that men favored Bush, women favored Gore; whites preferred Bush, nonwhites preferred Gore; the more affluent voted strongly for Bush, the less affluent heavily favored Gore; rural and small-town America went for Bush, urban America for Gore.

The geographical diversity of the presidential vote was colorfully evident in a map published in *USA Today* two days after the November 7 election. Counties carried by Bush were colored in red. Those carried by Gore were colored in blue. And while Gore's counties were clustered in several parts of the country, the bulk of the map was a sea of red. On quick inspection, it was not difficult to design a cross-country trip from the outskirts of Washington, D.C., to the outskirts of Los Angeles without passing through a single county carried by Gore.

But a more intriguing aspect of the election was how it essentially divided the nation into distinct halves—a Republican-oriented L-shaped sector that includes the South, the Plains, and the Mountain states plus Alaska; and a Democratic-oriented bicoastal–industrial heartland sector that includes the Northeast and the industrial Midwest and skips westward across the "L" to encompass the Pacific Coast states plus Hawaii (see figure 11-1).

The "L" is much more rural and geographically expansive, though it does include the heart of the fast-growing Sun Belt. The "L" comprises 26 states with 223 electoral votes. The bicoastal–industrial midland sector is more urban. It includes 24 states and the District of Columbia with 315 electoral votes.

This alignment has been in the making in presidential elections for several decades. From 1968 through 1988, Republicans frequently won the White House by dominating the "L" so conclusively that they were free to roam at will for votes in the Democrats' domain. But in the 1990s, Clinton reversed the equation, showing such strong appeal in the bicoastal–industrial midlands that he was free to make forays into the "L," ultimately making the Republican base look like a piece of Swiss cheese.

For many years, the disparity between the two sectors was merely a phenomenon of presidential elections, since Democrats dominated congressional voting across the country. That changed, though, in 1994, when the Republican tidal wave that swept the GOP into control on Capitol Hill came rolling out of the "L."

In 1996, Republicans won the presidential and congressional voting within the "L" (albeit the former quite narrowly), while Democrats had the edge in presidential and congressional voting outside the "L" (with the advantage quite large in the balloting for the White House).

But it was the 2000 election that marked a full coming of age for this "tale of two nations." The "L" was decisively Republican, the rest of the country decisively Democratic. Giving Florida to Bush, the Texas governor swept all but one state in the "L" (narrowly losing New Mexico). Gore won 19 of 24 states in the bicoastal–industrial midlands. Bush enjoyed a huge 218-to-5 electoral vote lead in the Republican sector of the country. Gore posted a 262-to-53 advantage in the Democratic sector.

Bush won the South, the Plains states, and the Mountain West by a margin of 5.3 million in the popular vote. Gore won the Northeast, the industrial Midwest, and the Pacific West by more than 5.8 million votes. Republicans won 44 more House seats within the "L" than the Democrats (107 to 63, with one independent). Democrats won 35 more House seats than the Republicans in the rest of the country (149 to 114, with one independent). Republicans hold 18 more Senate seats than the Democrats (35 to 17) in the "L." Elsewhere, Democrats hold

18 more Senate seats than the Republicans (33 to 15). Add the two sectors together, and you get roughly a dead heat in balloting for the federal executive and legislative branches.

In this first election of the new millenium, each party essentially dug in and milked its base. For Republicans, the cornerstone of the "L" is the South, followed by the Mountain West. The South—the 11 states of the old Confederacy plus Kentucky and Oklahoma—is now the epicenter of the national Republican Party, much like it was once for the Democrats. Bush carried the region by nearly 3.7 million votes on November 7 and swept every state, including Gore's home state of Tennessee and Clinton's home state of Arkansas.

The GOP holds 26 more House seats across the South than the Democrats and 8 more Senate seats. Many of the Republicans' top leaders on Capitol Hill are from Dixie, including former Senate Majority Leader Trent Lott of Mississippi and House Majority Leader Dick Armey of Texas.

While much smaller in population, the Mountain West is every bit as Republican as the South. Bush's three top states percentage-wise were in the Rocky Mountain region—Wyoming (where he drew 69% of the vote) and Idaho and Utah (each won by Bush with 67%)—and Bush outpolled Gore by roughly 1 million votes in the region as a whole. At the congressional level, GOP hegemony in the Mountain states (including Alaska) is almost monolithic. Republicans hold 13 more House seats in this region than the Democrats and a dozen more Senate seats.

Meanwhile, the two basic building blocks of the Democrats' bicoastal–industrial midlands sector are roughly 2,500 miles apart—the states of the "Amtrak Corridor" and the Pacific West. The Amtrak Corridor runs from Washington, D.C., to Boston, Massachusetts, and encompasses eight states and the District of Columbia. Gore not only swept them all by a combined margin of 4 million votes, but the Corridor was also the site of his top three states nationally—Rhode Island (where he polled 61% of the vote), New York and Massachusetts (each won by Gore with 60%), plus the District of Columbia (which he won with 85%).

Figure 11-1.
Inside and Outside the "L"

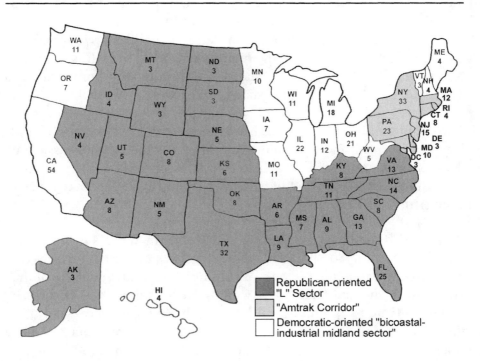

Republican-oriented "L" Sector

"Amtrak Corridor"

Democratic-oriented "bicoastal-industrial midland sector"

Design by Catherine Giambastiani

The Corridor has also been vital to Democrats at the congressional level, providing them with 18 more House seats and 10 more Senate seats than the Republicans, including the one in New York now held by former First Lady Hillary Rodham Clinton.

Yet it was returns from the Pacific West late on election night that enabled Gore to pull ahead in the popular vote count and for the

Democrats to pull closer to parity in the House. Gore swept the quartet of Pacific Coast states (California, Oregon, Washington, and Hawaii) by 1.5 million votes, while the Democratic advantage in House seats in this part of the country grew to 20, with a gain of a half dozen seats in this election alone. In the Senate, the Democratic edge stands at 6 seats in the Pacific West.

THE EVER-CHANGING MAP

But even as closely divided as the nation was in this election, the political map is constantly evolving. Although socially conservative, West Virginia went for Bush—the first time since the New Deal that the state voted Republican for president other than in GOP landslide years. On the other hand, the presidential vote in Florida was nip and tuck, even though Republicans had carried the state in 9 of the 12 previous elections since 1952, including the two in which Bush's father headed the GOP ticket.

There is no doubt that the election of 2000 was one of a kind. Whether it will be remembered as "great" will be for history to judge. The length of the current Era of Ill Feelings, however, should be quicker to ascertain. The original Era of Good Feelings was quickly followed by a brand of politics that was entirely different—a highly partisan era dominated by Andrew Jackson, whose encouragement of grassroots participation made it a Democratic era with both a large and a small "d."

With Republicans winning the White House in spite of a loss in the popular vote, they could hope that this is the start of a Republican era, with both a large and a small "r." Yet, if history does repeat itself, this Era of Ill Feelings will be followed by a period of less partisanship, with a more civil, bipartisan mode of governing. At this point, though, one can only hope that will happen.